Talk for Writing in Secondary Schools

How to achieve effective reading, writing and communication across the curriculum

Julia Strong

 Open University Press

Open University Press
McGraw Hill Education
8th Floor
338 Euston Road
London
NW1 3BH

email: enquiries@openup.co.uk
world wide web: www.openup.co.uk

and Two Penn Plaza, New York, NY 10121–2289, USA

First published 2013, updated 2020

A catalogue record of this book is available from the British Library

ISBN-13: 978-0-3352-5019-6 (pb)
ISBN-10: 0-3352-5019-x (pb)
eISBN: 978-0-3352-5020-2

Library of Congress Cataloging-in-Publication Data
CIP data applied for

Typesetting and e-book compilations by
Transforma Pvt. Ltd., Chennai, India

Talk for Writing in Secondary Schools

This handbook is dedicated to all the teachers across the curriculum whose enthusiasm for the Talk-for-Writing approach, and generosity in letting me use their material, have made this handbook possible. In particular, I would like to thank the following people from Brighton and Hove – Carole Sullivan, Teaching and Learning adviser; Vicky Hawking, English adviser and English teacher at Cardinal Newman; Zeb Friedman, Maths adviser and AST maths teacher, Varndean School; and Sue Pickerill, Science adviser and science teacher, Varndean School – for not only piloting the approach but for doing so in such a model way, building up the approach and making it their own. But most of all, thanks to Pie Corbett for creating the Talk-for-Writing approach and asking me to help him develop it; and for his endless inspiration, humour and passion to help teachers help children learn to express themselves effectively.

Julia Strong, www.Talk4Writing.com

Note: AQA examination-related materials are reproduced by permission of AQA Education (AQA).

Christine Counsell first published the Fire of London materials (see page 172) in the following pamphlet: Counsell, C. (1997) Analytical and Discursive Writing in History at Key Stage 3, London: Historical Association. Counsell's work has focused on how to integrate oral and written work to secure a strong relationship between thinking and knowledge-building within a disciplinary framework. The following publication sets out the most recent version of the resources, and models ways of using them in practice to secure historical argument: Counsell, C. (2011) 'Generating historical argument about causation in the history classroom: exploring practical teaching approaches', in Ghusayni, R., Karami, R., & Akar, B. (Eds.). (2012) Learning and teaching history: Lessons from and for Lebanon: Proceedings of the Third Conference on Education, Lebanese Association for Education Studies, 25-26 March 2011. Beirut: Arab Cultural Centre.)

Praise for this book

"Few schools make the most of the relationship between talk and writing. Often isolated teachers experience success with it, but their knowledge is rarely scaled up to the whole school. In this book Julia Strong draws upon her extensive and acclaimed experience of helping teachers raise their expectations of the quality of students' writing. The examples show the importance of respecting subject difference and of making the most of the disciplinary characteristics of texts within each subject. Strong thus avoids the dangers of a generic literacy that ignores the way knowledge is structured within disciplines. Instead, she gives senior managers the thoughtful, nuanced guide that is necessary for building whole-staff debate and sustained, shared reflection."

Christine Counsell, Senior Lecturer, University of Cambridge Faculty of Education, UK

*"**Talk for writing in Secondary Schools** offers a practical, systematic approach which clarifies for teachers how to help students talk the subject and write the subject.*

The manual is a rich source of practical ideas to use immediately and directly in the classroom. Offering active learning techniques that empower students to produce better independent writing, as well as building confidence in expressing ideas and concepts in different subject areas, it can transform our approach to literacy and really raise achievement."

Carole Sullivan, Teaching & Learning Lead and Vicky Hawking, Literacy Lead, Brighton & Hove Secondary Partnership

*"**Talk for Writing** is a wildly successful approach to writing for pupils of all ages, well known and practised in primary schools, but now, with this publication by Julia Strong, completely accessible for all secondary teachers. Writing is integral to every subject, usually only the domain of English departments, yet, following the talk for writing approach using this book, teachers will be able to a) significantly raise their students' test results and b) give them powerful writing skills which can be applied to any subject. The book is a comprehensive manual for raising standards in writing across the secondary curriculum outlining every stage of the process and including cutting edge formative assessment, how to coordinate talk for writing across the whole school and advice about policies. Every subject is given pages and pages of high quality examples of the 5 stages, all drawn from Julia's work with teachers, and no subject is marginalized. The book is practical, reader-friendly and includes a pack of handouts and superb online resources. The use of talk for writing across the secondary phase is a very exciting prospect: I highly recommend using this book to make it happen."*

Shirley Clarke, Education consultant, Associate of the Institute of Education, University of London, UK

"This is an excellent resource for schools. High quality writing and the inspiration to make this happen has never been more important. This book will help teachers and school leaders maximise the possibility for young people to improve their writing skills. Julia Strong has extensive and successful knowledge in school improvement and this shines through her highly original and exciting approaches."

Graham Tyrer, Headteacher, Chenderit School, Banbury, UK

" 'Silent classrooms do not lend themselves to progress,' the Foreword to this important new book reminds us. What follows is an exceptionally well-informed and practical guide to how high quality talk can lead to high quality writing. I strongly recommend it for all teachers across all subjects."

Geoff Barton, Headteacher of King Edward VI School, Suffolk, UK, author and speaker

Contents

Foreword

In the 1960s, James Britton and his colleagues at the Institute of Education brought into being the notion of 'language across the curriculum'. It has been over 50 years since that idea was first developed and yet still the vision escapes most secondary schools.

Each subject has its own vocabulary and sentence patterns. The rhythms and tune of the language of mathematics are different from the patterns of argument needed by the historian. How can we help students acquire the language of so many different subjects?

It seems obvious that talk is central to learning. To deepen understanding, talking through problems plays an important role. Silent classrooms do not lend themselves to progress. Discussing, explaining, questioning and using talk and writing to tussle with ideas are all aspects of the struggle towards clarity and deepening of thought.

But what about the sort of language that students need to express their ideas when writing? It is a mistake to believe that this is the domain of the English teacher. How can an English department be responsible for helping students acquire the language children need for music, PE or science? Each subject has its own language which is tied up inextricably with meaning. An English teacher cannot teach children the vocabulary of science, let alone the patterns of language needed to express scientific thought. Only a science teacher can do that – but how?

The acquisition of vocabulary seems simple enough. The science teacher (or music teacher, maths teacher. . .) can use scientific specific vocabulary in many different contexts so that students begin to understand what the words mean. Very specific modelling of 'scientific talk' helps students hear how a scientist thinks. This modelling will inform the children's talk and, perhaps, their writing.

This book takes the idea of modelling language further by emphasising 'Talk for Writing. Building on techniques used in this country and many others around the world to raise the standards of writing in primary schools, this early work in secondary schools is the beginning of what will become a revolution in the teaching of 'language across the curriculum'.

The very specific techniques used in Talk for Writing are powerful tools that help students internalise the structures and sentence patterns needed to express themselves in different curriculum areas. It is almost like learning a series of slightly different dialects, each with their own phraseology. The approach is simple, highly effective and accessible to all secondary teachers.

Only 10 years ago, just six primary classes in the country used Talk for Writing, whereas now thousands do. Indeed, every primary school in the country has been touched by its influence. This movement has spread because it works. The same will happen in secondary education. There is no reason why almost all children should not be able to express themselves in different subjects. With some training, a shift in practice and the belief in the power of teachers to transform children's lives, this can be achieved. Julia Strong's book will play a central role in this revolution.

Pie Corbett

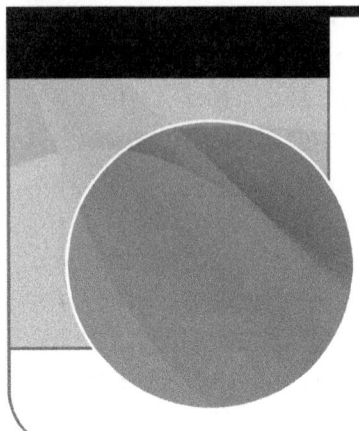

Guided tour

The online that accompanies this book is a useful addition for anyone reading the book as well as for anyone wanting to provide staff training on the Talk-for-Writing approach. It provides footage of a training day with teachers, over 70 downloadable and amendable handouts (including exemplar text), and PowerPoint slides to adapt for your own training sessions.

The book, the slides and the video all follow the same structure: an introduction laying the foundations and introducing the Talk-for-Writing approach followed by the five steps to amending units.

Making learning visible is key to the approach. Icons throughout the text and the online help to guide the reader, as shown below:

	The Talk-for-Writing approach spins around the concept of providing students with model text. The **exemplar text icon** indicates where such text is provided. More examples are available online.
	Teachers are encouraged to devise talking-the-text activities to enable students to rehearse what they are going to write. The **talking-the-text icon** is used to indicate such activities.
	Boxing up text is a simple device that can be used for analysing and planning any text. The **boxing-up icon** shows where the approach is illustrated within the book.
	Underlying the approach is the concept of internalising useful words and phrases. Teachers are encouraged to devise oral activities that will warm up the words of a unit. The **warming-up-the-words icon** is used to flag up these activities.

	Teachers are also encouraged to devise oral activities that will warm up the phrases of a unit. These activities are flagged up by the **warming-up-the-phrases icon.**
	Students are encouraged to store useful words and phrases as they arise within units of work just as a magpie hoards shiny objects. Hence the **magpie icon.**
	Emphasis is placed on analysing the ingredients that contribute to the effectiveness of exemplar text and co-constructing these ingredients into toolkits, as indicated by the **toolkit icon.**
	Teachers are encouraged to scaffold students' understanding of each feature of the toolkit for the type of text they want them to write. The **toolkit ingredient icon** flags up such activities.
	The **handout icon** indicates where a handout has been included to illustrate the approach. Editable complete versions of all the handouts are also available online.
	Embedding learning activities are encouraged throughout a unit of work as well as at the end. Such activities are highlighted by the **embedding learning icon.**
	www.mheducation.co.uk/professionals/open-university-press/olc/t4w-secondary-school

Subject index of handouts

The following is an index of handouts and exemplar text related to specific subjects. All of the handouts are available online and can be amended to suit curriculum needs. Most of the examples can be adapted to suit the needs of a wide range of subjects.

Handout and steps	Title	Art	Design & Technology	Drama	English Language	English Literature	French	Geography	History	Computing/ Business	Maths	Music	PE	RE	Science & Geology	All
Introduction																
H1 Page 4	Overview of how to adapt a unit															1a
H1a online	Unit planning toolkit															
H2 Page 9	Non-fiction text ingredients															2
H2b online	Non-fiction text ingredients game				2a											2a
H3 Page 16	Shared writing phrases															3
H4a Page 13–14	Text map and text for Fox		.		4a											
H4b page 18	Overview of Text-for-Writing process															4b
Step A Pages 33–37	**Building in progression**	Art	Design & Technology	Drama	English Language	English Literature	French	Geography	History	Computing/ Business	Maths	Music	PE	RE	Science & Geology	All
H4c/H4d page 34	Ai. Exemplar text		4c/d			4c/d		4c/d		4c/d		4c/d			4c/d	4c/d
H5 Page 35	Aii. Framing learning										5c		5b		5a	
Step B Pages 38–69	**Warming up the words**	Art	Design & Technology	Drama	English Language	English Literature	French	Geography	History	Computing/ Business	Maths	Music	PE	RE	Science & Geology	All
H6 Page 39	Never-heard-the-word							6c	6d	6f	6a		6b	6g	6e	6
H7 Page 47	Activating prior learning							7a			7b					

Step C Pages 70–103	Warming up the phrases	Art	Design & Technology	Drama	English Language	English Literature	French	Geography	History	Computing/ Business	Maths	Music	PE	RE	Science & Geology	All
H8 Page 50	Sorting technical terms											8a			8b	
H9 Page 51	Generating related vocabulary	9b/c										9a/d				
H10 Page 53	Labelling activities		10													
H11 Page 55	Sorting and generating	11a													11b	
H12 Page 56	Generating examples and mime												12			
H13 Page 58	Word root detective										13					
H14 Page 62	Dominoes		14c		14b						14d		14a		14e/f	
H15 Page 66	Word loops												15			
H16 Page 68	Exam command terms														16	
H17 online	Generic sentence signposts															17
H18 Page 72	Raiding the reading															18.
H19 Page 78	Clumping signposts						19									
H20 Page 79	Sorting sentence signposts				20			20	20					20		
H21 Page 82	Formal and informal				21											
H22/H23 Page 84	Sequencing text and graphs														22/23	
H24 Page 87	Sequencing writing frames			24												
H25 Page 88	Sequencing text and mime														25	
H26 Page 91	Advanced sequencing					26a	26b									
H27 Page 93	Phrases for evaluation	27														

		Art	Design & Technology	Drama	English Language	English Literature	French	Geography	History	Computing/Business	Maths	Music	PE	RE	Science & Geology	All
H28 Page 94	Hook phrases for evaluation	28		28		28									28	
H29 Page 94	Bloom's Taxonomy															29
H30 online page 99	Analysing sentence signposts														30a/30b/30c	
Step D Pages 104–197	Internalising the text including text maps	Art	Design & Technology	Drama	English Language	English Literature	French	Geography	History	Computing/Business	Maths	Music	PE	RE	Science & Geology	All
H31 online page 109–115	Internalising exemplar text				31a/31b										31c/31d	
H32 Page 128	Comparing text: what = good														32	
H33 Page 132	Exemplar text for what = good					33										
H34 online Page 137	Using icons to talk the text		34a/34b													
H35 online Page 143–145	Using advanced exemplar text					35a										
H36 Page 153, 155	Analysing exam exemplars														36a/36b	
H37 Page 163, 165, 169	Sorting activities for non-chronological essays								37a/37b							
H38 Page 173, 174, 179	Sorting activities for chronological writing								38a/38b							
H39 Page 186–188	Building up exemplar text						39a–f									
Step E Pages 198–204	Consolidating learning	Art	Design & Technology	Drama	English Language	English Literature	French	Geography	History	ICT/Business	Maths	Music	PE	RE	Science & Geology	All
H40 Page 199	Revisiting learning frames														40	
H41 Page 201	Framing learning										41					
H42 Page 209	Promoting Reading															All

Part 1
Introduction

CHAPTER 1

Introducing the Talk-for-Writing approach

(This chapter is supported by **Handouts 1, 1a, 3, 4a & 4b**, **Slides 1–2 & 12–22**, and the introduction to the film clips online.)

This Talk-for-Writing guide takes you step by step through how to establish an effective whole-school approach to achieving quality communication – both written and spoken – across the curriculum and, through the process, help students to read better. This approach is all about helping teachers of all subjects adapt their units within a consistent framework so that students can transfer their learning from one subject to another and become confident communicators. It illustrates how every teacher can help students internalise the pattern of language of their subject through focused talk activities related to exemplar text. This enables students to independently generate the speech and sentence patterns that are key to whatever subjects they are studying. In short, it is all about putting language in to get language out.

Students talking the text

The book is structured so that the reader understands how the Talk-for-Writing approach could apply to their subject area before considering how to spread it across a department or school.

Part 1 introduces the approach and outlines the foundations that need to be in place to underpin literacy across the curriculum.

Part 2 demonstrates how to adapt any unit of work to the approach using these five steps:

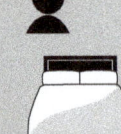
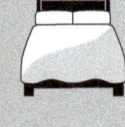

- **Step A: Creating exemplar text that builds in progression** – how to get the best exemplar text for each subject;

- **Step B: Warming up the words of a unit** – a wide range of fun activities to select from in order to warm up the technical words of a unit in any subject;

- **Step C: Warming up the phrases of a unit** – ideas on how to warm up the phrases that will be central to coherently expressing whatever subject you teach;

- **Step D: Internalising the tune of exemplar text** – moving from the simple imitation of text to more sophisticated approaches to talking the text, learning from model examples;

- **Step E: Consolidating learning** – some end-of-unit suggestions for consolidating learning to embed the ongoing consolidation of learning throughout a unit.

This section will be useful to teachers of all subject areas because it is full of practical examples from across the curriculum and includes extracts from over 70 handouts. All of these handouts are available online and can be amended.

If you are the person leading literacy in your school, you first have to trial the approach in whatever subject you teach so that you understand it in practice before you begin to develop a whole-school approach. The wide range of flexible examples from across the curriculum will enable you to see how it can be adapted to suit all areas. This is essential if a whole-school approach is to be successfully implemented: teachers have to be able to see how it works in their subject if they are to be convinced that it is worth adapting their practice.

Handout 1 online is an overview of the 5 steps, while **Handout 1a** is useful for training days as it raises key questions to reflect on when using the approach. You may want to download these and make notes as you read.

Part 3 focuses on how to use Talk for Writing to achieve an effective whole-school approach that supports students in becoming powerful communicators across the curriculum because they can transfer skills learnt in one area to another. This section includes the structures you need to put place, how to run successful training, and how to embed the approach. The appendix is a maths case study on how the approach has been adapted in maths across an authority.

The power of the Talk-for-Writing approach lies in its ability to enthuse teachers and students alike across the curriculum. Teachers can see how it will help them to make their students powerful communicators of their subject and students can see how it supports their understanding and achievement:

- *"The Talk-for-Writing approach in modern language lessons has been inspirational. Not only does it make lessons far more exciting and engaging for both learners and teachers but it also greatly enhances performance in writing tasks."* – Juliet Park, Director of Languages Yewlands Academy, Sheffield (author, speaker, trainer)

- *"I was inspired by your Talk for writing presentation and have tried some of the ideas in my science lessons. I feel that it is a natural next step for us. If you are interested, I have video interviews with year 11 students who used the approach and found it enormously helpful."* – Matt Renshaw, science teacher, Lancashire

- *"There was something about the 'Talk for Writing' project that struck a chord with me. This was comparing maths to written communication in a direct and explicit way. It felt like an epiphany in the hall listening to Julia Strong explaining about Talk for Writing. This was the answer and, as I began to work with aspects of this approach, I started to feel as of this was the magic wand I had been looking for to move my students and me onwards to the land of written mathematical communication."* – Zeb Friedman, Maths adviser and teacher, Brighton and Hove

- *"In science, I know the whole process of photosynthesis as Miss Shabir modelled it to us. In my exam I am going use this to help me to revise."* – KS3 Science student, Yorkshire

- *"I enjoyed talking about the options and telling the class why some were good and some were bad. It helped me write a detailed answer that argued my case well."* – KS4 Geography student, Brighton

A note on terminology: The examples included come from schools in England and Wales but the approach could be adapted to suit the curriculum requirements of any country. I have tried to cut down the use of English-centric terminology but, for the sake of brevity, this jargon is sometimes used. For those unfamiliar with the English education system, Ofsted is the acronym given to the education inspection system, Ofqual oversees the examination system, while KS3 refers to the first 3 years of secondary school (Years 7,8 & 9) and KS4 (Years 10 & 11) to the two years that lead up to the formal exams called GCSEs.)

Before introducing the Talk-for-Writing approach, it's worth reflecting on why developing an effective approach to literacy across the curriculum has proved so hard.

Why being a school literacy coordinator is no easy task

Schools have been trying to coordinate literacy across the curriculum effectively since at least the Bullock Report of the mid-1970s, and it is ever-increasingly key to the demands of inspectors, but exactly how to do it remains challenging.

A seemingly ever-present problem is that pupils tend to go backwards when they transfer from primary to secondary: the writing advances they were making in Years 5 & 6 are often not built on and many complain that they are just doing things they have already done. As Ofsted's telling document *KS3 The Wasted Years* (2015) states:

"Inspectors found that **too many secondary schools did not work effectively with partner primary schools to understand pupils' prior learning and ensure that they built on this during Key Stage 3**. Worryingly, some secondary leaders simply accepted that pupils would repeat what they had already done in primary school during the early part of Key Stage 3, particularly in Year 7."

We need to build pupils' skills as writers and communicators not just across the curriculum in a simple coordinated way but from sector to sector. This is where Talk for Writing can help.

The elephant in the room is that forty-five years have passed since the Bullock Report, and literacy across the curriculum always appears in some guise or other in inspection requirements, but remarkably little progress has been made.

Since this book was first published there are, perhaps two really useful publications relating to it. One is from Ofsted, the government organisation responsible for inspecting schools in England, and the other is from the Education Endowment Foundation, an independent charity that aims to improve the educational attainment of the poorest pupils schools in England by providing evidence-based resources designed to improve practice and boost learning.

In January 2019, Ofsted published an overview of the research evidence underpinning its new inspection framework called *Education Inspection Framework – Overview of research*. This draws on a range of sources, including both their own research programme and a review of existing evidence bases and, as such, will be of significant interest to all school managers, not only those in England who are inspected within this framework.

Given the focus of this book, the most relevant part is section 1: *Quality of Education* which begins with four inspection grade criteria which very much emphasise the importance of having a broad curriculum that is not diminished by the pressures of high-stakes testing, alongside teaching the curriculum in such a way that the most disadvantaged can access it: sentiments that we would strongly endorse. This section of the overview provides an extremely useful insight into curriculum design, memory and retention, as well as teacher effectiveness and assessment. Not surprisingly, it reiterates the centrality of reading and vocabulary to educational success alongside the related research findings.

In July 2019, the Education Endowment Foundation's (EEF) published *Improving Literacy in Secondary Schools*. Like all its publications, all the points are well supported by research into what works. It provides a very useful outline of the steps secondary schools need to take to support literacy across the curriculum. In particular, it emphasises the importance of prioritising what it calls disciplinary literacy across the curriculum (in this book this is referred to as 'the tune' of subjects). Perhaps this lies at the heart of schools' fatigue with constant calls for literacy across the curriculum. Because the emphasis has always been on curriculum links we have failed to see that the cure lies in recognising how improving literacy begins at home – teachers need to focus on the literacy that underpins the particular subject they are teaching and then see how this can be joined together coherently, as Talk for Writing advocates.

This, perhaps, answers the question of why the literacy co-ordinators job is so challenging. Because secondary teachers haven't been helped to see that their subject has its own literacy requirements, they don't see it as part of their job. I've never met a teacher who didn't think literacy was important but I've met an awful lot who think it is someone else's job and in secondary schools that someone is the English department.

At the heart of the problem is the fact that many, possibly most, secondary teachers are much better at teaching the facts and skills related to their subject than how to express that knowledge effectively. Some are frank and admit this: 'In all honesty, I hadn't really thought about how the students were going to express their ideas before . . . It's the way the approach engages disaffected pupils that makes it so successful' (Science teacher from the Brighton & Hove Talk-for-Writing pilot). Such dislocated thinking was perhaps exacerbated because the National Literacy Strategy separated teaching and learning from literacy across the curriculum; in reality, they are inseparable. The more you consider the key elements that underpin effective teaching and learning, the more you realise that they are exactly the same as those that underpin literacy across the curriculum.

Moreover, because many teachers don't know how to make literacy across the curriculum work in practice in their subject, made worse by the fact that many attempts at implementing it have been far too English focused, there is an understandable air of resentment. Teachers have often been pressured into doing things that aren't relevant to their subject, such as being handed writing mats to display on all work surfaces that only focus on the language of creative writing, or management declaring extended writing weeks for all subjects. Although lengthy extended writing is a significant feature of the English curriculum, it is not a feature of most curriculum areas. I have tried to listen carefully to the reading, writing, and speaking requirements of each subject area and have adapted this approach accordingly. As one teacher commented on the evaluation sheet after a day's training on Talk for Writing: 'At last, a literacy consultant who really understands the phrase "Across the curriculum" rather than trying to make us all English teachers'.

Finally, an often side-stepped reason why a focus on literacy is not always flavour of the month is that many teachers are insecure as to how best to express themselves in writing. If you have been the teacher in charge of checking the quality of reports written by teachers, you will know what I mean. Perhaps because of this insecurity, we often set students writing tasks that we don't try to write ourselves. As soon as you try writing the tasks yourself, you become acutely aware of the difficulties involved; it can make you realize that far more support needs to be offered to the students. Nobody likes facing such truths and, if we are not careful, the literacy coordinator can be seen as the enemy. You only have to check the body language on a whole-school training day on literacy to know that this is true.

An overview of Talk for Writing and why it is the key ingredient

I first started running conferences on literacy across the curriculum in 1997 and have provided more school training on it than I care to recall. Throughout, I have tried to gather as many good ideas as possible and incorporate them into a coherent approach to achieving literacy across the curriculum that could really made a difference to student achievement. For many years now, I have been aware that in secondary schools it's all about achieving a coordinated approach while at the same time making the approach flexible enough to be relevant to the subject that each teacher teaches – in essence, it's all about helping the teachers help the students to express the tune of their subject. The one approach that has really made it all come together into a coherent whole is Pie Corbett's 'Talk for Writing' because it pulls together the essence of how children learn within a motivating and engaging framework.

Educationalist James Britton famously said: 'Reading and writing float on a sea of talk.' Pie Corbett expresses it similarly: 'You cannot write it if you cannot say it; you cannot say it if you haven't heard it.' It is worth reflecting on the significance of this to our teaching practice. How central is focused talk to how subjects are taught within your school? What opportunities are there for the students to hear exemplar text, of the sort we hope they will come to be able to write themselves, read aloud?

Talk for Writing is all about teaching in such a way that the students are helped to tune into the language of whatever subject is being taught. It provides a pattern for students to imitate, and then innovate on in a variety of ways so that they internalise it and are able to apply it independently.

This is achieved by well-planned interactive tasks that step by step help students internalise the pattern of language of the subject (see **Handout 1**). These focused-talk activities are related to exemplar text, which helps the students generate the sentence patterns that are key to the subject so that they can express themselves coherently. Students are first involved in imitating the text before being shown how to innovate on the pattern so that they can achieve their own version. With practice, they fully internalise the approach so that they can write independently in the style required. This helps students not only to express their knowledge more clearly, thereby gaining higher marks in tests, but also to engage more with their learning and thus become more effective, confident learners.

Originally devised by Pie Corbett, with myself employed as critical friend, Talk for Writing was first developed for primary schools, where it has been shown to at least double the rate of pupil progress. In schools in challenging circumstances, where it has been applied systematically, the proportion of children attaining the expected levels at the end of primary school has increased from around 30% to well over 90%. With the help of a range of authorities, schools, and teachers, I have adapted it to meet the needs of the secondary curriculum and the approach has been enthusiastically taken up within the secondary sector.

Sometimes, in our attempts to help, we make things too complex. It is often the most simple of things that are the most effective. There are six key non-fiction text types. These quite rightly formed the basis of the approach to text adopted by the National Literacy Strategy when it was introduced in 1998 and primary teachers found them very helpful. As part of teaching text type, teachers were shown how always to help children think about the audience and purpose of any piece of writing before attempting to structure it, since it is the audience and purpose that dictate form. In some ways, each text type has a different structure and it is possible to construct skeletons reflecting the different shape of all the text types and their varied hybrids. (For a useful handout outlining the typical ingredients of the key non-fiction text types, see **Handout 2** online.) But looked at from another angle, all writing, whatever it is, has the same simple structure:

- a beginning
- a middle
- an end.

So rather than thinking about what separates the text types, we retained the Strategy emphasis on audience and purpose creating form, but increasingly concentrated on what features the different text types had in common and how this could be built on across the curriculum, as illustrated below.

Grid showing what features the six key non-fiction text types have in common

	Instruction	Recount	Explanation	Information	Persuasion	Discussion
Typical structure	chronological	chronological	chronological/ logical	logical	logic of emotion	logical
		topic sentences	topic sentences	topic sentences	topic sentences sometimes	topic sentences
	headings		headings	headings		
Typical language features	impersonal	impersonal/ personal	impersonal	impersonal	personal	impersonal
	time connectives	time connectives	causal connectives	causal & time connectives	emotive connectives	causal, time, & comparing connectives
		descriptive	description to illustrate	description to illustrate	description to promote	description to illustrate

This realisation led to Pie Corbett moving away from the text skeletons that had developed from the literacy hour to suggesting that you could box up any text using a very basic grid, and then analyse the text to co-construct a toolkit. Each text type will have different ingredients in its toolkit, as illustrated throughout this handbook.

If you box up any typical explanation text for, say, science, history or English, in its most simple form it would look as follows:

Boxed-up grid for explanation text

Beginning	• Introduce what is being explained • Include a hook to interest your reader
Middle	• Put key points in paragraphs in logical order • Link points clearly so the reader can see how one thing leads to another • Include detail where necessary to make explanation clear
End	• Include technical terms and explain if necessary • Conclude your explanation by rounding it off logically in a memorable way

Boxing up allows you to understand the structure of any type of text and to use similar ingredients to help you structure a similar text. This approach underpins the Talk-for- Writing approach, and it's very simplicity has made it easy for students to grasp and apply to any writing task in any subject, so that they can plan their writing right across the curriculum.

The Talk-for-Writing process

One of the best ways to understand the essence of Talk for Writing is to look at the initial Talking-the-text-type pilot. (Watch video clip **Part 1.i** online to illustrate this process.)

Before the project, pupils were asked to score their attitude to writing. This is one Year 3 boy's response:

- Do you like writing? – '*1/10. Because it isn't fun*'

- What is hard about writing? – '*I am not good at writing*'

- Are you a good writer? How do you know? – '*No, because I am not good at sbeling*'

However, by the end of the pilot, the same boy answered very differently:

- Do you like writing? – '*10/10. Because it is cool*'

- What is hard about writing? – '*nuffing*'

- Are you a good writer? – '*YES*'

The key difference is that the boy now feels positive about writing because he has experienced success. This new-found confidence, based on being provided with well-planned steps to move his learning forward should, if continued systematically, enable him to fulfil his potential and become a successful communicator. So what did the teacher do to cause this transformation? The Year 1 samples from the pilot below hold the key.

Following an engaging lesson in which a woman with a real bat had talked to the 5-year-old children about bats, the class was asked to write down what they now knew about bats. All the focus had been on providing interesting content to write about without any support for how to express it. One girl, whose writing was progressing well, wrote:

> Bats Han up side down.
> Bats like new homes.
> Bats like to eat inses.

This provided the 'cold text' baseline from which to measure progress because it established what the child at this stage could do. You can see that she can write in simple sentences, remembering to begin with a capital letter and end with a full stop while leaving a space between each word. But, after she had been taught Talk-for- Writing style for 3 weeks, she could write like this:

Hedgehog Facs.

> Hedgehogs are not pets.
>   What are they like. They hav e sharp spins on ther bakes but undernif they are soft.
>   What do they eat? They eat slipuriy slugs crushey bittls tickley spids and juciy catppl. They like frat too. They gring wort. Badgers are the alle anmls that eat hedgehogs.
>   Did you now. Hedgehogs are nkctnl that mens they come out at nit. Hedgehogs hibnat that mens they sleep in the winter. Their nest is called a hibnacl. Ther babys are coled hogllos.
>   And . . . they can sime!

Now when you analyse her writing skills, you can see that she not only knows how to structure her writing into logical paragraphs but she also knows how to engage her reader with a hook at the beginning and an interesting ending. She knows how to use rhetorical questions to introduce her ideas and to add touches of description to make it interesting. In addition, if she uses a difficult technical word, she knows she should explain it to her reader. And, because she has not been afraid to use challenging vocabulary, she has used words that she cannot spell.

The three stages of the Talk-for-Writing approach: moving from imitation to innovation to independent application

So what had the teacher done? She had achieved this progress by following the three stages of Talk for Writing to provide a language template for the child to build on. Watch the video clip **Part 1.ii** to illustrate this progress.

Stage 1. Imitation

First, the class had imitated (learnt out loud) an exemplar text which they had not seen but which the teacher had orally presented to them using a text map, like the one on the next page, and movements to help them recall the words, as illustrated below.

![Foundation stage children talking the text]

Foundation stage children talking the text

Text map for Fox Facts

The text would have been similar in structure to the one the child finally wrote, because it is the work she had done around this exemplar text that enabled her to make such progress.

Once the class had internalised the text and could repeat it word for word along with the related actions to help them remember the text, the teacher would then have shown them the text on screen. And, of course, all the children could now read the text easily because they were already familiar with the pattern of the language:

Fox Facts

Foxes are not pets.

What are they like? They are elegant dog-like creatures with sharp noses, bushy tails and reddish-brown fur . . .

What do they eat? They eat small furry animals, feathery birds and they are very fond of tasty plump chickens too. But they also eat squiggly insects and juicy berries.

Did you know that foxes are nocturnal? That means they come out at night. Foxes are famous for being cunning and pouncing on their prey. Their homes are called dens. Their babies are called cubs.

And they can swim!

Then, using a flip chart so the children could see the text on screen and the planning as it developed, the teacher would have shown them how to box the text up by involving them in analysing the text. For example, she would have asked them what the topic of each paragraph was and then written these headings down the left-hand side of the grid as illustrated below. The class would have ended up with something like the

Boxed-up colour-coded text to illustrate structure and key features

Beginning: Start with a striking **introduction** to hook your audience	Foxes are not pets.
Middle: paragraphs in logical order • **appearance**	What are they like? They are elegant dog-like creatures with sharp narrow noses, bushy tails and usually have reddish-brown fur.
• **diet**	What do they eat? They eat small furry animals, feathery birds and they are very fond of tasty plump chickens too. But they also eat squiggly insects and juicy berries.
• **habits**	Did you know that foxes are *nocturnal*? That means they come out at night. Foxes are famous for being cunning and pouncing on their prey. Their homes are called *dens*. Their babies are called *cubs*.
End: Conclude with an interesting **ending**	And they can swim!

Start a new paragraph for each idea and put them in a sensible order

Turn the topic of the paragraph into a question to interest the reader

Use detail to help reader picture what you are describing

Use connectives to join your ideas

Explain difficult words

Useful phrases for information writing

left-hand column on the flip chart. The full text would have been on the screen and the class would have been involved in colour coding it so they understood the different ingredients. The related annotations would probably just have been spoken, discussed with the children and turned into the toolkit to guide this type of writing, or they may have been added to the text on screen.

Helping the children consolidate what they have learnt is key to learning (see page 198). Toolkits are central to this embedding of learning – drawing out the essence of the features that contribute to making the writing effective. But they must be co- constructed. Just handing students lists of success criteria serves little purpose, as they have to have been involved in developing the list and understand the significance of the ingredients, to enable them to use them effectively.

Since the teacher is teaching 5-year-olds, she probably would have co-constructed a very simple writing toolkit to support them when writing information text based on their colour-coded exemplar text. The toolkit for older children would look something like this.

The information writing toolkit

Think about including the following ingredients:

Plan it: order the information logically	• Box up information logically inparagraphs • Introduce topic clearly with a hook to engage reader • Round information off with interesting conclusion
Link it: make it fit together well	• Begin each paragraph with a topic sentence to introduce it • Link points clearly using connectives, sentence signposts or pronouns • Read your writing through to check that it flows
Express it: make it clear and interesting	• Choose effective phrases to help the reader understand • Use detail to illustrate yourpoints • Vary sentence lengths to keep itinteresting • Use technical language appropriately and explain if necessary
Check it:	• Read it through, check for accuracy and improve it • Make certain your spelling and grammar are correct • Make certain it informs the reader in an interesting and engaging way

Stage 2. Innovation

Once the children had internalised the text and analysed it, they were shown how to innovate on the text through shared writing. So the teacher would have chosen another animal and, with the colour-coded fox text still on screen to show what they are innovating on, would have involved the class in writing a different version on another animal, for example a badger. Her shared writing would probably have begun like this:

Badger Facts

Badgers are not pets.

What are they like? They have long bodies but little short legs and their fur is mainly black with distinctive white-striped heads . . .

As you can see, the teacher is using the model as a basis for the new piece of writing and would have involved the children in constructing the writing saying things like:

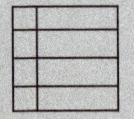

- Turn to your partner and . . ./ finish that sentence off

- Which do you think would work?

- In your pairs – quick . . ./ add a little more information.

- Let's just read that and see how it sounds.

- It's going to be much more powerful if . . .

(For more examples of useful phrases to use for shared writing, see **Handout 3 online**.)

Shared writing is absolutely key for students if they are to understand the writing process and, hopefully, this is something that is already a part of regular practice in English lessons and can be strengthened further to support this approach. If shared writing is well done by the English department, then the other departments will be able to build on this foundation and hopefully do a little shared writing themselves following some in-school training (see page 221).

Could use a flip chart?

As the shared writing was progressing, the teacher, or teaching assistant, would have been flagging up useful words and phrases and displaying them. An excellent resource for doing this is to use a washing line as your 'writing wall', as illustrated below and explained on pages 23–24. Also see the short clip at the end of the introduction on the video.

If all the useful words and phrases generated by the shared writing are displayed, then when the children have a chance to write their own version, there will be lots of visual help to support them.

The picture opposite shows Pie Corbett illustrating shared writing at the innovation stage. You can see that the exemplar text is on screen: he is using it as the model on which to base his new version. On the washing line is the toolkit and the boxed up planning.

The teaching assistant (out of shot) is flip-charting all the good alternative vocabulary that the class suggests to support them when they write their own version.

One very useful tip about spelling for anyone writing on the flip chart (and for the students when they are writing in their books) is that as soon as you are unsure how to spell a word, just have a go and put a dotted line beneath the word (just like your computer does to signal a wrong spelling). It is vital that students do not only write down words that they think they can spell because this

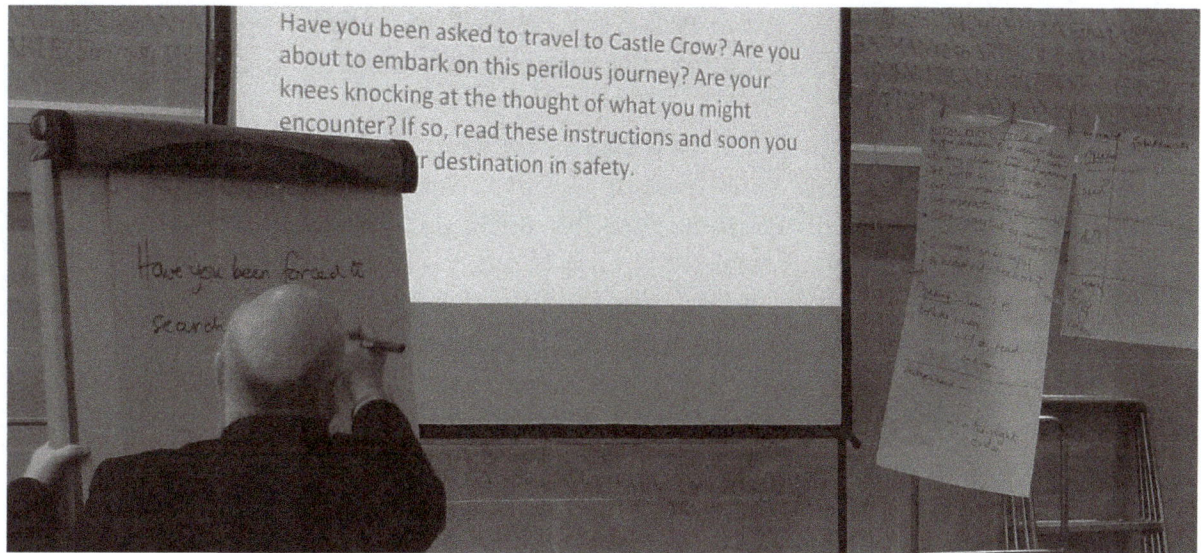

Pie demonstrating shared writing

will seriously limit their vocabulary. This method frees up the writer to select the best words – if you constantly break off from writing to check spelling, you break the flow of the writing. At the proofreading stage, the spelling can be checked. Throughout the process, the teacher would have regularly read the writing out to the class so they could hear it and decide if it works. All the time she would have been modelling what a good writer does.

Once the shared writing had been completed, the children would then have had a go at doing their own information piece on badgers using the shared writing and planning toolkit to help them know what to do and the words and phrases displayed to help them select the best language.

Once they had had time to write, the children would have been asked to share their versions with a partner and together they could have read through the writing and decided what worked well and what might need improving. The author would then have made the changes they wanted to make.

The teacher would have taken in the work and marked it, using this as a key opportunity for formative assessment to decide on what aspects of the work would need more focus if the children were to succeed in this type of writing. The writing toolkit can provide a very useful tick list here to check if all the students are managing to include appropriate ingredients effectively and, if not, what needs to be done to help them to take the next steps in improving their work.

Stage 3. Independent application

When the work is handed back, this is the best opportunity to work on those aspects that need attention. A visualiser, or any other thing that enables you to put text up on screen instantly, is an invaluable asset here, as you can display work that you want the students to see and use this as an opportunity to discuss what works well. Again, ensure that the students have an immediate opportunity to polish their work and put the improvements suggested into practice, otherwise time spent marking will be time wasted. Depending on how well the students have managed the task, you may be able to move immediately to the independent application stage.

In this example, the children would have researched an animal of their choice on the internet using a few selected simple sites suitable for young children so they could gather some information related to the paragraph headings, and then they would have had a go at writing their own version. By this stage they would have internalised the pattern of language required, so that all their focus could be on how to make their writing informative and engaging. In this way, using a series of focused supportive teaching steps, the 5-year-old girl's ability to communicate has been transformed. Below is a useful overview of the three-stage process that underlies the Talk-for-Writing approach with the key features highlighted.

Handout 4b: An overview of the Talk-for-Writing teaching process

(also available online)

Imitation stage	Class will have been introduced to language and phrases of topic through **warming up words/phrases** activities.
	a. Initially class not shown text but rather **learn text together orally** supported
	  – aurally by hearing the text presented by teacher
	  – visually by the **text map** and
	  – kinaesthetically by the movements to act out the meaning.
	b. Class shown text and **analyse text together** by
	  – **boxing it up** to show structure
	  – **highlighting text** to bring out key features and creating posters of key phrases.
	c. Class use this understanding to **co-construct the toolkit** for this type of writing.

Innovation stage	Teacher may use more **warming-up words/phrases** activities to help students internalise the language of the unit and expand the range of language they can use. • Using original text, planning, posters and co- constructed toolkit to visually support learning, the teacher then demonstrates through **shared planning** and **shared writing** how to innovate on the text to write a similar piece of writing about a related topic. • The students write their own version before sharing it with a partner, discussing how to improve it using the toolkit to support them. Student writes comment on their work saying how well they have completed the task.

	• Teacher takes in work and decides which aspects need strengthening and focuses on these when the work is handed back, so class has to improve their work immediately in the light of what they have just been shown.
Independent application stage	• Using exemplar text, planning, posters and co- constructed toolkit to visually support learning, the students then apply what they have learnt to a similar piece of writing. • Over time they will be able to write this sort of writing without any of the visual aids because they will have internalised the toolkit in their heads.

If the English department reinforces students' understanding of the different text types in this manner, then all departments will be able to build on this approach and adapt it to suit the particular tune of their subject. A very useful book for the English department when teaching Year 7 is *Talk for Writing Across the Curriculum – How to Teach Non-fiction Writing 5–12 Years* by Pie Corbett and myself, which includes fully worked units for each key non-fiction text type. In the words of one head of English in Essex, it is 'Fantastic!'. Encouragingly, Shirley Clarke, the leading expert on putting formative assessment into practice, has commented: '*This book will become the bible for knowing how to teach and transform non-fiction writing . . . with the combined talents of Pie Corbett and Julia Strong it was always going to be good – but it is no less than brilliant.*' It sold more than 10,000 copies in its first year, so somebody must like it!

A book which complements *Talk for Writing in Secondary Schools* is *Transforming Learning Across the Curriculum* (2020) by Pie Corbett and Julia Strong which includes 18 chapters written by practising teachers from Y5 to A-level showing how the Talk for Writing process has significantly enhanced teaching and learning in their subjects.

In secondary schools, the best way to implement the approach across the curriculum is to think about the type of writing that students will be required to do for GCSE in a subject and then build up these skills whenever possible through KS3 units so that by the time the students reach Year 10, they are ready to become effective communicators of each subject. Moreover, by applying a systematic approach towards helping students understand the type of writing that is required, students can easily transfer their learning from one subject to another.

2 Laying the foundations

(This chapter is supported by **Handouts 2a & 2b**, slides **3–11**, and film clips **from Part I** online. Suggestions for how to present this material on a training session are given on page 214.)

For any whole-school approach to literacy to be effective some key foundations need to be in place. This chapter provides a brief overview of these. It begins by summarising how research shows that formative assessment is at the heart of effective teaching. Then, since interaction is key to formative assessment, the next section suggests ways of setting up classrooms to aid interactivity. Reading provides students with a rich source of language as well as information, so the third section summarises the importance of building a school community that reads. The final section focuses on the importance of exemplar text and why developing teachers' understanding of this matters. Exemplar text underpins Talk for Writing.

1: Putting formative assessment at the heart of teaching

Education research is absolute in its findings that formative assessment is key to effective teaching and learning. Professor John Hattie of Auckland University spent more than 15 years analysing education research covering more than 80 million students in 50,000 studies. What emerged is that raising the quality of pupil–teacher interaction is central to effective learning and he identified the following key elements:

- **Teacher clarity** – being explicit about what to do

- Setting work that is **one step ahead** of the current level

- **Pupils assessing themselves** by reaching a view on their levels of understanding

- **Teacher credibility** – the students' perception that the teacher can enhance their learning

- Using **formative assessment** to decide next steps

- **Reciprocal teaching** – pupils take turns in teaching class

(John Hattie's *Visible Learning* published by Routledge, 2009)

These interactive elements are the key features of formative assessment. They also underpin the Talk-for-Writing approach so that formative assessment is at the heart of the process. It is all about first motivating the students to want to learn, then breaking down learning into small steps and co-constructing the learning with the students to embed what they have learnt while using assessment to guide the next piece of teaching. In this way, the students move confidently from imitation to independent application, because they have been fully involved in their learning.

Two invaluable, short and easy-to-comprehend books which illustrate how to make formative assessment work in secondary schools are Shirley Clarke's *Formative Assessment in the Secondary Classroom* (Hodder Murray, 2005), which introduces the basics of the concept very clearly, and *Active Learning through Formative Assessment* (Hodder Education, 2008), which is a more sophisticated application of the approach.

The importance of flexible planning

Some schools have been sucked into a culture of over-planning at the expense of formative assessment. Not only can this completely take over the lives of teachers and drive some out of the profession, it can also curb students' progress.

Children get in the way of your planning. It is only when you teach a group that you can judge how quickly you can move on or how much you need to slow down to make certain the foundations are in place. Your planning has to be flexible so that you can respond to the needs of the class – this is what formative assessment is all about. Each time you teach a lesson and when you are marking books you are working out what needs to be focused on next; in this way formative assessment guides your planning. Any other approach is counterproductive, as recent Ofsted overviews have emphasised.

2: Ensuring classrooms are set up to facilitate real interaction

(Watch the video clip at the end of **Part 1. Introduction** to illustrate this process.)

Since interaction is the key to successful learning, it is worth reflecting on our teaching styles and how our rooms are set up. Research tells us that the most effective ingredients to maximise learning involve the students in

- practising by doing

- explaining to others

- focused discussion.

(See pages 210–11 for a useful training day activity on this.)

The Talk-for-Writing approach is based on these ingredients: the more that classrooms are set up to facilitate this sort of interaction, the easier it will be for the students to make progress. Interestingly, many classrooms are still set up as if an exam were about to take place with serried ranks of tables facing the front. Such a set-up emphasises the notion that all communication revolves around the teacher and encourages a tennis match style of questioning, rather than encouraging group discussion. To facilitate interaction, we need to arrange our classrooms to

(a)   maximise sight-lines so that all students have a good view of the white-board and can interact with the teacher;

(b)   facilitate easy interaction between the students while minimising disruption.

The best way to check sight-lines is to stand in front of the screen, hold your arms out at 45° and then any tables to the front far right or left that are outside of your arms will need to be moved if at all possible. The front far right or left will be the worst place to sit in a classroom because you can't see what is going on without turning sideways.

Research has shown that the best way to facilitate interaction is to rearrange the tables into L shapes radiating out in front of the screen as the centre of vision, with no table outside of the sight-lines. It is then easy to seat four students at each L shape. Such a shape makes it practical for students to work independently, in pairs or as a group of four and it is easy for the teacher to support the group.

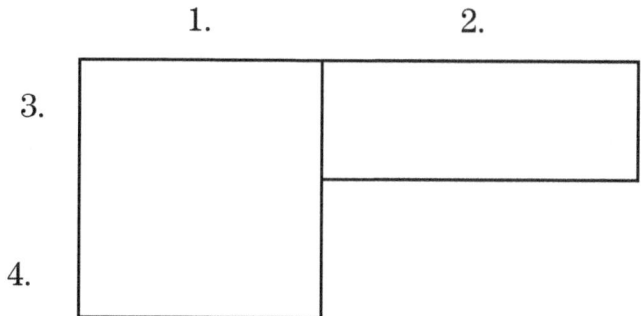

A whiteboard is a great piece of equipment for demonstrations and showing film clips but it is not interactive, despite its name. Students need to be involved in focused-talk activities in pairs and small groups to help them use the language and become familiar with the phrases they will have to present or write. Moreover, you often need to display several things at once when modelling text for a class. So, alongside the whiteboard it is best to have a flip chart to enable you to flag up the key learning points effectively. You can now get wipe-clean flip charts (just ask Google).

The key thing is to be able to display your flip charts easily. An excellent cheap way of doing this is to set up a washing line at the front of the classroom, preferably to the left of the board as brain research tells us that we remember best when we look up and left! Then the students can see the whiteboard, the flip chart with the structure of the text boxed up and the resulting key ingredients of the text displayed on the washing line at the same time. When discussing and later writing, they will then be well supported by the ingredients to include. Try the washing-line approach and you will wonder how you managed without one all these years.

Pie teaching a class in front of an audience of teachers. A pupil is talking about what he has written. The class teacher, like Pie, uses a whiteboard, a flip chart and a washing line

A visualiser, or any other piece of equipment that enables you to immediately put up on screen examples of work the students have just completed, is an excellent way to facilitate formative assessment through embedding learning, as the students can see examples of 'what = good', discuss them, analyse them, learn from them and steal ideas for future use.

Partner work will be key to the focused talk that underpins thinking, so it is useful to establish, through discussion, rules that will help paired and group discussion work. It's a good idea to break away from the 'hands up' approach to answering questions and use the 'think, pair, share' approach instead so that all students have a chance to reflect on the questions and discuss the issues with a partner or group before anyone answers in front of the whole class. It's also a good idea to vary the students' partners so that they have to explain things to a different person. A useful piece of software for this is available at www.superteachertools.com/, which provides group and random name generators. Somehow the fact that the computer has sorted the groups makes it easier for the students to accept.

3: Laying the foundations – building a school community that reads

Anyone who is good at writing will have been helped by the quality of the text that they have read. Reading is a great way to extend vocabulary; but it also helps us to extend and vary the pattern of language that we use. And, of course, it allows you independently to access all the information, ideas and stories that mankind has accumulated and refined across the centuries. Every student should leave school not only being able to read well but loving reading, so that they will continue to extend their knowledge and interests throughout their life.

I could write a handbook on the importance of building a school community that reads and how to set about doing it but fortunately I don't need to do so, as all the information is available from the National Literacy Trust (NLT) website.

As a result of the first National Year of Reading in 1998–99, the NLT received government funding which enabled it to develop Reading Connects and Reading Champions. Reading Connects pulled together all the great ideas from schools on how to get the whole school reading; Reading Champions focused on getting the boys on board. The funding has now dried up but all the resources are still accessible. So it's well worth looking at these ideas and then getting together a small group of enthusiasts to get the whole school reading. If we want to turn our students into avid readers, then all the staff will need to be involved in promoting reading. Very soon your pool of adult enthusiasts can recruit an army of students to help you with the task. The Reading Connects secondary handbook can be downloaded from http://www.literacytrust.org.uk/resources/ practical_resources_info/360_reading_connects_secondary_school_handbook, and more related material can be accessed at http://www.literacytrust.org.uk/ schools_teaching. If you are particularly concerned about involving boys, then Reading Champions, which was developed in the same way by the NLT, is just what you need. Visit http://www.literacytrust.org.uk/reading_champions. A useful resource from Ofsted is 'Good practice resource – Literacy across the curriculum: Aston Manor Academy' (http://www.ofsted.gov.uk/resources/good-practice-resource-literacy-across-curriculum-aston-manor-academy). Among other useful aspects, this illustrates how one school has built a reading community.

4: Establishing why exemplar text matters

Below is a list of typical writing tasks faced by a 15/16-year-old student around exam time (**Slide 10**):

Science: Investigate the factors that will increase the rate of a chemical reaction.	**History**: Why did more and more Americans begin to turn against the Vietnam War?
Geography: What traffic management scheme would best suit this city?	**Art**: Compare the work of two artists that have impressed you.
English Literature: 'Lady Macbeth was the driving force behind the murder of Duncan.' Do you agree?	**Maths**: Describe the 'magic square' process, highlighting appropriate methods used.
Design & Technology: How did your solution fulfil the original brief?	**Physical Education**: Devise and evaluate a fitness programme.
English Language: Summarise the information given about how tornadoes are formed, their general characteristics and their effects.	**Religious Education**: 'We should not feed the hungry.' Discuss, showing that you have considered more than one viewpoint.
Drama: Evaluate your performance work.	**Music** (listening test): Explain how the composer describes a train journey.

If you think about the very wide range of different text types involved, it becomes clear that we need to support students in developing their writing skills in a coherent manner so that they can transfer what they learn in English, for example, about how to write explanation, to science. This can be achieved if all teachers in a school build up their units to illustrate and exemplify the features of exemplar text as appropriate to the subject they are teaching. In this way, students will be helped to internalise a number of flexible writing toolkits in their heads, which will enable them to apply themselves confidently to any writing task. And, of course, it will also help them become fluent readers because prior knowledge (familiarity with the pattern of the language) is key to becoming a good reader once you have grasped the basics of phonics.

Exemplar text is the key to students understanding what they are trying to do. It is therefore essential that every subject helps students to analyse the type of text their subject requires and teaches all the stages needed to help the students imitate and then independently access and write this type of text. It is no good teachers thinking that the English department will cover all this for them, as the exact tune of each subject, the technical language used and the way the concepts are specifically expressed will not be covered in English, as this sentence from a science exemplar illustrates: 'Trypsin is a large globular protein molecule consisting of two polypeptide chains held together by three types of bonds: Hydrogen, Ionic, and Disulphide.' You don't learn how to write a sentence like that in an English lesson!

A useful starting point for a literacy coordinator is to work out just what sort of writing is required by each subject in your school. The following list was produced by teachers at Chenderit School, Oxfordshire:

- **Art:** Analysis and evaluation of images

- **Business studies:** Select material appropriate to purpose; understand and evaluate text

- **Drama:** Read scripts and work with text; analyse writer's intention; evaluate and compare texts

- **Technology:** Coursework: understand task set; analysis; comparison

- **Humanities:** Analysis of data and sources; how to answer question backed up by evidence; describe and explain

- **ICT Computing:** Describe abstract concepts; clarity about features needed to solve problems

- **Maths:** Compare and contrast info from graphs; interpret data; solve problems showing how you reached your answer

- **Music:** Extract info quickly from question; form inferences from question; bullet point structured analysis and use key words effectively

- **French:** Understand grammar terminology; extended writing; imaginative writing; silent reading

- **PE:** Extended answers to questions; writing relevant, informative sentences

- **Science:** Read with interpretation; explain; form an opinion with evidence; compare information

- **SEN:** Understanding the language of questions

Exemplars for a wide range of these text types are provided within this resource with suggestions for how to involve the students in building up the toolkits that will help them write the texts successfully. It is also worth considering the idea of colour-coding the key underlying features of exemplar text across the curriculum.

Why consistently colour-coded exemplar text is useful

If exemplar text can be consistently presented so that where there are things in common, this commonality can be seen as the students move from subject to subject, then exemplar text becomes even more powerful. As explained on page 9, all written text has a lot of similarities. Although the different subjects will have different text requirements and these texts will make different demands on the reader and writer, anyone attempting to write a paragraph or a longer piece of text will need to do the following:

- Plan it – order points logically or chronologically, usually in paragraphs, with a beginning a middle and an end.

- Link it – usually through topic sentences and linking points clearly by using connectives, sentence signposts or pronouns appropriately.

- Express it – select appropriate words and phrases to make the text accurate and engaging, and explain technical terms; vary sentence lengths to keep the reader engaged.

As you can see, this approach does not focus on grammatical technicalities but rather on the underlying general features that make writing work; teachers and students alike can understand it! What will help students most is if there is not only exemplar text for every subject clearly illustrating 'what = good' for the type of text required, but also if the key generic features in common can be consistently colour coded. Best of all is when the students are involved in identifying these features and the colour-coded exemplar is jointly developed to confirm their understanding, as illustrated throughout this handbook.

The exemplar text below has been 'colour coded' to emphasise how it has been planned, linked and expressed. Because this book is printed in black and white, I have had to use shades of grey! Colour would be clearer. The PowerPoint slides on the online are colour-coded to illustrate this point.

'Colour-coded' exemplar text for music

> **GCSE music question: What *compositional devices* have you included which match the *compositional strand*? (6 marks)**
>
> The compositional devices I have used fall under the **strand** of the **Western classical tradition**. In section A, **complex harmony** has been used creating a **primary and secondary contrast** within **chordal** use. **Antiphonal parts** have been added which are passed within the **string section,** creating links to early **Bach Brandenburg Concertos**. The overall composition uses a **ternary structure** cementing links with **classical controlled structure.**
>
> (Exemplar text for GCSE music by Barrie McArdie, Queensbury School, Bradford)

(See **Handout 4b** online for examples of colour-coded exemplar text from a range of subjects).

From this point on, all exemplar text is 'colour coded' at some stage in each unit. The key to the coding in this book is shown in the right-hand column below.

Key for colour coding the key underlying features of exemplar text

Key feature	*Colour coding used online*	*How represented in this book*
Plan it	• **Headings in bold** • Topic sentences underlined	• **Headings in bold** • Topic sentences underlined
Link it	• Connectives and sentence signposts highlighted in shocking pink	• Connectives and sentence signposts highlighted in dark grey
Express it	• Useful phrases for this type of writing highlighted in green • Technical terms in blue	• Useful phrases for this type of writing highlighted in pale grey • ***Technical terms in bold italics***

This simple approach to thinking about text will help the students work out how to plan, link and express everything that they write. Obviously, there is a range of different features that some departments will want to focus on, for example, point – evidence – comment/explanation for subjects that require discursive writing. Departments can flag up such bespoke requirements in different colours but the key point is that a fixed set of colours is used to clarify understanding of the underlying general features. If you have ever shadowed what the day in the life of a secondary student is like in lessons, you will understand why this could be useful.

Katherine Mobberley, Assistant Headteacher at Chenderit School in Oxfordshire, which has been noted for the quality of its literacy teaching, focused on whether colour coding exemplar text actually did help students as part of an action research project she was involved with. As you can see from the quotes below, she was somewhat astounded by the difference it made:

- *'The effect of this was instantly amazing and therefore I used a similar method with my Year 7 who were writing a report on the uses of ICT in society.'*

- *'The results with all three classes astonished me. I had expected improvements, but not on the scale seen.'*

- *'The Year 13 class had produced a similar evaluation a few months previously without the support. Five out of the six students had found this section particularly difficult, and three of the six had not submitted the work by the deadline, because they found it very difficult. The average mark for the class was 3/9. By the time this project was undertaken, five students were continuing with the course. Within 24 hours of completing discussing the colour-coded exemplars, all five students had submitted their work and the average mark for the class was 6.8/9, with two students gaining 8/9. As a result of this, the students were motivated to return to their previous piece of coursework which had not yet been submitted and were able to significantly improve their overall mark.'*

Hopefully, every department in your school will start colour-coding exemplar text in a consistent manner to help the students transfer their learning from one curriculum area to another. The more consistency there is in the way a school supports students in developing their writing skills across the curriculum, the more chance there is of students being able to develop effective writing skills.

Once students have been shown exemplar text, they can be shown how to analyse its structure and key features by 'boxing it up', as illustrated by the information text on foxes on page 14.

Again it is hoped that all teachers will help students analyse the exemplar text in this manner so the students can see easily how text is structured. As the text is analysed, its key features can be colour coded and turned into a toolkit for writing this sort of text, as illustrated on page 15 and throughout this handbook. The more the students are involved in building up these toolkits, rather than having them presented to them Blue-Peter style fully formed, the more they will understand them. The skills that lie behind each type of writing can be built up in this manner throughout KS3 so that the students will have co-constructed these toolkits and internalized them in their heads. Therefore, when asked to produce a certain sort of writing, they will know what to do and should be able to do it effectively.

The content of the text will obviously change depending on the topic focused on and the audience it is pitched at but the underlying expressions and linking phrases will often reappear. It is these key phrases that represent the underlying 'tune' of the subject that the students need to become familiar with if they are to be able to express their knowledge effectively. Therefore, these phrases need to be built up progressively in the opening years of secondary school. Throughout this book, how to pull out these phrases into posters to support the students is illustrated.

Part 2

The five steps to adapting units of work to the Talk-for-Writing approach

Part 2 focuses on how to adapt units of work in any subject to the Talk-for-Writing approach using the following five steps:

 Step A: Creating exemplar text that builds in progression – some hints on how to get the best exemplar text for each subject;

 Step B: Warming up the words of a unit – focusing on a wide range of fun activities to select from in order to warm up the technical words of a unit in any subject

 Step C: Warming up the phrases of a unit – ideas on how to warm up the phrases that will be central to coherently expressing whatever subject you teach.

 Step D: Internalizing the tune of exemplar text – moving from the simple imitation of text to more sophisticated approaches to talking the text, learning from model examples;

 Step E: Consolidating learning to build in progress – some end-of-unit suggestions for consolidating learning to embed the ongoing consolidation of learning throughout a unit.

There is a wide range of suggestions in each section illustrated by subjects from across the curriculum, so that hopefully all teachers will find something that makes sense to them.

CHAPTER 3

Step A: Creating exemplar text that builds in progression

(This chapter is supported by **Handouts 4c, 4d & 5**, **Slides 22–28**, and the video clip from **Part 2: Step A**. Suggestions for how to present this step on a training session are given on page 215. It is a good idea to read pages 25–29 before reading this chapter)

It is vital that progression is built into unit planning both for the content of a subject and how that content is expressed. A good way to ensure the latter when establishing the Talk-for-Writing approach in any subject is to consider the type of text that is required of A* students in that subject at GCSE and teach progressively towards helping the students express themselves similarly (see page 152–61 for an example of this approach for science). If possible, it is best if this understanding can be shared within each department so that everyone in each area is agreed on the type of writing they are ultimately looking for and progression can be planned in across the years. Then they can start collectively adapting the units for each year to build up these skills if the units don't already do this sufficiently.

The requirements of each subject are very different. Some, like English and the humanities subjects, require extended writing, often of a discursive nature, but most of the other subject areas do not. Some of the practical subjects don't really require any writing in the opening years of secondary school, but what all subjects do require is for students to be able to orally explain coherently what they are learning. Once you are clear about the direction in which you want the expression to develop, it is much easier to develop your units across the years to build up these skills.

Devising exemplar text to build in progression within each unit

For any unit of work, it is a good idea to begin by establishing what the exemplar text for the main written aspect of the unit would look like given the intended audience, in order to ensure that the unit builds up the tune of this text. If the unit does not require writing, then focus on the oral expression that you want the unit to develop to raise the level of the students' understanding and their ability to communicate in your subject (see PE example below). In this way, all students will develop their communication skills and, when writing is required, they will be able to write relatively easily because the pattern of language will be in their head.

PE example of using exemplar oral text to support learning at KS3

- Show two-minute clip of gymnastics routine

- Ask the students to discuss

Box up the students' responses under the following headings:

Good points		
Not so good points		
How performance could be improved		

- Model for the students how to present these points

- Ask the students to rehearse their version in pairs

- Ask a budding gym coach to present to class

(Developed by Chris Sergeant, PE teacher, Pendlevale College, Nelson, Lancashire)

You may be able to find an exemplar text from a textbook but you will probably have to write it/adapt it yourself. Make certain it contains good examples of all the language features you want to focus on, for example:

- **a clear logical structure**

- <u>well-expressed topic sentences</u>

- helpful sentence signposts and connectives guiding the reader through the text

- useful phrases that help make the topic clear

- *appropriate **technical language**, explained if necessary.*

(See **Handout 4** online for a range of exemplar text at A* GCSE level. In addition, Chapters 6 and 7 include a wide variety of exemplar texts for different subjects.)

As part of your whole-school approach, it would be very useful to set up an exemplar text support group so that people can ask for help with this important task. This idea is explored further in the final section (see page 220). Exemplar text is usually better when a few people have worked together to improve it. But remember your support group must contain good listeners, ready to hear and reflect on the type of writing each subject requires rather than turning everything into 'English' text. As history teaching expert Christine Counsell has so clearly explained, literacy coordinators need to work with subject teachers to identify the 'natural literacy' in their subjects, not impose their version of literacy on them: *'Subjects matter. They are not just settings for the deployment of someone else's skills.'*

When the exemplar text for a particular unit has been established, the unit can be tweaked, as illustrated in the following steps, so that the students build up familiarity with the pattern of language.

Framing and motivating learning

Once you've established your exemplar text for the unit that helps build in progress, it's useful to have some sort of way of framing the learning of each unit that builds in progression. Secondary schools organise their timetables differently, but if you have ever tracked a student for a day, you will notice that their learning is often very disjointed as they probably move from subject to subject every hour or so. Most units build on units of work the students may have done before, and those in Year 7 often build on what has been learnt in primary school, though primary teachers rightly believe we tend to forget this. Therefore, it is a good idea to help the students recall prior knowledge and build on it. Many teachers have found **Framing-learning grids**, which were originally developed by David Wray and colleagues as part of the EXIT project, a really useful way of doing this. They are also good because they make clear what the students are going to learn, motivate them to want to learn it, and provide them with a useful way of briefly recording the key things that they have learnt. In addition, they are an excellent revision tool as well as being a useful device to inform any adult who wishes to support the students' learning.

A typical framing-learning grid looks like this:

Handout 5a: Framing-learning grid for perpetual (non-stop) motion and energy (science)

Starter question: The higher you climb up a mountain, the colder it becomes. Why? Discuss in pairs for one minute and be ready to present your theories.

What do I already **know**?	What am I going to **find** out?	What have I **learnt**?
	• What are the main types of energy? • What happens to particles when heat energy is applied to them? • How is heat transferred through a solid • How is heat transferred through liquids? • How is heat transferred through space? • Do some solids transfer more heat than others?	

(Developed by Julia Strong with the support of Julian Klafkowski, science teacher, Prescot School, Knowsley)

To interest the students and help refresh their memories, the grid begins with an open-ended starter question: The higher you climb up a mountain, the colder it becomes. Why?

Go round the room listening to their ideas. If no pair appears to have the right answer, just say that the unit will explain it all. Then the grid is introduced. In the second column, the teacher will have listed the key questions the unit will be solving in the order in which the information will be taught. These questions may help jog the students' memories. In the first column, they jot down anything they may already know about this topic. The third column is filled in following discussion after each section has been taught. It is easy to adapt these frames to suit any topic.

Some departments have adapted these frames as a way of consolidating learning or of helping students identify things they are still unsure about. For example, the PE version below has been devised for the end of a unit to help the students revise.

Handout 5b: Revision frame for the human skeleton (physical education)

What do I know? Jot down the key points for the following:	What extra do I need to add?	Tasks to test myself on
Functions: – . . . – . . . – . . . – . . . – . . . Classification – . . . – . . . – . . . – . . . Anatomy of bone – . . . – . . . – . . . – . . . – . . . – . . . Growth of bone – . . . – . . . – . . .		1. Label the diagram of a skeleton: – bones – classification 2. Label diagram of structure of bone

(Adapted by Julia Strong from the work of A. Watson and D. Jane, PE department, Tupton Hill School, Chesterfield)

Such approaches help the students reflect on their learning because they can demonstrate progress over time, as illustrated below, and show what the next stages are to help them progress. It is also a good way of helping the teacher engage in dialogue about what the student needs to focus on. They can also be used with learning partners, to help the students to help each other.

You may also want to suggest that teachers sometimes begin a unit with a short, interesting text about whatever it is they are about to teach. The more students hear good English well read, the more chance they will have of being able to imitate such language. An excellent source of such material for science, English or geography is Bill Bryson's *A Really Short History of Nearly Everything* (Random House, 2003).

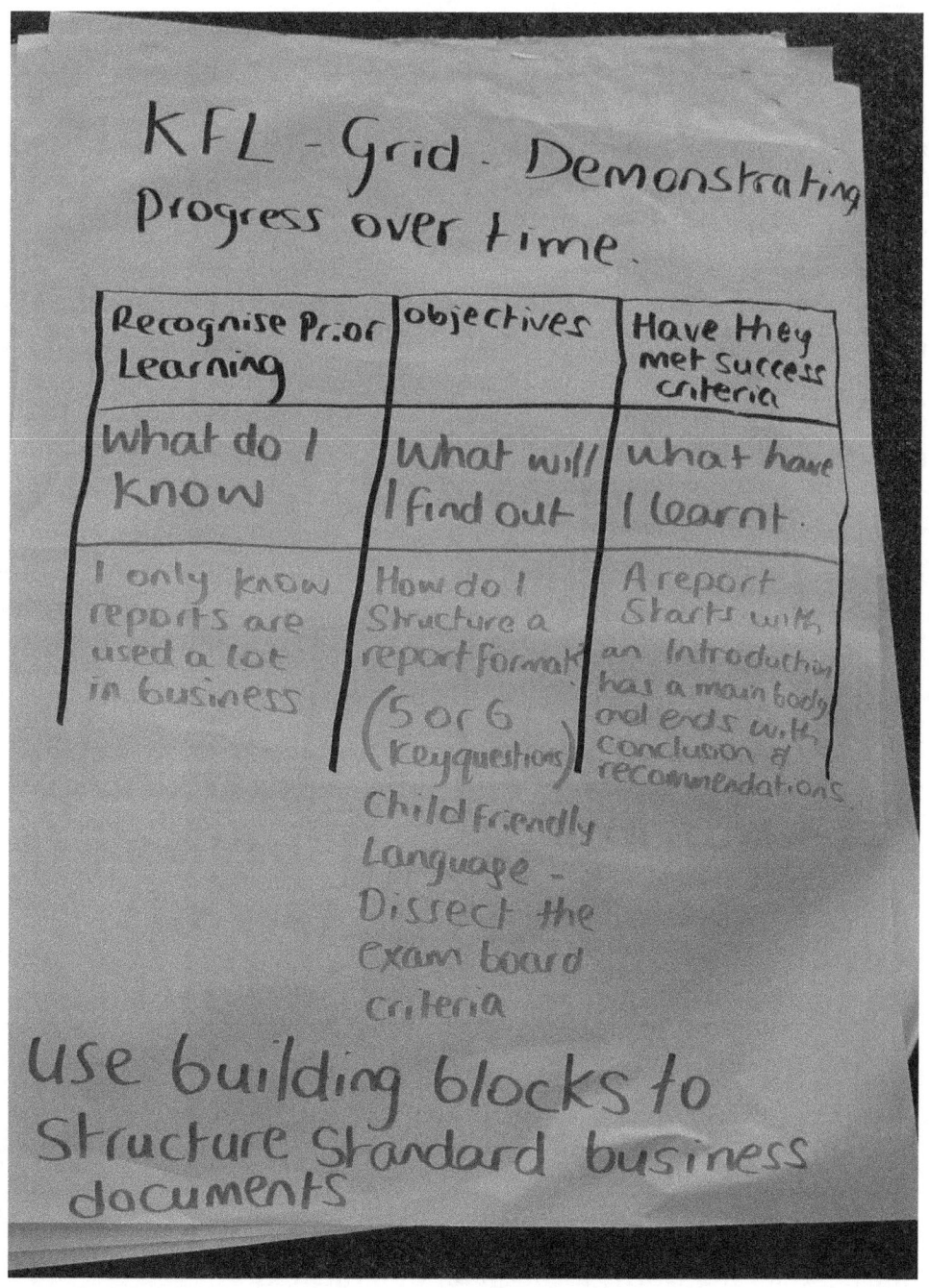

KFL workshop feedback

4

Step B: Warming up the words of a unit

(This chapter is supported online by **Handouts 6–16**, **Slides 29–35**, and the video clips from **Part 2: Step B**. Suggestions on how to present this step on a training session are given on page 216.)

Every unit will spin around a number of technical terms or new words that relate to the topic. It is therefore important that all teachers focus on ensuring that the students become confident speakers of this vocabulary. If we're not careful, such words are turned into undigested lists on the wall or unread glossaries at the back of exercise books. If the words are to move into the pool of language that students can use with confidence, so that they can reflect on the concepts they relate to, then engaging oral activities need to be devised to warm up these words. The students have to say the words out loud and not be afraid of them; they need to hear the words being used in context and use them in sentences themselves. Most of the following activities are based on sorting or linking concepts and many make great starter activities for lessons.

Step Bi: Using never-heard-the-word grids to flag up the key technical terms of a unit

A useful way of introducing the key technical terms of a unit is to flag them up with a never-heard-the-word grid as in the handouts below (use the Never-heard-the-word template – **Handout 6** – online to create your own).

- List up to 30 words on the sheet, flagging up with an asterisk any word that means one thing in everyday English and something completely different in the subject of the unit. This will help to draw attention to such tricky words.

- Give every student a copy of the sheet and present it as a challenge. You may want to tell them not to worry if they get none of the words right at the beginning of the unit but the aim is for everyone to get full marks when they revisit the sheet at the end of the unit.

- Say each word clearly and then repeat it in a sentence which provides context but doesn't give away its meaning. It's important for students to understand that you know a word by the company that it keeps.

- Allow enough time after each word for the students to tick the 'never heard the word before' column, 'heard it but not sure of its meaning' column, or to quickly jot down a meaning and/or example/image.

- Ask the students to put their score at the end of the activity. This will bring to the front of the students' minds vocabulary they may have heard before but had forgotten about and flag up all the key vocabulary coming their way soon. It also gives you a good idea of which words must be focused on.

- Let them know that you are not going to go over any of the words now but you will introduce each word in context as it's needed for the unit. (If you try to go over the words now, probably most of the class won't listen even if they are quiet.)

Below is an example for maths followed by a poster of the words to help build familiarity with the terminology throughout the related unit.

Handout 6a: Never-heard-the-word grid for numbers and the numbers system (maths)

Listen carefully while the words below are read to you and used in context – then fill in the appropriate column.

Warning: Beware of tricky words that have a very different everyday meaning from their meaning in a maths context. These tricky words are **highlighted** and marked with an **asterisk***.

Key words	Never heard the word before	Heard it but not sure of its meaning	Know what it means and can explain in context – jot down your ideas here
1. exponent			
2. greater than or equal to			
3. less than or equal to			
4. significant figures			
5. power* . . . etc.			

(Adapted from material developed by the maths department at Bishop Stopford School, Enfield) (See online for complete handout)

Displaying the words as word-wall posters

Enlarge the words from the never-heard-the-word grid onto a poster and display them (preferably on your washing line, as this makes it very easy to change the display to suit each class you teach). This poster acts as the interactive word wall for this unit, which can be added to if additional technical terms arise as the unit progresses. Devise ways of encouraging the students to say these words as often as possible throughout the unit as explained later in this chapter. Make the students aware that being able to use these words appropriately is important. As the unit develops, co-construct with them a toolkit ingredient like that below to help embed the fact that using technical language effectively is a key aspect of their learning.

Express it

Use technical language appropriately, explaining it if necessary

---

Technical vocabulary for the numbers system

Poster

• exponent	• powers	• percentages
• greater than or equal to	• roots	• ratio
• less than or equal to	• index	• proportion
• significant figures	• indices	• proportional to
• decimals	• index law	• calculation
• upper bound	• index notation	• compound interest
• lower bound	• standard index form	• constant
• integers	• fractions	• reciprocal

Never-heard-the-word grids and related word-wall posters are easy to devise for any unit for any subject, as the extracts below show. These are available in full on the resources online.

Handout 6b: Never-heard-the-word grid for fitness training (PE)

Key words	Never heard the word before	Heard it but not sure of its meaning	Know what it means and can explain in context – jot down your ideas here
1. multi-stage fitness			
2. Cooper's run			
3. stamina			
4. stork balance			
5. sit ups . . . etc.			

(Adapted from material developed by the PE department at Caerleon Comprehensive) (See online for complete handout)

Handout 6c: Never-heard-the-word grid for key words in the coming term (geography)

Key words	Never heard the word before	Heard it but not sure of its meaning	Know what it means and can explain in context – jot down your ideas here
1. arable			
2. latitude			
3. longitude			
4. relief			
5. scale . . . etc.			

(Adapted from materials developed by Lawrence Collins, Head of geography, Lincoln Minster School, Lincoln) (See online for complete handout)

Handout 6d: Never-heard-the-word grid for the language of international conflict (history)

Key words	Never heard the word before	Heard it but not sure of its meaning	Know what it means and can explain in context – jot down your ideas here
1. tension			
2. European powers			
3. offensive			
4. nationalism			
5. conflict . . . etc.			

(See online for complete handout)

Handout 6e: Never-heard-the-word grid for a unit on health (science)

Key words	Never heard the word before	Heard it but not sure of its meaning	Know what it means and can explain in context – jot down your ideas here
1. bacteria			
2. vaccination			
3. active immunity			
4. addiction			
5. alcohol . . . etc.			

(Developed with the support of Julian Klafkowski, science teacher, Prescot School, Knowsley) (See online for complete handout)

Filled-in never-heard-the-word grid for the technical language relating to circles in geometry (maths)

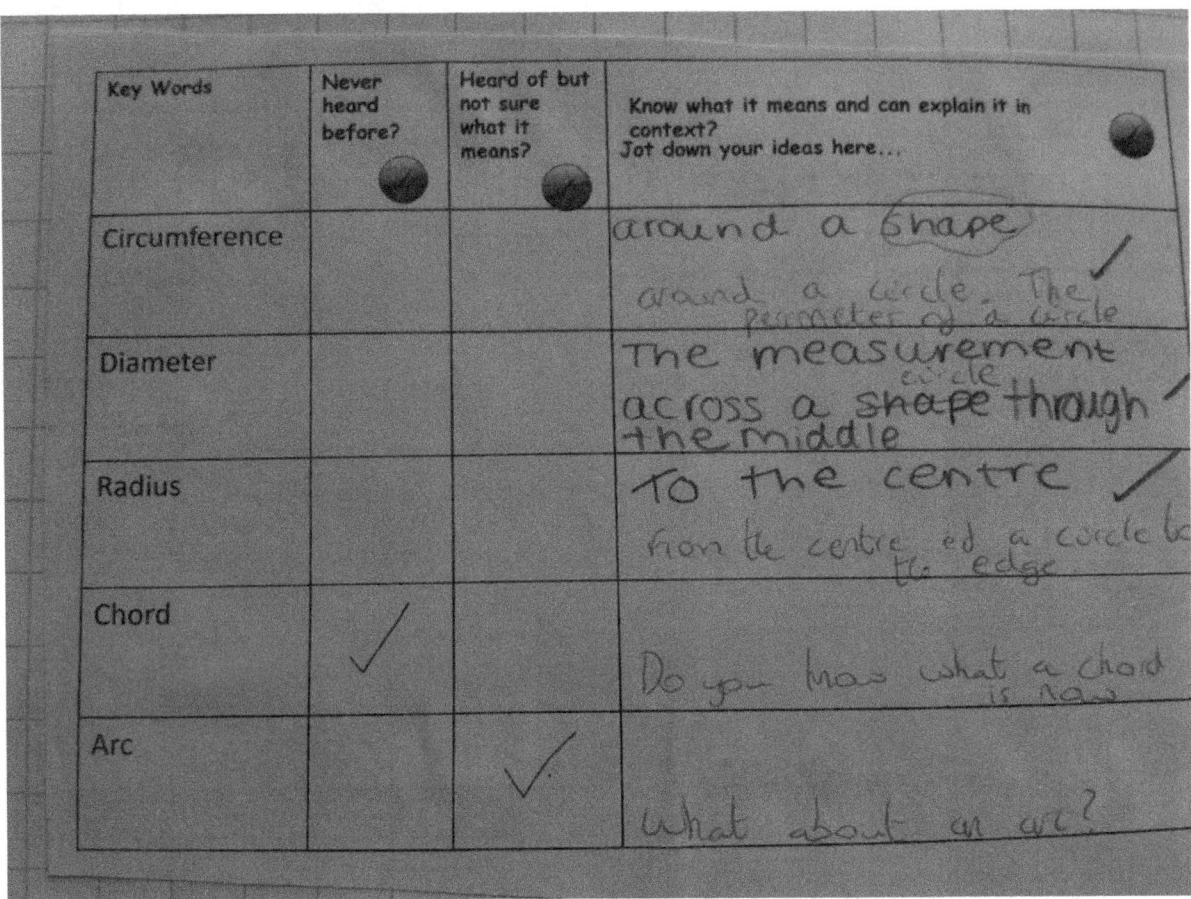

Key Words	Never heard before?	Heard of but not sure what it means?	Know what it means and can explain it in context? Jot down your ideas here...
Circumference			around a shape ✓ around a circle. The perimeter of a circle
Diameter			The measurement circle across a shape through the middle ✓
Radius			To the centre ✓ from the centre ed a circle to the edge
Chord	✓		Do you know what a chord is now
Arc		✓	what about an arc?

(Maths example from Helen Hindle, Portslade Aldridge Community Academy)

Apart from using these grids in the standard mode explained above, subject areas have adapted them to suit different purposes. For example, a French department devised a very interesting alternative formative assessment version that maximises the students' involvement in their own learning. In a workshop session, the teachers went on to develop all the steps necessary to support the students in this unit of work. This whole unit is in Step D (page 185), since it focuses on building up the phrases of a text to create a complete exemplar text.

Never-heard-the-word grids are an excellent way of embedding learning, as you can use them to introduce the key vocabulary of a unit and then challenge the students to use all of the terms effectively by the end of the unit and be able to spell them. Return to the grid at the end of the unit and test that they can now explain all of the terms. They are an instant hit on training days and teachers often devise very interesting ways of building on the idea, as illustrated by the Business department at Northumberland Church of England Academy here.

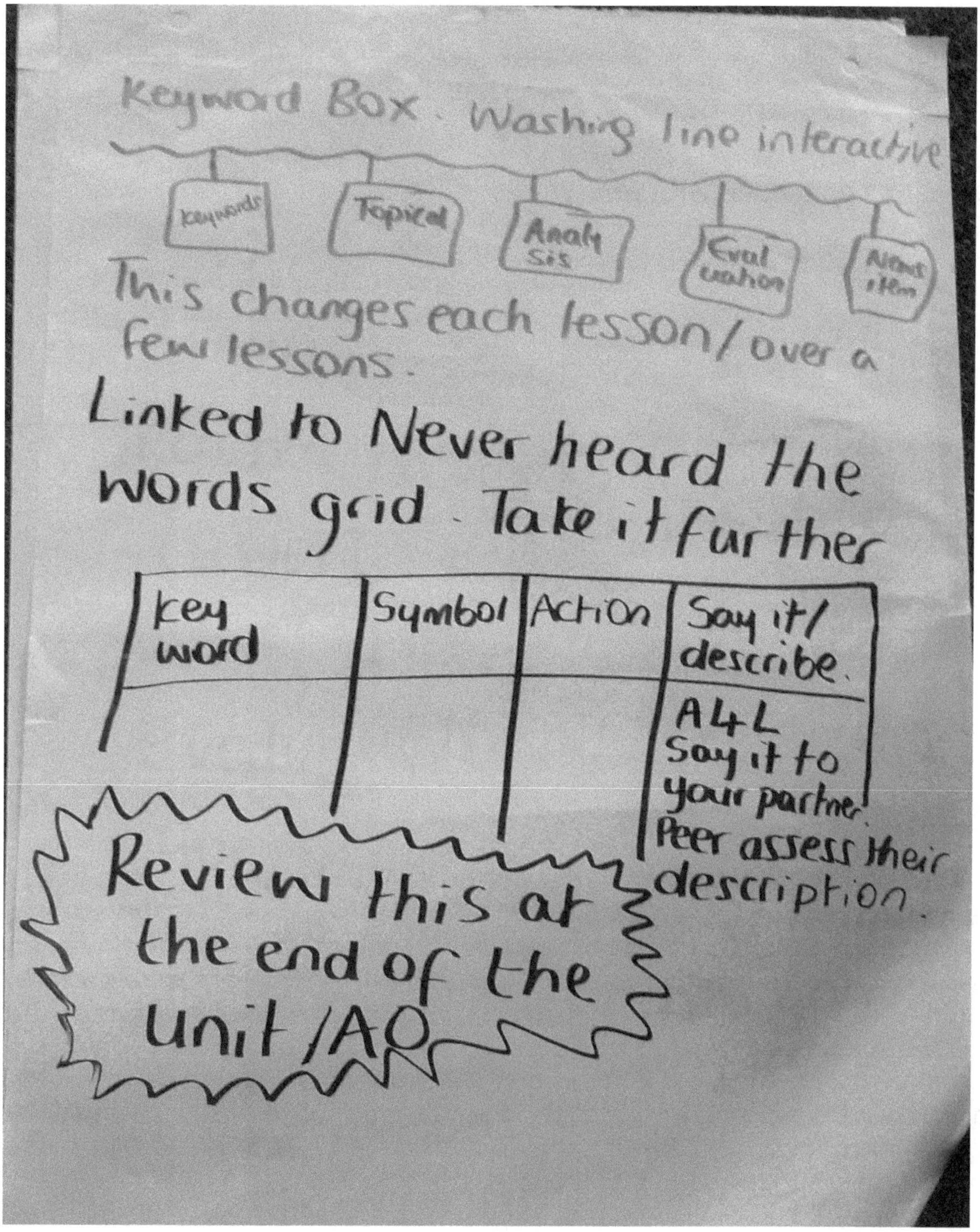

The handwritten workshop notes read:

Keyword Box. Washing line interactive

[Pegged cards: keywords | Topical | Analysis | Evaluation | Alternative item]

This changes each lesson/over a few lessons.

Linked to Never heard the words grid. Take it further

key word	Symbol	Action	Say it/ describe.
			A4L Say it to your partner. Peer assess their description.

Review this at the end of the unit /AO

Never-heard-the-word grid workshop feedback

Building confident users of technical vocabulary

The slide below is very entertaining but also rather worrying. It is all too easy to ramble on at the front about a topic that is pleasantly familiar to us and forget that we might as well be speaking in an unknown foreign language for all the understanding we are conveying. It's reasonable to assume that the child who wrote 'Three kinds of vessels are arteries, veins and caterpillars' had written down the definition of capillaries somewhere but nothing had happened to make him or her realise that the word they were hearing as 'caterpillars' was actually this new weird word 'capillaries'. We all stick with the words we are comfortable with unless something happens to make us confidently use a broader range of words.

Building confidence with new words

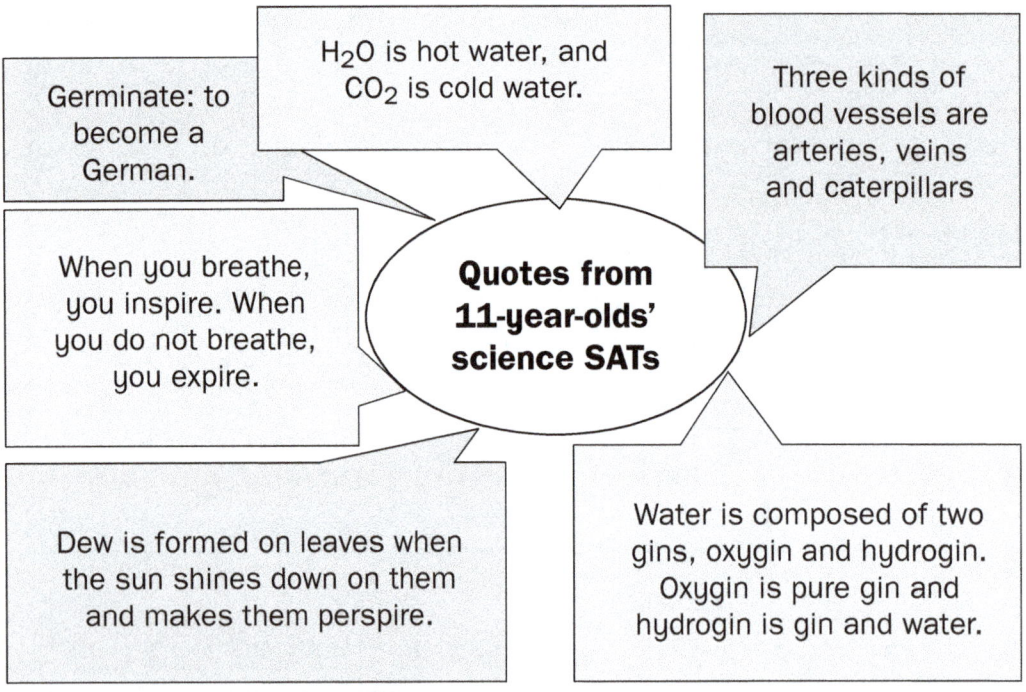

New words PowerPoint slide

Once you have flagged up the range of technical terms the students will encounter in the unit, the key thing is to devise a range of interactive vocabulary-building activities to go with the unit that focus on the students having to say the words out loud rather than writing down definitions. Copying definitions keeps them quiet but doesn't help them internalise the meaning of the words. It's worth reflecting on how much the vocabulary activities in any unit actually involve the students in saying the words in a range of contexts, which is the key to building confidence in using vocabulary appropriately. If they don't, then replace them with the type of activities suggested here.

A word of warning. Many of the vocabulary activities in off-the-shelf units look like the slide shown opposite.

Trying to match the words on the page with their definitions is self-defeating. The activity ismore of a time-filler than anything else. The process involved iscounterintuitive as the more links you make, the more confusing the sheet becomes. Being able to physically sort the words and the definitions with a partner is important, as this helps to clarify thinking and leads to discussion, which in turn helps to familiarise the students with the vocabulary. And to ice the cake, these off-the-shelf activities are often laid out so that the text is very small and squashed into the corner of the page just like my example, which I have kindly not attributed!

Avoid awful off-the-shelf vocabulary activities

Nincotine, alcohol and drugs: Match the correct definitions to the words below

Words	Definitions
addiction	An addictive chemical, found in cigarette smoke
alcohol	A sticky black substance found in cigarette smoke. It clogs the alveoli and stops the lungs working properly. It can cause cancer.
antibiotics	A poisonous gas found in cigarette smoke and produced in incompletecombustion.
carbon monoxide	Breathing in smoke from other people's cigarettes.
depressant	A legal drug found in beer, wine and spirits. It is produced by yeast during fermentation.
drug	The amount of alcohol found in half a pint of beer, a small lass of wine or a measure of spirits.
hallucinogen	The need t keep taking a drug. The user feels ill unless able to take more of a drug.
illegal	A substance that when taken into the body will affect the way that the user thinks or feels.
medicine	A drug which, if used correctly, can make the body work properly or get better.
nicotine	Medicines used to fight bacterial infections.
passive smoking	Describes bacteria that may not be killed by an antibiotic.
resistant	Against the law.
solvent abuse	Breathing in the fumes from some glues, paints and lighter fluids.
stimulant	A type of drug that slows down the body's reactions and makes the user drowsy and relaxed.
tar	A type of drug that speeds up the body's reactions and kames the user feel like they have lots of energy.
	A type of drug that causes the user to see things that are not really there.

What's wrong with this sort of activity?

Off-the-shelf vocabulary slide

There is a wide range of activities that can help students become confident users of vocabulary. Every teacher will already have a number that they traditionally use. The more interactive these are, the more liable they are to be effective. Here are just a few suggestions to encourage the students to talk the language so that every unit contains oral vocabulary activities. After each technical vocabulary building activity, the idea is that the teacher co-constructs with the students how this contributes to the toolkit for whatever type of text you are aiming at. You will probably end up with a toolkit ingredient similar to this:

Express it

Use technical language appropriately, explaining it if necessary

Step Bii: Clumping activities to activate prior learning

When teachers first meet a class in Year 7 and they know their subject has been taught in primary school, a useful vocabulary activity would be to devise a sorting activity with the key topics they will have studied listed as headings followed by a range of vocabulary for them to sort under the heading they think it fits best. This helps build in progression by immediately getting the students talking about their learning and helps the teacher know how much they know. The examples below are for geography and maths.

Handout 7a: Activating prior learning in geography

Can you remember all the vocabulary and place names below from geography work in primary school?

Task 1. (In groups) Take the heading **British Isles**. Select all of the place names and geographical terms that are relevant to this heading. Remember you have to have a reason to support your decisions. Next change the heading and decide which words you should now take out and which ones you add in. Do the same for all the headings.

1. UK	2. Europe	3. Africa	4. Asia
5. The World	6. Climate	7. Landscape and forms	

the Tropics	River Nile	volcanoes	Kenya
the Sahara	Egypt	drought	hospitals
rivers	earthquake	erosion	health

(Adapted from material developed by Lawrence Collins, Head of geography, Lincoln Minster School, Lincoln) (See online for complete handout)

Applying a similar approach in maths

A good way of bringing back to students' minds the words they encountered in primary school for, say, two- and three-dimensional shape is to set up a sorting activity to be completed in pairs. It would be useful to have all these words up on the screen in alphabetical order and to have read the list to them before they start the activity to remind them of what the words sound like.

First, they have to clump the words below, which would appear on separate cards, into the four categories given. If they don't know what a word means, they should put it to one side. Some words may 'fit' in more than one clump – just ask them to choose the best fit and these can be discussed later. Then, since these

terms are best understood visually, ask them if they can come up with an image to represent each word in each clump.

Handout 7b: Clumping activities to activate prior learning

Words related to circular shapes	Words related to multi-sided shapes (more than 3 sides)	Words related to triangles	General 2D/3D words
radius	square	triangular	regular
diameter	rectangle	three-sided	edge
circumference	kite	isosceles	face

(See online for complete handout)

Ask the students in pairs to check if they have the same groups and that their images look similar. The more opportunities the activity provides for them to actually say the words, the better.

Step Biii: Sorting activities to warm up the words

Sorting activities in pairs is an excellent means of strengthening understanding and confidence with technical vocabulary because it focuses on the students saying the words. Every subject has some key terms that the whole subject tends to spin round. Clearly, the more secure the students are with this vocabulary, the easier it will be for them to build their understanding of the subject, so time spent embedding this vocabulary pays off. For example, music spins around the seven terms on Handout 8a. The students in pairs are being asked to match the word not to its definition but to the characteristics that sum up its meaning and then see if they can think of two good examples of music that would illustrate what it means. The more students are involved in generating examples of the words they are working on, the more they will understand them.

Top tips:

- Remember to mix up the terms and definitions on screen before cutting them up so the matching pairs cannot be fitted together like a jigsaw.

- Store the sets in re-sealable plastic bags and the resource will last for years. If the sets get mixed up, do not despair. Many students will be more than willing to keep your resources sorted for you.

Handout 8a: Sorting activity for key terms in music

Tempo	Characteristic 2. Is the music fast or slow? Does it speed up, slow down or stay the same?
Rhythm	Characteristic 1. Are the sounds long, short, detached, in a constant pattern, not predictable?
Mood	Characteristic 6. How does the music make you feel? Is it calm, sad, dreamy, scary, dramatic, humorous, energetic, exciting, etc.?
Melody	Characteristic 3. Does the tune flow smoothly or move in steps or leaps? Does it have a predictable or unpredictable end?
Texture	Characteristic 4. How complex is the music? • single line unaccompanied? • single melody and accompaniment? • complex, interwoven music?
Pitch	Characteristic 5. Is the music high or low?
Dynamics	Characteristic 7. How loud or soft is the music. Does it get louder? Does it get quieter?

(Adapted from material developed by a music teacher at Newfield School, Sheffield)

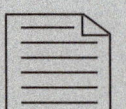

Handout 8b: Sorting activity for key terms in science

microbes	a very, very small organism (living thing) which often cause diseases
bacteria	a type of microbe that can grow rapidly by dividing into two new cells
micro-organism	a tiny organism that can't be seen without a microscope that often causes diseases
virus	an extremely small microbe that can invade other cells and copy itself inside the body cell

(Developed with the support of Julian Klafkowski, science teacher, Prescot School, Knowsley) (See online for complete handout)

Step Biv: Generating and embedding related vocabulary

The more that students can be involved in building up the related vocabulary, the more liable they are to become confident users of the terminology. So once the students understand the meaning of the key terms, they can start to apply them. The example below, like the one above, is for music, but it could easily be adapted to suit any subject.

Each pair of students is given a sheet of paper with the key terms on. The students then listen to extracts from Ravel's *Bolero* and Dukas' *The Sorcerer's Apprentice* and jot down all the words relating to each term in turn that came to mind when they listened to the music.

Handout 9a: Generating related vocabulary (music)

Key musical terms	Opening Ravel's *Bolero*	Opening Dukas' *The Sorcerer's Apprentice*
tempo		
rhythm		
mood		
melody		
texture		
pitch		
dynamics		

Once the students have had time to develop their own lists, the teacher – preferably on a flip chart – can create the class grid using the best of their words and adding in any key terms that haven't been included that the teacher wants the students to become familiar with. In this way, every teacher can create a 'word wall' for the unit they are teaching and display it on the washing line when they want to refer to it and add words as the unit develops. If this word wall is not relevant to the next class, it can be covered up. In this simple way, the washing line becomes the 'work in progress' area for each class and supports their learning. Lists on walls that are always displayed and rarely referred to just become wallpaper and, of course, you haven't got enough walls to display all the words and phrases you need for all the classes you teach.

Below is an example of the same approach but this time for art appreciation.

Handout 9b: Generating related vocabulary (art)

Key terms	Portrait by Van Gogh	Portrait by Picasso
use of light		
use of colour		
texture		
level of realism		
context		
mood		
impression of character		

The example below shows how the related words can be provided as a sorting activity to help familiarise students with the language of art evaluation. Some of the words would fit more than one category, which makes it a better activity since this leads to more discussion about the words.

Handout 9c: Matching related vocabulary to key terms (art)

Artist's intention	exaggerate express	distort explore	recreate evoke	reflect suggest
Mood	happy frightening	sad awesome	haunting entertaining	evocative nostalgic
Form/ composition	balanced design	symmetrical angular	arrangement curved	composition foreground
Use of tone, colour, texture	vivid clashing	sombre pastel	bright matching	dull rough

(Adapted from material developed by the art department at Hampstead School, Camden, London) (See online for complete handout)

Below is a similar activity for music where the students' growing confidence with the key vocabulary can be extended further by means of sorting. The students are given 36 cards with musical terms on them. The nine shaded cards printed in bold with a capital letter are the categories into which the other 27 terms are to be sorted. Again, some words could fit into more than one category. The students are told they will need to explain their choices.

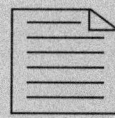

Handout 9d: Matching related vocabulary to key terms – music

Dynamic	acoustic	bass line	chorus
Electronic/digital	choral	cyclical	descant
Melody	harmonic	higher	improvisation
Mood	interlude	linear	lower

(See online for complete handout)

Step Bv: Labelling to help students apply their knowledge

An alternative approach is to get the students in pairs to label a diagram to show that they understand what it refers to. For example, in design and technology this approach could be used to help students apply the language of structural analysis. The students could be provided with 10 technical terms relating to structural analysis. They have to study the diagram and then select the six relevant terms and place them appropriately. Once they have completed their version, they should consult with another pair to check if they have reached the same conclusions and to see if they can explain their choices. Again the focus is on using the vocabulary in context.

Handout 10: Labelling a diagram – understanding the terminology of structural analysis (D&T)

Task: Select the six relevant terms from the list below and label the diagram appropriately.

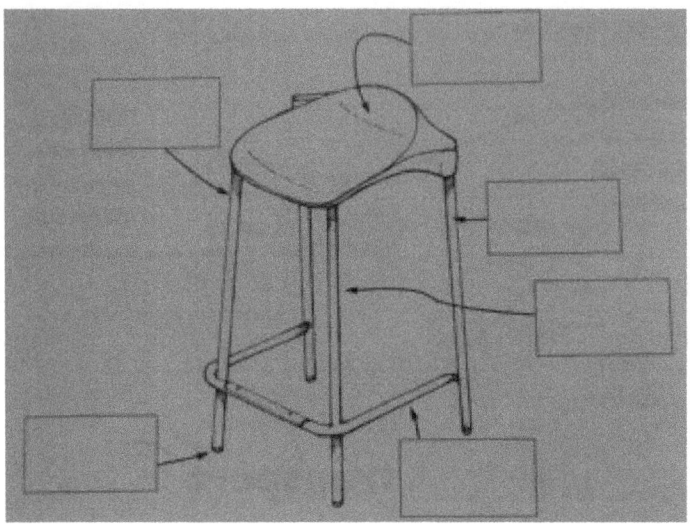

direction of force	weak point
stay	strut
tensional force	compression force
shell structure	frame structure
area of concentrated force	area of dispersed force
concentrated load	weakness point

(Adapted from material developed by Paul Drennen and Charlie Cook, D&T department, Hampstead School, Camden, London)

Step Bvi: Sorting activities to extend vocabulary

Another useful variety of sorting activity, again to be completed in pairs, involves the students in applying their knowledge. This should lead to more thinking and more focused discussion. In the first example below, the students are provided with the key terms and a range of related words and are asked to sort the words into clumps related to the key terms. This is aimed at extending the range of words students use when describing colour. Following the activity, the students are asked to generate any additional words they know to describe shades of colour within these categories. These can then be displayed as posters including their additional terms. The more they are challenged to apply what they have just been learning, the more they will be able to recall and develop what they have learnt.

Handout 11a: Sorting terms and generating more examples (art)

Orange	Red	Blue	Yellow
Green	Purple	Brown	

violet	azure	olive	cerise
rose	gold	lemon	chocolate
royal	fawn	emerald	cornflower

(Adapted from material produced by the art department at Cefn Hengoed Community School, Swansea) (See online for complete handout)

In the science example below, students are asked to match up the type of energy and what causes it with an example of the resulting energy. The students are then asked to see if they can generate one more example for each type of energy. This involves the students in applying their knowledge and should lead to more thinking and more focused discussion.

Handout 11b: Matching activity and generating examples (science)

Type of energy	How it occurs	Example
Kinetic energy	caused by movement	• waves
Strain energy	caused by something being stretched	• wound-up spring
Sound energy	caused by sound waves	• thunder
Thermal energy	caused by heat	• fire

(Developed with the support of Julian Klafkowski, science teacher, Prescot School, Knowsley) (See online for complete handout)

Step Bvii: Using mime to help recall the meaning of words

Another useful alternative approach is to involve the students in miming examples like the GCSE PE sorting activity below. First, the students are given all the information about the four different types of motor skills on separate cards and are asked in pairs to match the key terms with their working definitions and an example. They are told that there is no example for motor skills, as this is the generic term and all the examples are motor skills.

Handout 12: Sorting terms, generating more examples and miming them (PE)

Key term	Working definition	Example
motor skills	ability to perform certain movements with control and consistency	
open motor skills	ability to perform movements affected by the environment or by others	making a tackle in football
closed motor skills	movements performed in stable conditions where performer has almost total control	a free throw in basketball
fine motor skills	involves movement of small muscle groups	flick of the wrist as the ball is released
gross motor skills	involves movement of large muscle groups	a sliding tackle

(Adapted from material produced by K. Ford, PE department, Old Hall School, Rotherham)

Next, the students in groups of four are asked to come up with three more examples for one type of motor skill. If the students were then asked to feed back their suggestions, the chances are the class wouldn't listen, but if you asked each group to mime their examples and the class had to identify the activity, then they would probably stay involved. The more they are involved in generating the examples, the more they will understand the concept.

Mime is an extremely powerful learning technique because, when you mime something, you have to go through the sequence you are miming in your head – in effect, it makes you talk to yourself about whatever it is you are trying to mime. So for anything that can be sequenced, mime is very powerful.

Step Bviii: Warming up the words through talking the text

An excellent way of warming up and consolidating the key vocabulary of a unit is to integrate key words into an exemplar text and internalise the text in Talk-for-Writing style. This is explained on page 104.

Step Bix: Helping students remember seriously difficult key words

Learning should be all about understanding rather than remembering. However, the terminology can sometimes get in the way of this learning. It may be useful to pay special attention to difficult technical terms that are key to your subject and frequently lead to misunderstanding, for example terms like 'mean', 'median', 'mode' and 'range'. A little rhyme like the one below, to be sung to the tune of 'Hey diddle diddle, the cat and the fiddle', can help fix the shades of meaning in the head:

> Hey diddle diddle, the median's the middle.
> You add and divide for the mean.
> The mode is the one that happens the most
> And the range is the bit in between.

> (Rhyme courtesy of Andy Harrison, maths teacher at
> William Hulmes Grammar School, Manchester)

An alternative useful method is to use icons to support understanding. Ask students to devise an icon to represent what each term means. Share some of the best ideas, then students can use someone else's idea or stick with their own. The important thing is that they have a clear image in their head of what the word means.

Challenge students to come up with a rhyme, mime or pictogram to help them remember tricky words

Step Bx: Playing word root detective to help understanding of key difficult vocabulary

If your subject spins around rather obscure technical terms with similar roots, then this approach may be useful. For example, most technical mathematical terms relating to shape or number are rooted in Greek or Latin and can thus seem rather strange. Understanding these roots can help students become more confident users of the words and more capable of decoding similar words. Rather than providing them with the meaning of the roots, they will remember it more if they have been actively involved in solving the problem as demonstrated below. The groups of words and their related prefix/suffix should be printed on card and cut up. The students match the words to the card that helps unlock the meaning and then have to try to explain what each word means, using images where possible.

Handout 13: Mathematical word detective – match the words with the card that helps unlock their meaning

unit, uniform	uni = one
bisect, binomial	bi = two
triangle, triple, trillion	tri = three
quadrangle, quarter, quartile	quad = four
pentagon, pentagram	pent = five
hexagon	hex = six
heptagon	hept = seven
octagon, octahedron	octa = eight
nonagon, nonahedron	non = 9
decimal, decagon	dec = ten
centimetre, centilitre	cent = hundred
polygon, polyhedra	poly = many
equivalent, equilateral, equals	equi = the same as
intersection, interquartile	inter = cut across/between
polygon, octagon, pentagon, decagon	gonia = angle
polyhedron, octahedron, tetrahedron	hedra = face of a geometrical solid
concentric, excentric	centric = centre
concave, convex, concentric	con = with

(Adapted from material developed by the maths department, Cardinal Heenan School, Liverpool) (See online for complete handout)

The more the students can start applying their understanding of the meaning of the words, the less scary the words will be. So a useful additional activity here is for the students to see if they can generate at least two more words containing the same root – these words don't have to be mathematical, e.g. tri – tripod, triplets, triplicate.

If all the words can then be displayed and are referred to throughout units they appear in, the more the students will internalise this tricky vocabulary and cease to be afraid of it.

Step Bxi: Consolidating understanding through linking activities

There are many ways that you can use linking activities like mind mapping or graphical organisers to help students relate words logically. The examples below all relate to maths but the approaches can be applied to any subject.

Mind mapping words

Take one key word and ask the students to come up with a mind map of all the link words they can think of, as illustrated below. This activity can be done individually or in pairs and is a useful way of getting students to manipulate the language of any subject.

A page from a student's book from Andy Lyon's maths class, Queensbury School, Bradford

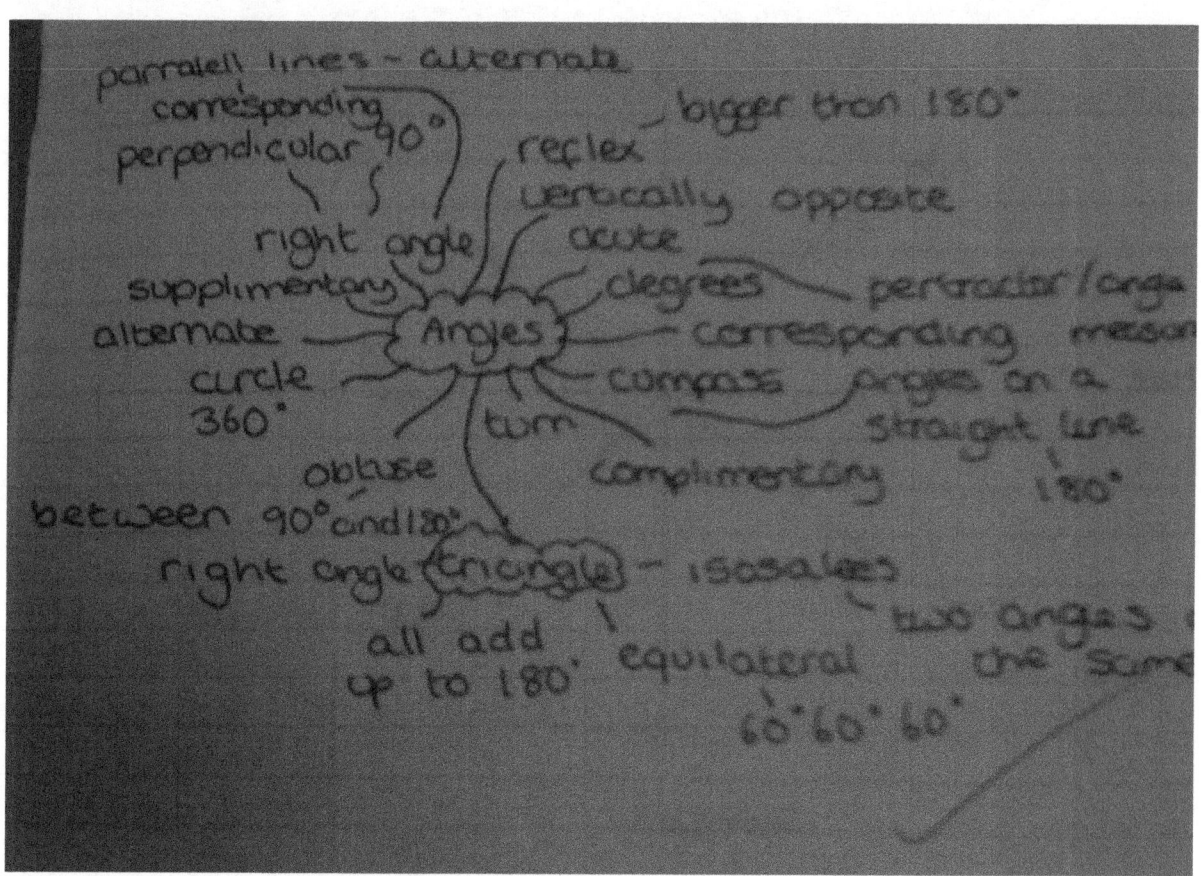

Alternatively, graphic organisers can be used to help students express their understanding.

A page from a student's book from Andy Lyon's maths class, Queensbury School, Bradford

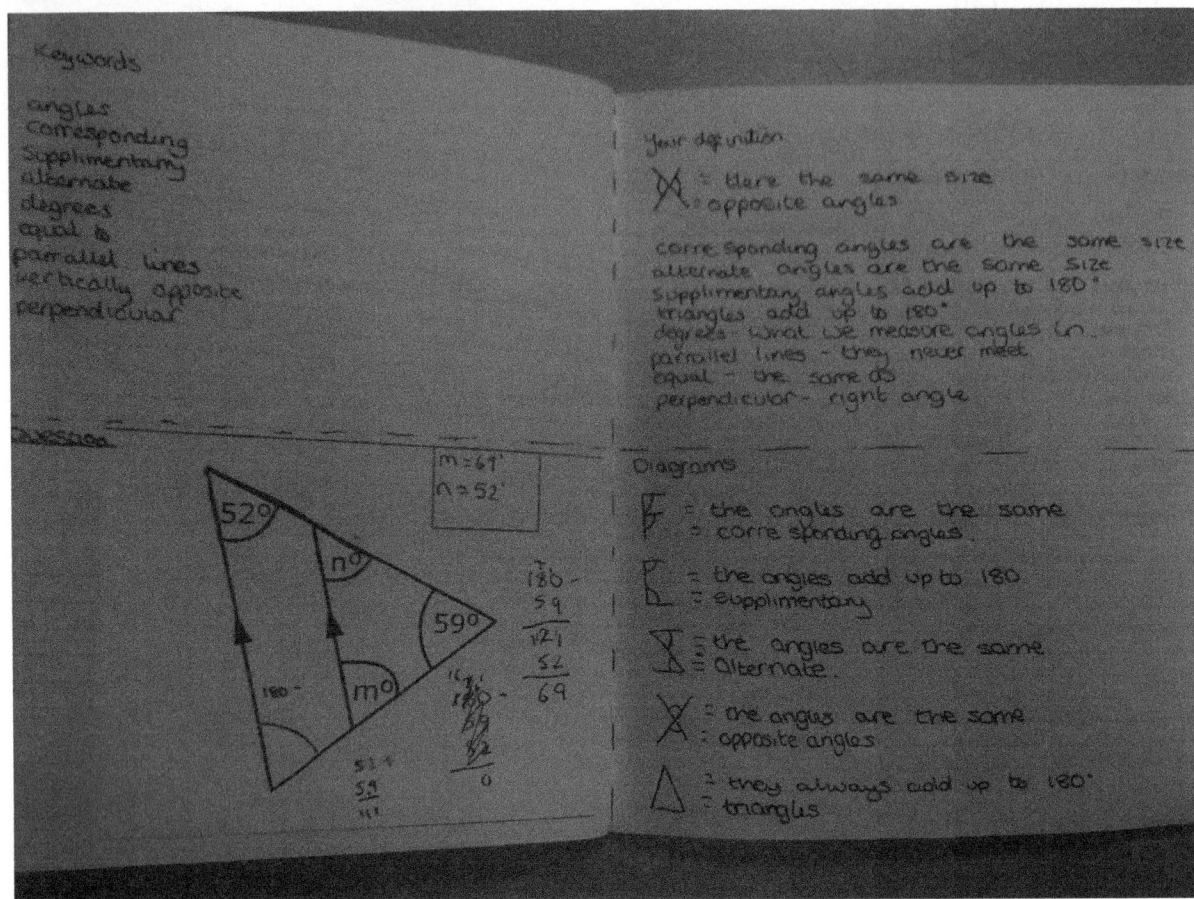

These approaches can be reinforced by quick-fire revision activities like the one below to help students recall some significant information. In the example below, students in pairs decide on the missing figure and then check with another pair that their answers are correct.

- The angles of a triangle always add up to . . .

- Angles on a straight line add up to . . .

- Angles around a point add up to . . .

- Acute angles are less than . . .

- Obtuse angles are more than . . . but less than . . .

- Reflex angles are more than . . . and less than . . .

Andy Lyon, when he was KS4 maths coordinator, Queensbury School, Bradford, found that a focus on key words and their meanings made a very significant difference to his students' mathematical understanding. Apart from some of the techniques above, he also:

- encouraged students to use technical language both in their speaking and writing

- praised students when they used the key words

- devised quick-fire activities to keep the conversation going, for example:

  - choose any two of the key words and explain their meaning to your learning partner

  - homework – tell five people about . . . find a definition of . . .

Step Bxii: Consolidating the key technical terms through linking word dominoes

(Watch the video clip **Part 2: Step B: Word dominoes** to illustrate this progress)

Word dominoes (i.e. cards with two words on them that are like a domino, as illustrated below) can be an excellent way of consolidating students' confidence with using the key vocabulary of any unit. The students have to see if they can find another domino that they can link to either of those words but they can't put a domino down unless they can explain the link between the terms. For example, if the dominoes were for the technical vocabulary of football, like the example below, then 'hand ball' could be placed next to 'penalty' if the link was explained as follows: 'If you touch the ball in the penalty area, the opposing team will be awarded a penalty kick.' Model how to talk the links for the class so they know how to play.

corner	hand ball

The idea is that the students play dominoes collectively in groups of two to four. It is best initially if all the dominoes are laid out on the table and any one domino is selected as the starter, for example **anaerobic: circuits**. The students can then see all the choices and decide which dominoes to link together to create a straight line of dominoes. Once they are familiar with the approach, they may be able to divide up the dominoes and play competitively but this is quite hard, especially when there are only a few dominoes left, as the choices become limited.

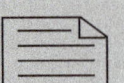

Handout 14a: Dominoes for the technical vocabulary of fitness training (PE)

multi-stage fitness	aerobic		anaerobic	circuits

Cooper's run	muscular endurance		atrophy	suppleness

stamina	aerobic		cardiovascular	sit and reach

stork balance	recovery rate		balance	fartlek

sit ups	plyometrics		multi-stage fitness	reaction time

boomerang	sprint		speed of skill	intervals

grip strength	agility		weights	vertical jump

Once one group has finished, get another group to check their links. The idea is to maximise use of the technical language of the unit. Apart from being an excellent end-of-unit activity to consolidate understanding of the key terminology, this can also be a good beginning-of-unit activity if the terms have already been covered and are needed for a later unit.

It is easy to adapt the key vocabulary from the never-heard-the-word grid for any unit into a set of dominoes to embed understanding of the key terminology. Here are some extracts from more examples from a range of different subjects – the complete examples are available online.

The first is a set of dominoes that would be useful for English teachers, since this was the language of the primary literacy hour and is still widely used. This could be used as a beginning-of-unit activity to see if the new intake is familiar with this terminology.

Handout 14b: Dominoes for revisiting the literacy language of primary school

sentence	plural	singular	sequence

third person	layout	imperative	opinion

instructions	informal	tense	introduction

pronoun	advertisement	conclusion	recount

(See online for complete handout)

Handout 14c: Dominoes for the key vocabulary of design and technology

design brief	model	customer survey	graphics

prototype	exploded diagram	design proposal	mock up

context	parts drawing	design ideas	final design

investigation	two-dimensional	cross-section	work plan

(Adapted from workshop material developed by D&T teachers from Northumberland) (See online for complete handout)

Handout 14d: Dominoes for the numbers system

proportional to	index notation		integers	index law

exponent	percentages		roots	compound interest

upper bound	decimals		powers	lower bound

constant	ratio		index	reciprocal

(See online for complete handout)

The following dominoes consist of specific concepts that relate to a particular unit of geology. The concepts have been selected so that there is only one match for each concept (i.e. it is a word loop). Working in pairs, students should discuss how to link these dominoes so that they form a circle.

Handout 14e: Word dominoes for an A level geology unit

mid-Atlantic ridge	liquid		mainly carbon dioxide and water vapour	solid

heat and pressure	early atmosphere		basalt and granite	

mantle	metamophoric example		igneous formed by	crust

(Adapted from work devised by two geology teachers from the science department at High Storrs School, Sheffield) (See online for complete handout)

Handout 14f: Word dominoes for a unit on health (science)

white blood cells	tar		virus	passive smoking

vaccination	tumour		resistant	nicotine

microbes	alcohol		immune system	cancer

infections	breathing rate		antibodies	bacteria

(See online for complete handout)

Express it

Use technical language appropriately

It's worth reflecting on why sorting activities like dominoes are so effective. They challenge students–activities that are too easy are tedious and not worth paying attention to. They are interactive and allow everyone to be involved and they have that necessary edge of competition as people vie to show their superior understanding. Very quickly whole classes get involved, as do large halls of teachers from all subjects as the picture of teachers playing dominoes illustrates. If an inspector called, they are definitely 'on task'!

Some advice on making dominoes

- Select around 30 key terms from your never-heard-the-word grid and word wall.

- List them so that potential matching pairs are on different dominoes.

- Make dominoes open not closed (i.e. a wide range of possible links, not a fixed loop).

- Provide at least two good matches for each word.

- Differentiate, if you want, by making the bottom half more difficult.

- Print so reversible, i.e. 'white blood cells/tar' reads 'tar/white blood cells' when you turn the domino over.

- There is a dominoes template online

Step Bxiii: Consolidating learning through linking word loops

Physical education, like many subjects, is full of sequences. These lend themselves to being expressed as word loops and then mimed. The following activities are particularly useful when students need to recall the sequence.

First, put all the stages of the sequence on dominoes like the cardiac cycle dominoes below. Provide the students in pairs with a set of these dominoes.

- Their first task is to sequence them and to be able to explain what is happening in the sequence.

- The next task is to mime how the cardiac cycle works.

Handout 15: Sequencing loop for cardiac cycle (PE)

vena cava	right atrium

tricuspid valve	right ventricle

pulmonary artery	lungs

pulmonary vein	left atrium

bicuspid valve	left ventricle

semi- lunar valve	aorta

(Adapted from material from the PE department, Tupton Hall School, Chesterfield)

Step Bxiv: Sorting and analysing activities to help understand the language of exams

Exam terminology is often confusing, as terms like 'explain' can be used in many different ways. It is therefore a good idea to see if the exam board provides guidance on their use of exam commands and then turn this into an interactive exercise as in the example here.

This activity is based on AQA's useful document 'Command Words for GCSE Sciences'. To help the students comprehend what it is the examiners are asking for, the information has been turned into a sorting activity requiring the students to act on the information, so that they learn by doing. The handout on the next page would need to be cut up into cards. This activity would probably be good for Year 9 so that by the time the students reach KS4 they are confident with the terminology of command terms for the exams.

- Ask the students in pairs to match the question command word with its explanation, and the example that illustrates what the command requires.

- When they have finished, ask them to check their conclusions with another pair, in particular focusing on how the examples illustrate what the command is asking them to do.

- Then, in their groups of four, every student should take two command words and practise being the visiting examiner who has come to explain what the terms mean. It may help them to convert the explanation of the meanings of the words into a text map to help them recall the information.

- Ask them to take it in turns to explain a command to their group and show how the example illustrates the points they are making. If you have some outstanding examiners, get them to present to the whole class. By putting the students in teacher role, they will gain confidence in responding to these tricky commands.

Handout 16: Understanding what the question is asking you to do

Command word	Explanation of its meaning (in context of science exams)	Example answer to illustrate what the command requires
1. Calculate	**Use the numbers given in the question to work out the answer.** Always show your working – marks may be awarded for the method even if the final answer is wrong.	• Mass of N $1 \times 14 = 14$ $(14/135) \times 100 = 10.37$ Percentage of nitrogen $= 10.4\%$
2. Compare	**Describe (explain) the similarities and/or differences between things.** Don't just write about one.	• Generating electricity for an immersion heater burns fossil fuels, which releases carbon dioxide into the atmosphere but solar energy doesn't release any extra carbon dioxide. Solar energy is a renewable energy source, which also means that we are conserving fossil fuels, which are in danger of running out. Solar energy does have disadvantages because it needs the daylight and some countries don't have enough hours of sunlight, like Scotland in the winter. This means there will be times when not enough hot water is available for the household, whereas an immersion heater can supply hot water all of the time.
3. Complete	**Fill in the gaps.** Answers should be written in the space provided, e.g. on a diagram, in spaces in a sentence or in a table.	(a) The particles in a **solid** vibrate about fixed positions. (b) The particles in a **gas** move at high speed in any direction. (c) The particles in a **solid** are arranged in a pattern.

(Adapted from AQA's 'Command Words for GCSE Sciences') (See online for complete handout)

To extend this understanding further, the students could then analyse the connective phrases and sentence signposts that suit each type of answer. For examples of how to do this, see the phrase activities on page 95.

A note on spelling

Try to establish that each department builds in spelling activities throughout each unit focusing on words from the never-heard-the-word grids, including setting spelling for homework and testing it. Then each department will be focusing spelling corrections on the key terms list and any other words the students are frequently using to express each subject.

Doubtless some students will be misspelling a wide range of common English terms, for example, endlessly confusing 'it's' and 'its'. It is probably best to set up a coordinated approach to sorting out spelling problems so that each department deals with their technical terms and frequently used terms, and flags up problems with other words as appropriate, while the English department deals with the more general words and perhaps informs the teachers of particular classes when it is having a blitz on careless errors and would want these to be flagged up by all departments. Also make certain that everything displayed in classrooms is spelt correctly. If you read the displays in classrooms or look at school booklets, there's a worrying number of spelling errors out there, including material that has clearly been produced by teachers.

Step C: Warming up the phrases of a unit

(This chapter is supported online by **Handouts 17–30**, **Slides 36–39**, and the video clip from **Part 2: Step C**, with sections on highlighting, sorting and sequencing. Suggestions for how to present this step on a training session are given on page 216.)

It is standard for teachers to think about the key technical vocabulary of a unit but it is not so common for teachers to consider the key phrases (sentence signposts and connectives) that are key to linking information about their subject. For example, phrases like *usually*, which signals generalisation; *whereas*, which signals contrast; or *equally*, which signals similarity. (See **Handout 17** online for a useful general handout of a range of different sentence signposts and connectives and what they signal.) As explained in the opening section on exemplar text, it is focusing on how to teach the linking phrases alongside the phrases that help everyone express themselves clearly and coherently that is the key to successful communication. Every unit of work will benefit from time spent focusing on speaking these linking and expressing phrases. For those subjects for which writing is key, this will lead to students being able to write about the subject more effectively; for the practical subjects at KS3, it will mean that the students can talk more clearly about the subject, which in turn will enable them to understand it better.

Once subject teachers have identified the sort of linking phrases that are key to their subject, these phrases should be focused on as appropriate in context throughout every unit. Over time, the students will become very familiar with the phrases that glue their expression of each subject together, which will help them express exactly what they are trying to say.

A wide range of activities can help students do this. Here are a few tried-and-tested ideas to choose from (many of which feature highlighting, sorting or sequencing) so that every unit contains at least one activity to warm up key phrases. These are excellent starter activities and can be used to build up a range of posters featuring the specific key phrases for the different text types that each subject focuses on. These posters will support the students in using these phrases so that they begin to automatically express themselves coherently. This approach is illustrated throughout this section.

Step Ci(a): Raiding the reading

Encourage teachers to look at any text that they will be using within a unit and think about the phrases that the students could 'steal' from this to use in their own work. A primary teacher who helped develop the Talk-for-Writing approach, and whose key subject focus happened to be science, told me that it was this raiding the reading that made him realise what reading was good for. The proportion of his pupils achieving the expected levels at the end of KS2 increased from about one-third to over 90%.

This process in primary schools is often now referred to as 'magpieing', but many secondary schools prefer the term 'hijacking' or 'nicking'. The idea is that you devise ways of drawing attention to useful phrases that the students note down to use later. An easy way of doing this is to provide pairs of students with a copy of an exemplar text and ask them to highlight any phrases that (a) join the text together and (b) help the writer to explain what is being written about clearly. If this is the first time they have done this, the teacher will need to model how to do it.

There are thousands of well-written non-fiction texts, such as *A Really Short History of Nearly Everything* by Bill Bryson (Random House, 2003), *Alex's Adventures in Numberland* by Alex Bellos (Bloomsbury, 2010), *The Map that Changed the World* by Simon Winchester (Penguin Books, 2002), and *Longitude* by Dava Sobel (Penguin Books, 1996). Encourage teachers to find a really good short piece of text related to whatever they are teaching and use this alongside their exemplar text as a source of additional useful phrases. In this way, the students will have been given access to real quality text and, if it has been read well to them and the trickier language explained, they will be able to understand it. The more they hear the pattern of good English, the more they will be able to produce it themselves. For example, if you wanted the students to write a short analytical account of what someone had achieved, you might select an exemplar text like the one below and ask the students to highlight the useful phrases for this type of writing. (See **Handout 18** online for a non-highlighted version of the text.) The highlighted text will look something like this:

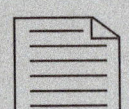

Handout 18: Raiding the reading – Ulug'bek and the Conquest of the Stars

Why is it that a man who accurately plotted the movement of the stars as long ago as 1437, is largely ignored by the West?

Ulug'bek, the grandson of the great conqueror Tamburlaine, was born in Afghanistan in 1394. Inspired by his teacher, Kazi Zade Rumi, he became interested in astronomy. By the age of 34, he had built an observatory in Samarkand – the best equipped anywhere in the medieval world. Nine years later, in 1437, he constructed a star catalogue detailing the accurate positions of 992 stars.

'Where knowledge starts, religion ends', was Kazi Zade Rumi's motto. Ideas like this led to Ulug'bek's untimely death. Because his findings conflicted with religious beliefs, he was assassinated on 29 October 1449. Shortly after his beheading, his observatory was destroyed by religious fanatics. Fortunately, one astronomer escaped with the star catalogue; a copy of which was discovered in Oxford's Bodleian Library in 1648.

In 1908, over four hundred and fifty years after the destruction of his observatory, a Russian amateur archaeologist unearthed a giant sextant on the edge of Samarkand. This was one of the major finds of the twentieth century. Now, next to the sextant, is Ulug'bek's memorial fittingly inscribed, 'Religion disperses like a fog, kingdoms perish but the works of scholars remain for an eternity', his comment that had so infuriated his opponents: Ulug'bek's findings have lasted for nearly 500 years.

Get the students to feedback their ideas, flag these phrases up on a flip chart and ask the students to remember to hijack them for future use. A good way of displaying such phrases is on a washing line. Remember to keep adding good phrases from the reading and get the students into the habit of raiding their reading and adding to the posters.

Poster A

Useful time connectives and sentence signposts for analytical recount writing

- *Why is it that*
- *By the age of*
- *Inspired by*
- *X years later, in . . .*
- *Ideas like this led to*
- *Because*
- *Shortly after*
- *Fortunately,*
- *In x, over xxx years after*
- *This was*
- *Now*

Poster B

Useful expressions for analytical recount writing

- *as long ago as*
- *is largely ignored by*
- *he became interested in*
- *in the world.*
- *untimely death*
- *his findings conflicted with*
- *have lasted for*

The resulting phrases can also be flagged up as co-constructed toolkit ingredients:

Link it

Use effective sentence signposts and connectives to introduce and link your ideas

Express it

Use well-expressed phrases to make your points clear

This approach can be used to introduce whatever type of text a teacher wants the students to be able to write. Thus, if it is explanation text, they could use a good short explanation text relevant to their subject and get the students to identify all the causal links and signposts. For example, 'because', 'as a result', 'therefore', 'leading to', etc.

If it's recount, then time phrases like 'An hour afterwards', 'It wasn't until', 'After that' and 'Three months later', as well as causal phrases, if there are any.

A useful side effect of preparing such work is that it attunes your mind to the important role that these phrases have in aiding communication. It becomes easier to flag them up as you talk or within text that you are teaching, so that you increasingly model them for the students.

Putting the students in teaching assistant role

It is useful to train up students as your 'teaching assistant' who can flag up these phrases on the flip chart for you, while you focus on teaching the class. Nothing will sharpen up thinking and help embed learning faster than being put in this teaching assistant role; so the more students you can involve in the process, the better. If you are lucky enough to have a teaching assistant, this can be an excellent role for them. The biggest problem for anyone flagging up phrases is that they might not know how to spell the words. Remember to encourage students and teacher alike to put a dotted line under any word they are uncertain about (see pages 16–17). This allows the scribe to get the phrases down quickly and the spelling can be checked later. Before displaying the posters for future use, check the spelling is correct. This is a wonderful way of freeing students up when writing so that they extend their vocabulary into words they are not certain of spelling and should be encouraged whenever students are drafting their writing.

Step Ci(b): Raiding the reading – supporting students with being tentative

One of the problems with evaluation or commentary is that it is often reflective and uncertain. Most students don't seem to like being tentative, probably because schools have often taught them (and their parents too) that there are only right and wrong answers. A useful activity to support students in being tentative is to find a good text related to your unit that is tentative and get them to raid the reading. Read the passage to them so that accessing the text is not problematical. Then the students in pairs could be asked to highlight the phrases, signalling uncertainty. Display these as a poster and build up the list as other tentative phrases emerge from different texts. (See page 183 for an example of a tentative exemplar text where the tentative phrases have been highlighted and turned in to a poster.)

Poster C

Useful tentative phrases for explaining something uncertain

- *Nobody knows even approximately . . .*
- *It is thought to be . . .*
- *It is probably . . .*
- *They are presumed to be . . .*
- *It is nearly impossible . . .*

- *It is suggested that . . .*
- *One possible explanation is . . .*
- *Another theory is . . .*
- *It is not known exactly . . .*
- *No one has yet been able to explain exactly why . . .*

Step Ci(c): Raiding the reading – supporting students in English with narrative writing

Raiding the reading is an ideal way for English teachers to build up students' understanding of how to write in the full range of narrative genres. For example, if the novel being read with the class includes suspense, the class can identify the key techniques the writer uses to achieve this suspense and then co-construct a suspense toolkit. This can then be strengthened by looking at how different writers achieve suspense and adding to the toolkit. The teacher can then model suspense writing with the class, selecting the ingredients from the toolkit that they think are most appropriate for the effect they want to achieve, before the students have a go themselves.

How to express suspense might look like this toolkit, which was developed by Pie Corbett:

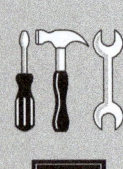

Suspense toolkit: to make your writing scary you can

- Begin with the main character enjoying themselves in a safe place
- Put the main character in a dark lonely place
- Put yourself in their shoes and see it in your head – then describe the place
- Use your senses (see, hear, touch, taste, feel)
- Include detail – use sets of 3
- Use 'empty' words – 'something'; 'someone'; 'it'
- Hear something scary – sinister sounds
- Use a sound effect
- Catch a glimpse of something scary – scary sightings

- Introduce an 'unknown danger'/threat (e.g. a warning or something coming alive) with a dramatic connective – 'At that moment . . .'; 'To his horror . . .'; 'Out of the blue . . .'

- Show how the main character feels – what they think; how they react; what they do

- Introduce an obstacle/block their escape

- Use repetition for effect

- Consider ending section with a question showing character's -worries – suggest what the MC is thinking – and worry the reader by making them think of their worst fear.

Step Cii: Clumping sentence signposts

The following type of activity is useful for any language teacher, but it could also be adapted for any subject area to help draw out the fact that different phrases can signal different things. For an example for French, following some introductory work on the topic of how much television children watch (so that the students will have some idea of what to say and how to say it) the teacher could provide the students with a discursive topic like 'Do children watch too much television?', to be answered in French, and then show the students in English how to box it up.

Boxed-up plan for 'Do children watch too much television?'

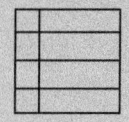

Beginning: Introduction to question	
Middle: • Arguments saying they do watch too much television • The other side of the argument – saying they don't • Additional points	
End: Conclusion	

The introduction and the three parts of the middle section can be represented by the four corners of the room and the teacher's desk can be the conclusion. Then give every student a different sentence signpost in French from the list below. Each student then has to decide what their phrase signposts, and go and stand in the appropriate part of the room. As the students gather in their area, they check if everyone in their area has got the right sort of sentence signpost (thus encouraging them to speak all the phrases and think about what they mean). Once the groups have checked that everyone is in the right place, each person then says their phrase. The students then return to their seats where they will be given the whole sheet to support them in the writing task. The students, in pairs, then try to present to their partner the arguments they would use, utilising some of the phrases.

Handout 19: Sentence signposts in French

Introductory remarks	In conclusion
• Tout le monde accorde à se penser que . . . (Everyone agrees that . . .) • Une question souvent évoquée est celle de . . . (A much discussed question is that of . . .)	• Pour résumer . . . (To conlude . . .) • En somme (In short . . .)
One side of the argument • La première constation qui s'impose, c'est que . . . (The first point to note is that . . .) • En premier, examinons . . . (First, let us examine . . .)	**The other side of the argument** • De l'autre côte . . . (On the other side . . .) • En revanche . . . (On the other hand . . .)

(Adapted from work provided by Andy Roberts, languages department, Fazakerley High School, Liverpool) (See online for complete handout)

Step Ciii(a): Sentence signpost sorting activities

Sentence signposts are key to good communication because they signal to the listener/ reader the direction in which the text is heading. Without them, clear communication is impossible. These often have to be taught like a foreign language because they are not very commonplace in the mumbles of everyday speech. They counteract the 'cos, like, well, anyway, innit' syndrome. Below is a range of ways of helping students become familiar with the appropriate signposts.

Once teachers have identified some key signposts for their subject, a good way of warming up students' ability to use these phrases is to devise sorting activities where they have to clump the phrases according to what they signal.

The activity below is best suited for subjects that include discursive writing. Because newspapers like *The Sun* do not like complexity but rather choose to present a simple answer to everything, the only sentence signposts they use signal either ridicule or agreement; it is useful for students to be aware of this trick but also to be wary of it. Quality discursive writing does not rely on these tricks but rather presents the complexity of issues fairly and reflectively.

The students in pairs first have to sort the sentence signposts so that all those signalling ridicule, agreement, neutrality or complexity are clumped together. Some of the phrases could be placed in more than one clump depending on the tone in which they are said. This is a useful discussion point following the activity.

Handout 20: Sorting sentence signposts (English and humanities)

Ridicule: anyone who thinks like this is an idiot	**Agreement:** all decent, sensible people think like this
Complexity: it's not easy to come to a definite view	**Neutrality:** there are different viewpoints, all of which need to be taken into consideration

On the other hand . . .	Now is the time to stand up . . .	A counter-argument is . . .	Surely . . .
This is just the sort of namby-pamby . . .	Alternatively . . .	There can be no one who still thinks that . . .	Are we going to let ourselves . . .?

(See online for complete handout)

Once the cards have been sorted, ask the students to read the cards out to each other in the appropriate tone of voice so they can hear what the phrases signal.

Flag up on posters any of the phrases that will be useful for work within the unit and display them on the washing line. These can be created to suit whatever type of text is most useful for the different subjects, for example:

Poster D

For and against discursive signposts

- *There is much debate about whether . . .*
- *Many people would argue . . .*
- *On the other hand, those who oppose this view would argue . . .*
- *From a different perspective . . .*
- *The majority view is . . .*
- *However, a minority of people felt that . . .*
- *Supporters of .... would argue that . . .*
- *However, this turned out not to be the case because . . .*

- *A key point in support of this opposing position is . . .*
- *A further complication is . . .*
- *Other sources suggest . . .*
- *A further counter-argument is . . .*
- *In hindsight, it appears that . . .*
- *A convincing argument against this is . . .*
- *Another issue to consider is . . .*
- *Experts at the time thought that . . .*

Uncertain versus certain (theory versus fact) signposts

Poster E

It could be argued that:

- *It is clear that . . .*
- *It is worth considering . . .*
- *The main cause is . . .*
- *A key reason why . . .*
- *Another possible cause . . .*
- *Research has established that . . .*
- *Research suggests that . . .*

Again it's worth reflecting on why sorting activities like these are so effective. Like the dominoes sorting activity, they challenge students. They are interactive and allow everyone to be involved, and they have that necessary edge of competition as people vie to show their superior understanding. Once again, very quickly whole classes become involved, as do large halls of teachers from all subjects as the pictures of staff sorting sentence starters illustrates. The more such engaging focused talk activities become part of units, the more the students will learn. And they'll enjoy the lessons.

Teachers engaged in a sorting activity

Step Ciii(b): Sentence signpost sorting activities – formal and informal

An alternative approach is to analyse the type of writing that the students are tending to do as opposed to the type that the subject requires. Often subjects require formal expression and the students' writing is too chatty and informal. Provide the students with the sort of audience they are trying to communicate with and include some in-role activities to help them speak these formal phrases.

A good way to begin is to devise a sorting activity where the students in pairs have to separate the formal from the informal for, say, report writing related to a particular topic they have studied, and where they have discussed

the audience. Then ask them to try presenting the report orally to their partner so that they actually start to speak the phrases. If some students are particularly good at this, they can present their report to the whole class. The more the class gets to hear the formal language, the more they will be able to replicate it themselves.

The activity below was devised to support formal report writing in English but can easily be adapted to suit the needs of any subject that requires formal writing.

Handout 21: Sorting formal and informal phrases (English)

Not suitable for a formal report (informal, personal, active, concrete and specific)	Suitable for a formal report (formal, impersonal, passive, abstract and general)
I decided to vote for the _____ bid because . . .	The meeting was held to discuss . . .
You hear each of the bids in turn and then . . .	Presentations were made on behalf of . . .
Anyway, once we'd heard the bids we . . .	The first organisation to present its bid was . . .
The daftest point they made was . . .	The main arguments supporting the bids were . . .

(See online for complete handout)

Flag up on posters any of the phrases that will be useful for work within the unit and display them on the washing line.

Step Ciii(c): Sorting images and graphical information to aid comprehension

Many subjects lend themselves to sorting visual information to aid understanding. There is a wide range of excellent sorting activities available for many subjects. The more students are engaged in focused discussion around concepts, the more likely they are to understand and recall them.

For example in maths, the Red and Black numbers Rules-R-us activity from the former Standards Unit, where the students engage in working out what the rule is given the pattern of the numbers they are looking at, is a brilliant way to help Year 7 students understand the logic of algebra because it is a simple way of making an abstract theory more concrete. Looking at the activity online, it seems as if it was originally devised as an activity for a student to do on his or her own to enable the teacher to assess their understanding, but I would recommend using it as a teaching aid as it works wonderfully as a discussion activity to aid

learning. If you type Rules-R-Us into the search mechanism of www.
nationalstemcentre.org.uk, the teachers pack for assessing pupil progress
comes up and this is within the Year 7 resources.

This is just one of many such resources developed by the National Strategies.
Many of these resources are still available at http://tlp.excellencegateway.org.uk/
resource, like the sorting activity below where students are given three sets of
different graphical representations for 10 different situations and have to sort
them so that the graphs representing the same information are clumped together.

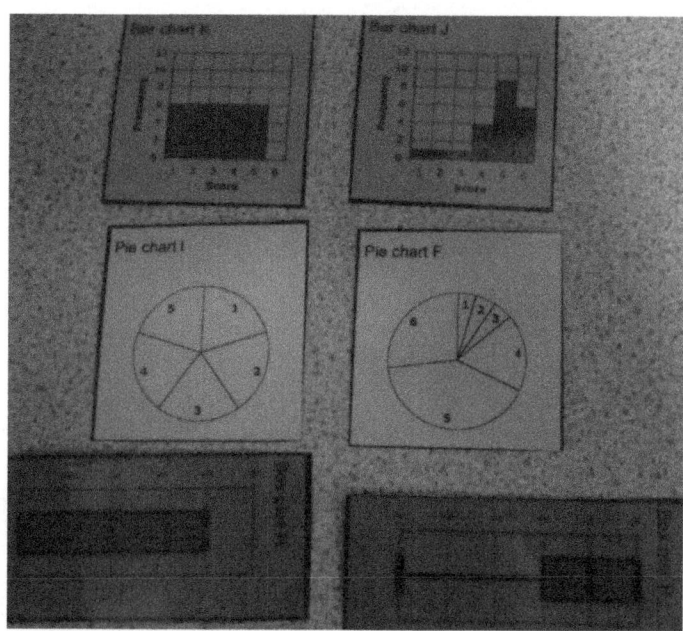

**Another very useful source of material is the Thinking Skills website:
http://www.ncl.ac.uk/cfl at/about/thinkingskills.htm**

Again, working in pairs to sort this information aids learning because the students
are constantly trying to express their understanding in words and, through doing
this, their understanding increases. Another very useful source of material is the
Thinking Skills website: http://www.ncl.ac.uk/cfl at/about/thinkingskills.htm

Step Civ(a): Sequencing text activities – matching text against a graph

Sequencing text against a graph is a way of helping students internalise the
pattern of language for recounting experiments. This approach is relevant to the
many subjects that require students to be able to interpret graphs. The example
below is for science.

Context for this example: This activity would follow an experiment in
which students had observed what happens to ice when it is heated. Provide
the students in pairs with the graph below and the accompanying text cut
up into eight sections.

Handout 22: Graph relating to heating ice

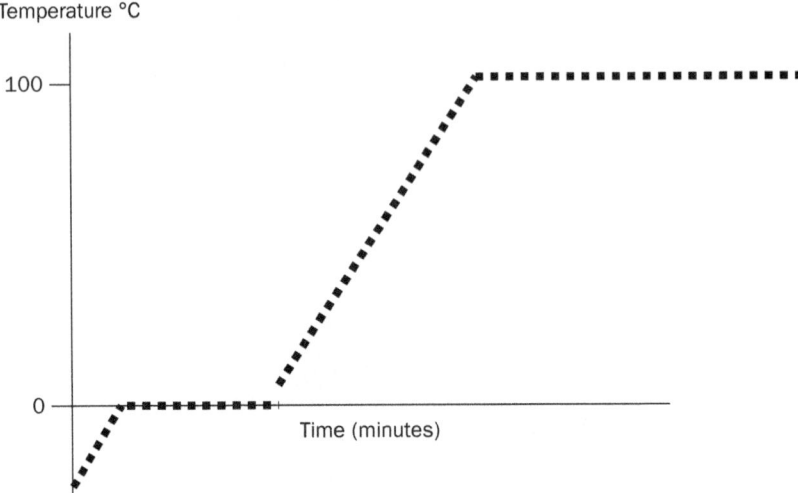

Handout 23: Sequencing text – what happens to ice when heated (science)

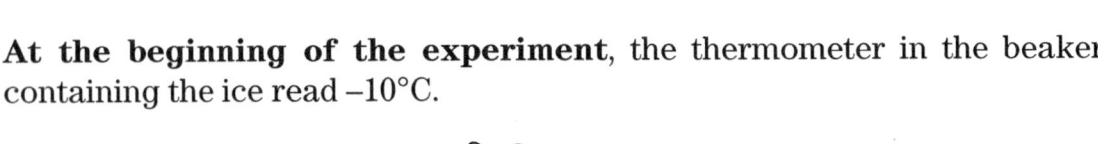

At the beginning of the experiment, the thermometer in the beaker containing the ice read –10°C.

– – – – – – – – – – ✂ – – – – – – – – – –

Once the lit Bunsen burner was placed below the beaker, the temperature rose steadily to 0°C.

– – – – – – – – ✂ – – – – – – – – – –

However, at this point, for a few minutes there was both ice and water in the beaker but there appeared to be no change in the temperature of the water.

– – – – – – – – ✂ – – – – – – – – – –

(Developed in collaboration with Simon Cossutta, science teacher, Cardinal Newman School, Brighton) (See online for complete handout)

Ask the students to:

- decide the order of the text and place it against the appropriate section of the graph;

- check that their text then reads coherently and be prepared to explain the order in which they have placed the text;

- look at the text and select which phrases might be useful to link or express other experiments.

Once they have completed this, you may want to display the text on the whiteboard as exemplar text, display the linking phrases and useful phrases as posters, and co-construct the related toolkit ingredient as illustrated below:

Exemplar text: What happens to ice when heated

At the beginning of the experiment, the thermometer in the beaker containing the ice read –10°C. Once the lit Bunsen burner was placed below the beaker, the temperature rose steadily to 0°C. However, at this point, for a few minutes there was both ice and water in the beaker but there appeared to be no change in the temperature of the water.

This can be explained by the fact that particles in a solid are packed closely together. As a solid melts, the energy transferred is used to pull the particles apart. As the particles in a solid are heated, they vibrate more and the temperature rises. This is because, when all the particles are pulled apart, they are freer to move. Thus as more energy is put in, they move faster and faster causing the temperature to rise. In other words, they have more kinetic energy.

The thermometer then showed a steadily increasing rise in temperature. After x minutes, the water reached 100°C (boiling point) and soon started to boil furiously.

Useful linking phrases recounting experiments

Poster F

- As
- After x minutes
- Causing
- Thus
- This is because
- This can be explained by the fact that
- In other words

Link it

Link the explanation together clearly using causal and time connectives as appropriate

Poster G

Useful expressions to describe what happened in an experiment

- *there appeared to be*
- *the temperature rose steadily*
- *as more energy is put in*
- *the energy transferred is used to*
- *a steadily increasing rise in temperature*
- *and soon started to*

Express it

Use well-chosen phrases to help the reader understand the explanation
Use detail to help make points clearer

Additional activity: Challenge the class in groups of four to mime what happens to the ice. In this way, they will have to interpret the text and the miming process will help fix the information in their heads.

Useful tips for this activity: Remember when cutting up text to rearrange the paragraphs on screen first before printing them off to be cut up, otherwise the text can be put together using the cut edges like a jigsaw. It is also a good idea to present the opening phrase of each section in a larger font. This makes it easier to discuss the text and refer to the different sections.

Step Civ(b): Sequencing text activities – writing frames

Many teachers have understandably tried to shortcut the process of helping students structure text coherently by using writing frames. The main problem with writing frames is that although they temporarily enable students to replicate a well-focused piece of text, the framework does not stay in their heads, so they need another writing frame every time they are required to do any similar writing. However, the sentence starters that form the basis of a well-written writing frame make a very good sequencing activity, since these are the connective and sentence signposts that join the text together. A useful tip to ensure the quality of the frame is to cut it up and then try to sequence it. If it is hard to sequence, the frame needs improving. Once you have ensured that the frame is coherent, you can present it as a sequencing activity as illustrated below.

The following sentence signposts for drama evaluation could be cut up and given to the students to place in a logical order. Activities like this help them to think about how text is structured and will help to fix the opening phrases in their minds. Again, remember to rearrange the order of the phrases before they are cut up so that they cannot be reassembled like a jigsaw.

Handout 24: Sequencing writing frames (drama)

The scene was very effective because . . .

— — — — — — — — ✄ — — — — — — — — — —

The impact of the scene was built up by . . .

— — — — — — — — ✄ — — — — — — — — — —

The staging helped make the scene work because . . .

— — — — — — — — ✄ — — — — — — — — — —

The dramatist had created credible characters by . . .

— — — — — — — — ✄ — — — — — — — — — —

In addition, the quality of the dialogue helped because . . .

— — — — — — — — ✄ — — — — — — — — — —

In conclusion . . .

— — — — — — — — ✄ — — — — — — — — — —

Express it

Use well-chosen sentence starters to guide your reader through the investigation

Step Civ(c): Sequencing text activities – the centrality of sentence signposts to coherence

One reason why many students' writing is poor is because the text is incoherent. One point does not lead to another and the reader is left confused and has to guess how the text would link up for it to make sense. Finding well-constructed text related to your unit for students to sequence can be a very useful way of raising their understanding of the centrality of sentence signposts in giving text meaning.

In the example below, the students would be given four paragraphs plus the text heading to sort into a coherent text. The opening words of each paragraph have been highlighted to make discussion of the order easier. You might want to put instructions like these on the whiteboard for such an activity:

- In pairs, sequence the text.

- Read the sequenced text aloud to check it is coherent.

- Be prepared to explain the order in which you have placed the text.

Handout 25: Sequencing text

Why Vaccinations Work

— — — — — — — — ✂ — — — — — — — — — — —

This allows your white blood cells to detect these types of micro- organisms and learn how to make antibodies to attack and kill them.

— — — — — — — — ✂ — — — — — — — — — — —

At a later time, you might be infected with a harmful form of the micro-organism. Because your white cells have already learnt how to defeat these germs, they can quickly detect the germs and make the antibodies to attack them.

— — — — — — — — ✂ — — — — — — — — — — —

The harmful micro-organisms, therefore, are killed before they can make you ill.

— — — — — — — — ✂ — — — — — — — — — — —

When you have a vaccination, the doctor injects a weak or dead form of particular micro-organisms into your blood.

— — — — — — — — ✂ — — — — — — — — — — —

Once the students have sequenced the text, ask a pair to explain which paragraph is the introductory paragraph and how they know this. The resulting discussion should bring out the key role of the connectives and sentence signposts in guiding the reader through the text. Put these onto a poster to encourage the students to use similar phrases.

Useful linking phrases for explaining something

Poster H

- *When* . . .
- *At a later time* . . .
- *therefore* . . .
- *This allows* . . .

Link it

Link the explanation together clearly using causal and time connectives appropriately

Display the colour-coded exemplar text in the right order on your whiteboard to help the students understand how the text works.

Why Vaccinations Work

When you have a *vaccination*, the doctor injects a weak or dead form of particular *micro-organisms* into your blood.

This allows your *white blood cells* to detect these types of micro-organisms and learn how to make *antibodies* to attack and kill them.

At a later time, you might be infected with a harmful form of the micro-organism. Because your white cells have already learnt how to defeat these *germs*, they can quickly detect the germs and make the antibodies to attack them.

The harmful micro-organisms, therefore, are killed before they can make you ill.

Step Cv: Using cloze procedure to help students understand why coherence matters

A useful alternative is to take any coherent short text related to the unit you are teaching and remove the key words or phrases that make it coherent. Then ask the students to see if they can fill in the gaps. A focused cloze procedure like this is an excellent way of helping students understand the centrality of sentence signposts in making text coherent. The same text on vaccinations has been used below to illustrate this point.

Why Vaccinations Work

In pairs, make this text coherent by adding a word or phrase into the gaps below:

_____you have a **vaccination**, the doctor injects a weak or dead form of particular **micro-organisms** into your blood.

_____your **white blood cells** to detect_____type of micro-organisms and learn how to make **antibodies** to attack and kill _____

_____, you might be infected with a harmful form of the micro-organism. _____your white cells have already learnt how to defeat these **germs**, _____ can quickly detect the germs and make the antibodies to attack them.

The harmful micro-organisms,_____, are killed before_____can make you ill.

Step Cvi: Miming text to help students internalise the sequence of events

A useful addition to sequencing text activities is to get the students to mime the content. This helps to fix the information in their minds because it helps them focus more carefully on the content and the sequence of events in order to interpret it in mime. Mime can be a powerful way of helping students retain information as well as being entertaining because it is active. So for the text above, once it had been sequenced completed the next task could be:

Vaccination role-play

- In groups of four, mime/act out how vaccinations work so that a 9-year-old audience could understand.

(Ground rules: no physical contact – all attacks and defences must be mimed)

- two people are the micro-organisms invading the body

- two people are the white blood cells

More challenging mime: As mentioned before, mime is extremely powerful and can be used to internalise extended sequences as well as short ones like the one above. For example, if you are teaching a Shakespeare play, once the students are familiar with the text, perhaps through having seen a film, read the text of a particular scene to them without giving them a copy, which may just faze them, and ask them in small groups to work out how to mime each section. This process makes even the most tricky groups really engage in trying to listen and interpret what is said. Afterwards, their recall of the scene and ability to interpret its significance is greatly improved. A similar approach could be used for any subject where sequence is significant.

Step Cvii: More advanced sequencing activities – how one thing leads to another

An alternative approach that works extremely well with any information that can be sequenced is to provide closed word dominoes, sometimes known as a word loop. These can be sequenced because there is only one correct order in which they can be placed if the information is to be presented logically. For this it is best to leave the left-hand side of the opening domino blank and the right-hand side of the closing domino blank, as illustrated by handout 26a. In this way, it is clear where the sequence begins and ends. This approach is an excellent way of achieving focused talk if the activity is done in pairs because the students have to discuss the order of events to establish the sequence and to recognise how a quotation is related to an event.

Below is an English example for *Macbeth*. Note that the second task below is an excellent way of getting students to consider the writer's purpose, which is key to developing critical thinking in literature.

Macbeth sequencing activity – introducing dramatic purpose

Task 1: In groups, sequence the cards into chronological order by selecting the quote that supports the event. Begin with the *enter three witches* card. Select your own quotation to accompany the final domino.

Task 2: Decide who says each speech and what Shakespeare's purpose was in including each speech.

Handout 26a: Sequencing events activity – Macbeth

	Enter *three* witches	'Fair is foul Foul is fair.'	Macbeth defeats the rebels
'Brave Macbeth – well he deserves that name –'	Macbeth and Banquo meet the three witches.	'All hail, Macbeth, that shalt be King hereafter.'	Duncan makes Macbeth the Thane of Cawdor.
'Stars hide your fires; let not light see my black and deep desires.'	Lady Macbeth reads the letter from Macbeth.	'too full of the milk of human kindness.'	Duncan arrives at Macbeth's castle.

(Adapted from work produced by the English department at Mexborough School, Mexborough) (See online for complete handout)

This approach would fit very well with information that needs to be presented in sequence, so it can be easily adapted to suit science, PE, D&T or IT, and doubtless other subjects as well. Below is a very different example sequencing a conversation in French.

Year 7 French – Unit 2: La Famille

Task 1: In pairs, match up the dominoes.

Task 2: Now practise reading them aloud, taking it in turns to be the questioner.

Task 3: Cover up the left-hand side of the dominoes and work out the answer to each question.

Task 4: Cover the right-hand side of the dominoes and work out what the question would have been.

Handout 26b: Sequencing conversation activity (French)

*	Comment tu t'appelles?		Je m'appelle Jean-Michel.	Ça s'écrit comment?
J-E-A-N M-I-C-H-E-L.	Il y a combien de personnes dans ta famille?		Dans ma famille, il y a quatre personnes.	Tu as des frères et des soeurs?
J'ai une souer mais je n'ai pas de frère.	Comment s'apelle ta soeur?		Elle s'appelle Christine.	Quel âge a-t-elle?

(Adapted from work by Gaby Simons, languages department, Burnham Upper School, Buckinghamshire) (See online for complete handout)

Step Cviii: Supporting students with the language of evaluation

If students have difficulty writing evaluative sentences, they will need to be supported in their attempts until such sentences become part of their speaking and writing repertoire. An effective way of doing this, which can be adapted to suit the needs of any subject, is illustrated below. A useful piece of equipment for doing this with is a pocket chart, a large plastic poster with long clear plastic pockets, which allows you to display strips of text with ease – the teaching resources company TTS provides good value versions of these. A whiteboard will do but the pocket chart is more flexible. A pocket chart enables you to have an image up on screen while you demonstrate a range of related sentence starters beside it. Alternatively, you could use a washing line for this activity.

If the students are evaluating, say, Van Gogh's *Wheatfield with Crows,* provide them with a range of possible sentence starters, such as:

- The darkness of the sky . . .

- The track cutting right across the centre of the picture . . .

- The inclusion of the crows . . .

Plus a choice of evaluative verb phrases, for example:

- creates a feeling of . . .

- suggests . . .

- implies . . .

- is almost as if . . .

- makes me feel . . .

If you want them to write or present a third-person formal evaluation, include 'makes me feel' and then ban it so they are aware that they must not express themselves in the first person.

Next, ask the students in pairs to select one sentence starter and any verb phrase that they want and then, preferably on mini-whiteboards, complete the sentence. Ask a number of students to read their sentences to the class. Everyone, with this level of support, should be able to produce a good third person evaluative sentence.

Build on this, creating a whole series of opportunities for the students to speak formal evaluative sentences. Once they have started to become confident, you could model being a visiting art professor who has come to explain all about Van Gogh's *Wheatfield with Crows* to the class. Then in pairs they can practise being the visiting professor.

The handout below of useful phrases for art evaluation could be used to extend this approach.

Handout 27: Phrases for evaluation (art, music, English, drama)

When trying to describe the effect of the work:	When taking imaginative leaps or being tentative (uncertain) about the work:
can be inferred from	I wonder what/if
connotes	It could be that
creates a mood of	It is as if
creates a feeling of	It is almost as if

(See online for complete handout)

Below is a more advanced version for any creative evaluation. A good way of helping students internalise the language below is to provide them with the handout and then ask them in pairs to be in teacher role, taking turns to be teacher, and use a wide range of the phrases when commenting on a work of art, drama or literature.

Handout 28: Hook phrases supporting evaluation/ analysis (art, drama, English)

Personal comment (first person):

- This gives me a feeling as though . . .

More distanced comment (third person)

This/which openers

- This shows that . . .

Which linking phrases

- . . . which conveys the idea that . . .

(Created by Vicky Hawking and Julia Strong) (See online for complete handout)

Step Cix: Supporting students with the language of learning – Bloom's taxonomy

An alternative method of helping students to extend their vocabulary and their understanding is to devise phrases as in the handout below giving examples of how to use Bloom's language of learning within your subject. Graham Tyrer, head teacher at Chenderit School, Oxfordshire, has added an additional layer 'Innovation' after 'Evaluation' to encourage students to be more creative with their thinking.

Handout 29: The language of learning – Bloom's taxonomy

Knowledge	list; define; tell; describe (who? what? when? where?); identify; show; label; collect; examine; tabulate; quote; name
Comprehension	summarise; describe; interpret; contrast; predict; associate; distinguish; estimate; differentiate; discuss; extend
Application	apply; demonstrate; calculate; complete; illustrate; show; solve; examine; modify; relate; change; classify; experiment; discover
Analysis	analyse; separate; order; explain; connect; classify; arrange; divide; compare; select; explain; infer

Synthesis	combine; integrate; modify; rearrange; substitute; plan; create; design; invent; compose; formulate; prepare; generalise; rewrite
Evaluation	assess; decide; rank; grade; test; measure; recommend; convince; select; judge; explain; discriminate; support; conclude; compare
Innovation	what if; supposing; say; let's say; imagine; picture; envisage; visualise; see in your mind's eye; think of; consider; conceive of; create in your mind

Step Cx: Analysing sentence signposts to understanding the difference between exam command terms

If the exam command terms are causing confusion in your subject, you may want to adapt the following approach to suit the demands of your particular subject. The example below is for science where the exam command terms are very specific.

Identifying useful phrases for responding to 'explain', 'describe', 'compare', 'evaluate' and 'suggest' type questions in science exams

This activity could be used to follow the vocabulary activity Bxiv, page 67, which helped students understand what the different command terms mean in science exams. This activity, which again is best completed in pairs, now helps the students internalize the sorts of phrases they will need to use when answering each type of question. Time spent helping students become familiar with the tune of the different sorts of answers that need to be written in response to the typical command terms of science questions will be time well spent, as it will save time later on and build confidence. If possible, it would be useful if students are familiar with the tune of all these different types of scientific texts by the end of KS3.

Provide the students in pairs with a copy of **Handout 30a** (see online) and ask them to highlight useful sentence starters/connectives for each type of science answer.

- Now ask the pairs to compare their conclusions with those of another pair.

- Get feedback from the groups and highlight the text on screen as illustrated below. You may also want, at the same time, to build up posters of the phrases highlighted, as illustrated for the Explain section.

Identifying useful phrases for responding to the different command terms

1. Explain – responses to explain-type questions

Example 1a

By the time the temperature is 22°C, the photosynthesis enzymes are working at maximum rate for the conditions and the graph is flat. It means that either light intensity or carbon dioxide is rate limiting at that stage, not temperature.

Example 1b

The molecules in the egg yolk have a 'head' part that dissolves in water, but a long 'tail' part that dissolves in oil. A large number of these molecules surround the oil droplet and so it can stay suspended in the water as an emulsion which is stable. The egg yolk molecules act as an emulsifier.

Example 1c

Because black is a good absorber of the radiation from the sun, in a given time, more of the sun's energy will be captured and transferred into the water, making it hotter.

Poster I

Sentence signposts and connectives for 'explain' answers

By the time
It means that either . . . or
Because
and so
making it

2. Describe – responses to describe-type questions

Example 2a

First of all the heat (stimulus) will be detected by the temperature receptors in the skin. The receptors will send an electrical impulse along the sensory neurone to the synapse in the spinal cord. A chemical messenger is released, which crosses the synapse space and triggers an impulse in the relay neurone. The same thing happens at the next synapse so that an impulse is sent down the motor neurone to the muscle, which is the effector. When the impulse reaches the muscle, it causes the muscle to contract and pulls the hand away from the heat. This is a reflex action, which does not have to be processed via the brain.

Example 2b

In the beginning, dust particles and gases are pulled together by the force of gravity. As the atoms of hydrogen gas are forced together, the nuclei collide and nuclear fusion begins. The star becomes stable as the forces acting inwards and the forces acting outwards are balanced. Eventually, it runs out of hydrogen, so the star starts to cool and becomes a red giant. Then it starts to shrink under its own gravity and, as the material comes closer together, the temperature rises and the star glows much brighter as a white dwarf.

3. Compare – responses to compare-type questions

Example 3a

Generating electricity for an immersion heater burns fossil fuels, which releases carbon dioxide into the atmosphere, whereas solar energy doesn't release any extra carbon dioxide. Moreover, solar energy is a renewable energy source, which also means that we are conserving fossil fuels, which are in danger of running out. However, solar energy does have disadvantages because it needs the daylight and some countries don't have enough hours of sunlight, like Scotland in the winter. This means there will be times when not enough hot water is available for the household, whereas an immersion heater can supply hot water all of the time.

Example 3b

The advantages of phytomining are that it would take less energy than the traditional method and it will be carbon neutral because the plants will take the same amount of carbon dioxide out of the atmosphere as they grow as they release when they are burnt. On the other hand, the traditional method is quicker as the plants take a long time to grow.

4. Evaluate – responses to evaluate-type questions

Example 4a

Fossil diesel is mainly used because it is quick to produce from crude oil and, up to this point, is cheaper than biodiesel.

However, biodiesel has a lot to recommend it, as it is a renewable resource, whereas crude oil is running out. In addition, it is carbon neutral because it takes in the same amount of carbon dioxide when the plants are growing as it gives out when burnt as fuel.

Although burning biodiesel does produce the same amounts of both carbon dioxide and carbon monoxide as fossil diesel, there is less sulphur dioxide, so there will be less acid rain, and fewer carbon particles – which cause global dimming. Also, waste oils can be used up to produce fuel.

Overall, I think we should be using more biodiesel, as it is important for us all to reduce our carbon footprint in an effort to halt global warming.

Example 4b

This trial involved large numbers, so that would have given valid results. It was also a good trial of the general population because, if poor uneducated women could make it work, it would be reliable. However, the trial was not very ethical by today's standards because we don't know that the women gave informed consent, and they were not told it was experimental or that there could be side effects. The trial was not well designed as there was no placebo control group and they did not do pre-trials to find the best dose and check for side effects. I believe that this was an unethical trial.

5. Suggest – responses to suggest-type questions

Example 5a

The particles might be small enough to pass through the skin and they might be toxic inside the body.

Example 5b

This could be a control group so that the researchers had a group with no cancer to compare their results with.

To reinforce student understanding prior to science exams, you may want to revisit this area and convert the highlighted words and phrases into an activity to help the students become familiar with the specific sort of sentence signposts and connectives that may be useful when answering the different types of command questions in science.

Ask the students to look at the lists of sentence signposts and connectives from the exemplar text for the different command terms, as reproduced in the handout below. Explain that there will probably be some explanation terms like 'because', 'this resulted in', signalling that one thing caused something else, in all of the texts. In other words, all of the terms include the concept of 'explain', but 'compare', 'describe', 'evaluate' and 'suggest' commands all call for a specific type of explanation. Then ask them to do the following:

- In pairs, highlight any terms below which are standard causal connectives, e.g. 'because', 'this causes', etc.

- Discuss your selection with another pair.

Handout 30b: Identifying useful connectives and sentence signposts for describe, compare, evaluate and suggest questions

'Suggest' answers	`Describe' answers
• might be • This could be • So that	• First of all • Which • And triggers
'Compare' answers (advantages and disadvantages) • Which • Whereas • Moreover	`Evaluate' answers • Because • up to this point, • However,

(See online for complete handout)

- Ask the groups to feedback which words they have highlighted. The list on the screen will look something like this.

Handout 30c: Useful connectives and sentence signposts for describe, compare, evaluate and suggest questions highlighting generic explain signposts

'Suggest' answers	'Describe' answers
• might be • This could be • So that	• First of all • Which • And triggers

'Compare' answers (advantages and disadvantages)	'Evaluate' answers
• Which • Whereas • Moreover	• Because • up to this point, • However,

(See online for complete handout)

- Now ask the pairs to see if they can add any additional phrases that could be added for the describe, compare, evaluate and suggest categories.

- Get the students to feedback their ideas and create posters for each specific command word, which can be built up as more text of this type is encountered. The more the students can become attuned to looking for the phrases that are often used in scientific descriptions, evaluations, etc., the more they will have the appropriate phrases in their heads and be able to use them appropriately and, of course, understand what they signal when they read them.

Your posters may end up looking something like this:

Useful phrases for describe-type questions

Poster J

- First of all,
- The same thing happens . . .
- In the beginning, . . .
- Eventually, . . .
- becomes . . .
- Then . . .

Additional suggestions

- After that, . . .
- It can be observed that . . .
- This is known as . . .

Poster K

Useful phrases for compare-type questions

- *Whereas . . .*
- *Moreover, . . .*
- *which also means that . . .*
- *However, x does have disadvantages because . . .*
- *Like . . .*
- *The advantages of . . .*
- *On the other hand, . . .*

Additional suggestions

- *The disadvantages of . . .*
- *The negative effects of . . .*
- *The positive effects of . . .*
- *An additional drawback is . . .*

Poster L

Useful phrases for evaluate-type questions

- *In addition, . . .*
- *Although . . .*
- *Overall, I think . . .*

- *However, . . .*
- *The trial was not . . .*
- *I believe that . . .*

Additional suggestions

- *In conclusion, . . .*
- *For these reasons, . . .*
- *There is not sufficient evidence . . .*

Poster M

Useful phrases for suggest-type questions

- *might be . . .*
- *This could be . . .*

Additional suggestions

- *This suggests that . . .*
- *This indicates that . . .*
- *It is possible that . . .*

Poster N

Useful phrases for explain-type questions (note these terms may also appear in describe-, compare-, evaluate- and suggest-type questions, as these all contain an element of explanation)

- *It means that either . . . or.*
- *Because . .*
- *making it . . .*
- *which . . .*
- *and triggers . . .*
- *so that . . .*
- *When . . .*
- *it causes a . . .*
- *As . . .*
- *There is less . . . so there will be less . . .*
- *As it is important . . .*

Additional suggestions

- *This results in . . .*
- *Which leads to . . .*
- *This will make . . .*

CHAPTER 6

Step D: Internalising the tune of exemplar text – the basic approach

(This chapter is supported online by **Handouts 31a–31e** and **Slides 40–41**. Suggestions for how to present this step on a training day are provided on pages 216–17.)

An excellent way of warming up the key words and phrases needed for a unit is to involve the students in talking the text type so they actually internalise all the language related to a particular topic; in effect, they become familiar with its tune.

Devise an exemplar text that illustrates the key terms, phrases and concepts that you want to focus on, and present it orally like the text on the fox for the imitation stage of Talk for Writing (see page 13). Rather than giving the group the text, display the related text map or graph and then say the text to them out loud and devise, with the group's help, a series of actions that sum up the technical vocabulary and concepts you want the students to internalise. Learn the text together with the actions so that everyone has internalised the passage like the science and maths examples below. In this engaging way, the class is involved in internalising not just the technical vocabulary of the topic, but all the sentence patterns and useful phrases that contribute to the tune of your subject, as highlighted below.

Exemplar text explaining a graph in science – to be learnt orally This *graph* is showing the relationship between *heart rate* and *time of exercise*. The heart rate is shown on the *vertical axis* and the time is shown on the *horizontal axis*. These are the *variables.* As one thing changes, the other changes. As the time of exercise **increases** (goes up), my heart rate increases (goes up). The *shape of the graph* is a *straight line*. The graph does not start at the *origin* as I always have a *heartbeat*, otherwise I would be dead!

(Developed by Sue Pickerill and Catherine Jessey, science teachers at Varndean School, Brighton)

Express it

Use technical language appropriately

Below is a more sophisticated example of the same approach, this time for a Year 10 class.

Exemplar text relating to enzymes

Enzymes have *specific shapes*. Their *active sites* fit with *specific substrates* to form the *enzyme–substrate complex.*

They act as *catalysts* in *reactions* to reduce the *activation energy* needed to start them and make them take place more quickly.

If the temperature gets too hot, enzymes *denature* and stop working.

(The group worked with the teacher to create actions that would help them understand not just the meaning of the technical words but how they are used in context, as illustrated below.)

- **Enzyme** – specific shape of hand
- **Substrate** – corresponding shape to 'fit' to enzyme
- **Enzyme–substrate complex** – fit enzyme and substrate hand gestures together
- **Catalyst** – speeds up a reaction = fast cat 'meeeoooooow'
- **Denature** – close up hand to show change in shape

(Developed by Sue Peckerill and Catherine Jessey, science teachers at Varndean School, Brighton)

They could then recite the passage using the actions to help convey its meaning. As a result of the process, the students became more able to express their learning clearly as illustrated by this Year 10 student's ability to write about the topic:

The structure of an enzyme is important because the specific shape allows molecules to fit into the enzyme active sites to create an enzyme-substrate complex, which is very important in order for the enzyme to work.

Express it

Use technical language appropriately

In many ways, this text sums up the nature of the tune of science. If you are hoping the English department might be teaching in such a way that they can express their science like this, you could be very disappointed! A teacher who understands the content also needs to teach the students how to express their knowledge effectively.

The approach can also be useful to help students memorise key formulas, as illustrated by this maths example relating to geometry.

> *In any right-angled triangle, the square of the hypotenuse is equal to the sum of the squares on the two other sides.*

The class learned the short text together with the actions so that everyone internalised the sentence. They could then recite the sentence using the actions to help convey its meaning. As a result of the process, the students became more confident in using and applying the language of mathematics. (This approach was developed by Andrew Lyon, KS4 maths coordinator, Queensbury School, Bradford.)

These sorts of Talking the text activities are very motivating for the students, as so much of their school experience is passive. GCSE PE teachers have found this method particularly useful for livening up the daunting vocabulary and concepts that students have to internalise for this subject.

Moving from imitation to independent application

The underlying pattern of any text that we want the students to write has to have been internalised if they are to write it successfully. Without such support, they will experience repeated failure which, in turn, will understandably make them dislike writing.

The simplest and most effective way of helping insecure students internalise the pattern of language of any subject or text type is to follow the three stages of the Talk- for-Writing approach, as outlined at the beginning of this handbook (on pages 12–19) and illustrated in Parts 1.i and 1.ii on the video clips, where the students learn an exemplar text word for word as it is told to them by their teacher with a text map to help them recall the details and actions to help them remember. The idea is that before they see the exemplar text written down, they have learnt it so that when they do see it they can read it easily and can therefore engage in analysing it. This approach can be beneficial in any subject that requires the students to write, whether that's writing a well-crafted paragraph or extended writing.

As explained in the introduction to this handbook, it will be most effective across the curriculum if the Talk-for-Writing approach is used by the English department and other departments can build on the approach as appropriate. A key resource to support English departments in doing this is *Talk for Writing Across the Curriculum* by Pie Corbett and myself which, as explained earlier, includes fully worked English-based units of work for each of the key non-fiction text types, including a series of warming up the word and phrase activities as well as the three stages of talking the text type. Below is one example of what the approach might look like for a unit of work in English.

Say that in the first term of Year 7 in English, the students are doing a unit on explanation, including a section on why some people are seen as heroes, pitched at a teenage audience. The teacher uses a learning frame to introduce the unit, and devises some activities to warm up the causal language of explanation first by raiding the reading of some explanation texts and then orally through role play, for example explaining why you are late for school, or haven't done your homework. Since the exemplar text is on David Beckham, they may also want to include a brainstorm on why Beckham is so world famous to warm up the content.

Stage 1. Imitation

The teacher then prepares an exemplar text of the sort of writing they want the students to do but does not show it to them at this stage. The teacher turns the text into a text map – a series of images to sum up the text – and displays this on the whiteboard. This text map is available as **Handout 31b** on the online.

Text map for *Why is David Beckham so famous?* (see p. 108)
The students are asked to stand up and 'perform' the text with the teacher imitating what the teacher says and the actions used. The teacher builds up the text line by line so that the students repeat the words and actions after they have been demonstrated (as illustrated by the videos online). Slowly the teacher builds up the whole text so that all the students are engaged in talking the text. The teacher must make certain that the class is using the right intonation and, as they get more secure in imitating the text, the teacher should back off and become quieter and quieter so that it is the student voice that dominates the talking of the text.

Once they have internalised the text as a whole class, which will not take long, the students are asked to perform the text in groups and finally in pairs. It is useful for them to jot down their own version of the text map, as we remember things much better from our own squiggles rather than those of other people. Once they have internalised the pattern of the text in this manner, they are then shown the text on the whiteboard. See **Handout 31c** online for a non-annotated version of the text.

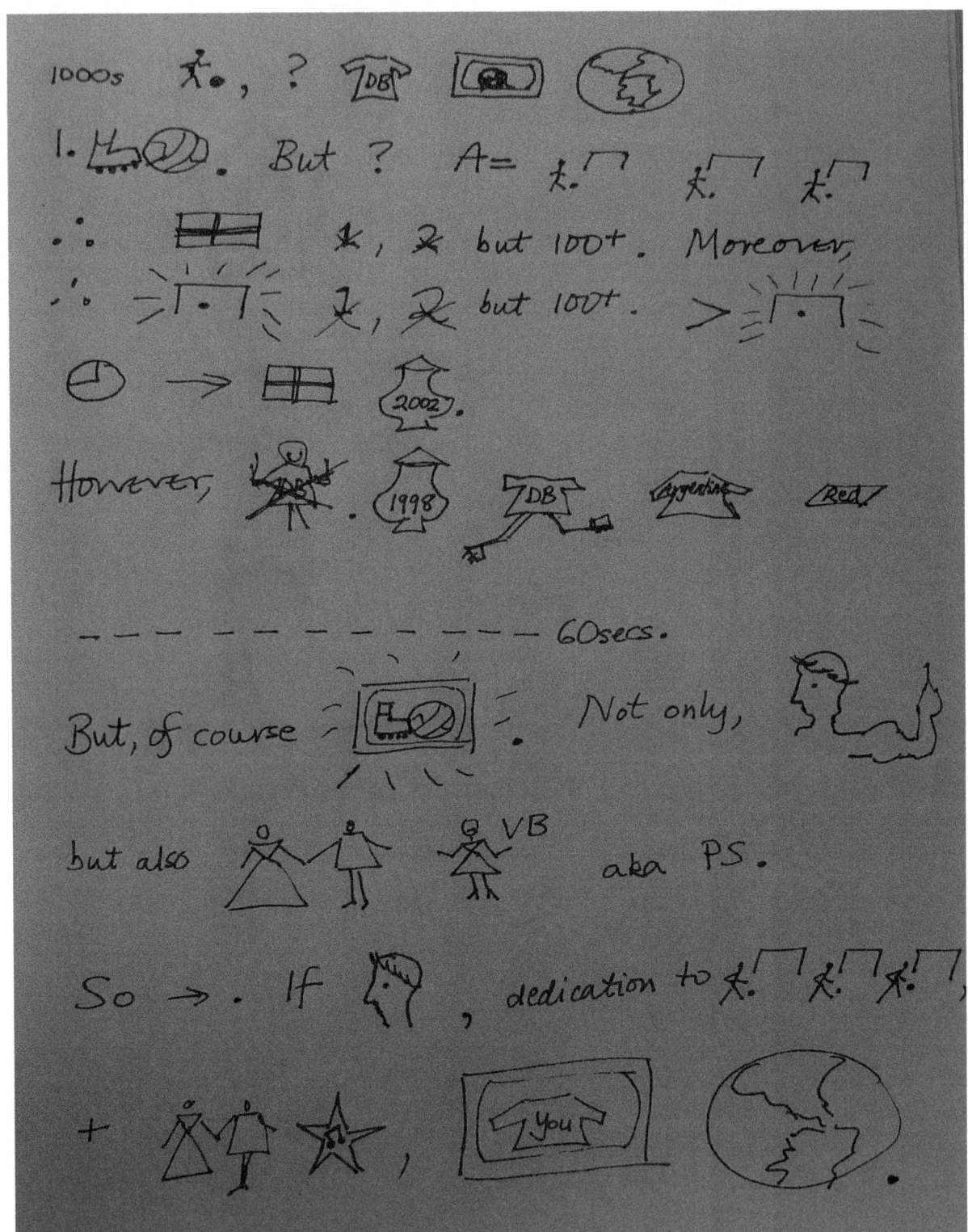

Text map for *Why is David Beckham so famous?*

Top tip

Do not use clip art to create the images on your text maps. The brain recalls things much better from symbols we have created ourselves, so the students need to be presented with hand-drawn examples and then create their own hand-drawn text maps.

Now, using a flip chart alongside the text on the whiteboard, the teacher shows the class how to box it up so they can see how it is structured

This boxed-up plan for explanation text can then be displayed on the washing line.

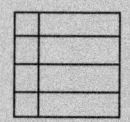

Boxed-up planning for *Why is David Beckham so famous?*

Beginning: introduce the question	Intro why is Beckham so famous in an interesting way to hook reader
Middle: Main reason + additional info supporting main reason	1. Brilliant at free kicks because practises obsessively Therefore played for Eng over 100 times and scored more than 100 goals – mention World Cup goal 2002
A reason against	However, not always hero – red card incident 1998
Additional reasons for	Great looking Married to ex-Spice girl now fashion icon
Conclusion	Sum up explanation and echo opening lines

Now the teacher gives each pair of students a copy of the text and asks them to highlight the following three features:

- any linking phrases (connectives or sentence signposts) that join the text together and tell the reader the direction it is going in;

- any technical language;

- any other phrases that might be useful for any piece of writing explaining why someone is famous.

If the class has not done this sort of work before, the teacher would do the first two paragraphs on the screen with them so they understand what to do.

Once they have finished, they discuss their highlighting with another pair and then, following feedback from the class, the exemplar text on screen would probably end up looking something like this:

Why is David Beckham so famous?

There are thousands of famous footballers, so why is it that David Beckham is probably the most famous football player in the whole wide world?

First, he's a genius at **free kicks**. But why is he so good? The answer has to be, practise, practise, practise. That is why he played for England not once, not twice, but over a 100 times. Moreover, that is why he's scored not once, not twice, but over a 100 times. His most famous goal, in the dying seconds of the match, **qualified** England for the 2002 **World Cup**.

However, he's not always been the hero. In the 1998 World Cup, David Beckham kicked out at an Argentinean player, and was given a **red card** – the longest 60 seconds of his life.

But, of course, he's not just famous for kicking a ball. Not only has he got the physique of a **Greek God**, but he's also married to **fashion icon** Victoria Beckham, otherwise known as Posh Spice.

So, there you have it. If you look like a Greek God, have the dedication to practise, practise, practise, and marry a pop star, you too could be the most famous football player in the whole wide world.

Turn the highlighted phrases into posters to support the students' writing.

Poster A

Useful causal linking and signposting phrases for explanation text

- *There are thousands of . . .*
- *so why is it that . . .*
- *First, . . .*
- *But why . . .*
- *The answer has to be . . .*
- *Moreover, that is why . . .*
- *However, . . .*
- *But, of course, . . .*
- *So, . . .*
- *If you . . .*

Poster B

Useful general phrases for explaining why someone is famous

- *the most famous . . .*
- *in the whole wide world . .*
- *not once, not twice, but over a . . .*
- *not always been the hero . . .*
- *he's not just famous for . . .*
- *you too could be . . .*

The exemplar text can then be used to draw out all the features for the explanation writing toolkit and the related posters that illustrate the features. This should be co-constructed with the class so they understand all the elements that will help them embed the process. You will probably end up with something like the following:

The general explanation writing toolkit – use these guidelines to help you

Plan it: order information logically	• Box up explanation ordering points logically and remembering audience • Introduce explanation with a hook to engage reader • Consider including points that may undercut your explanation • Conclude explanation effectively, e.g. round it off with an interesting fact or an echo of the beginning
Link it: make explanation fit together	• Link points clearly and logically using causal connectives and sentence signposts (see **Poster O**, p.110) • Read it through to check that it flows

Express it: make explanation clear and interesting	• Use well-chosen points to explain to the reader (see **Poster P**, above) • Use detail to help make points clearer • Vary sentences to engage the reader • Use technical language appropriately and explain it if necessary
Check it:	• Read explanation through, checking it for accuracy and improve it where it doesn't sound right. Check it is well punctuated and all words are spelt correctly • Make certain your writing explains clearly in a coherent and entertaining way

These 'writing ingredients' should be displayed, as they will be central to the later stages (the shared and independent writing) as well as informing self/peer evaluation and feedback from the teacher.

Stage 2. Innovation

Now that the students have internalised the pattern of the text and taken part in analysing it, the teacher can move to the innovation stage where they demonstrate how you can use the same basic pattern to explain why someone else is famous. So for the shared writing session the teacher could choose, for example, to explain why Nelson Mandela is probably the most famous leader in the world. The session might start with the class brainstorming suggestions for why Mandela is so famous to warm up the topic, followed by some raiding the reading from an information sheet on Mandela before beginning the shared writing. For the shared writing, the teacher would keep the David Beckham text on the whiteboard so the class can see the exemplar, and the boxed-up planning on the washing line together with the posters of useful phrases and the explanation writing toolkit. They would then, with the help of the class, craft the new text involving the students with phrases like

- Which do you think would work best?

- Let's just read that and see how it sounds.

- We've got _____ what else do we need? What could follow? You tell me.

- Which bits don't seem to fit?

- What would make it flow better?

For more examples of useful phrases to use for shared writing, see **Handout 3** online.

As the shared writing is progressing, a student could be flagging up useful alternative words and phrases and displaying them on the washing line so that when the students have a chance to write their own version, there is help at hand. Throughout the process, the teacher would have regularly read the writing out to the class so they could hear it and decide if it works. All the time the teacher would have been modelling what a good writer does.

The shared writing might end up looking something like this:

Why is Nelson Mandela so famous?

The world is full of leaders but most of them are forgotten almost as soon as they lose power. So why is it that Nelson Mandela is probably the most famous leader in the whole wide world, even though he retired in 1999?

The answer has to be that despite all the odds he became the first ever South African president to be elected in a democratic election after years of oppressive apartheid, a system of racial segregation enforced by the government to maintain white minority rule. Not only did he survive 27 years as a political prisoner and then become president, he also led the movement for reconciliation to help people of all races to live together in harmony in South Africa.

However, for a few people, he will never be a hero because he was a militant anti-apartheid activist, and the leader of the armed wing of the African National Congress.

But for most people he remains a great hero. To prove it, he has received not one, not two, but over 250 awards, including the Nobel Peace Prize, which he was awarded in 1993.

It's hard to imagine a more challenging and inspiring life. That is why Nelson Mandela is probably the most famous leader in the whole wide world.

Now it's time for the students to have a go at writing their own explanation of why Nelson Mandela is so famous. The teacher might want to provide them with a key facts sheet so they have additional information to back up their explanation. The teacher would display the shared writing as well as the boxed-up planning, the writing toolkit and the posters of useful phrases resulting from the shared writing so they have a model and ideas to guide their writing.

It's a good idea to ensure that there is time for the students to share their versions with a partner, so the students in pairs could have read through the writing and decided what worked well and what might need improving. Allow the authors time to make the changes they want to make. Also, encourage the students to write their own comment at this stage on how well they think they have completed the task.

Now the teacher can take in the work and mark it and use this as an opportunity for formative assessment to decide on what aspects of the work need more focus. The writing toolkit can provide a very useful tick list here to check if all the students are managing to include all those ingredients effectively and, if not, what now needs to be done to help them to take the next steps in improving their work. The teacher can add their comment to the student's comment to begin a dialogue on what they need to do to improve. The more students are encouraged to reflect on what they need to do to make progress, the more likely they are to progress.

Stage 3. Independent application

When the work is handed back is a key opportunity to focus on those aspects that need attention. A visualiser, or anything that enables you to put text up on screen instantly, is an invaluable asset here as you can display work that you want the students to be able to see and help them discuss what works well. Again the teacher would ensure that the students have an immediate opportunity to polish their work and put the improvements suggested into practice, otherwise time spent marking can be time wasted. The teacher could now focus on whatever aspects of the work need more extended attention and could then move on to the independent application stage.

It's important that the students are enthusiastic about whatever it is they are to write about, so it's best to leave the choice of which famous person they write about up to them. The teacher could perhaps ask the students to choose a very different hero or heroine and ask them to write an explanation about why this person is so famous. Again keep all the support materials in place. Hopefully, this time, the students will have internalised the pattern and all the additional teaching points and will be able to set about the task confidently and produce a well-crafted explanation.

Applying this approach across the curriculum

This three-stage approach is not only applicable to English teaching in secondary schools but can easily be adapted to suit the needs of a wide range of other departments even if they only tackle a certain sort of writing, say, once a term. For significant text that reappears throughout a subject's curriculum, for example investigations in science, it is probably worthwhile investing time in this process so that by the end of KS3 the students have thoroughly internalised the patterns of language required by investigations.

Say that in the first term of Year 7 the students are going to investigate the effect of exercise on heart rate. You have framed the unit with a learning frame, introduced the technical vocabulary with a never-heard-the-word grid and integrated some activities to warm up the words and the phrases into your teaching of the scientific content. The students are now at the stage where they need to write up the investigation.

Imitating the exemplar text

Prepare an exemplar text of the sort of writing you want the students to do but do not show it to them at this stage. (The text used here to illustrate the approach

is only the opening sections of the investigation, not the full investigation.) Turn the text into a series of images to sum up the sequence and display that on the whiteboard (see the example below). Again do not use clip art to create your images/symbols and discourage the students from doing so when they create their own text maps. The brain recalls things much better from symbols we have created ourselves because of the hand–brain connection.

Text map for science investigation. This is available as **Handout 31d** online.

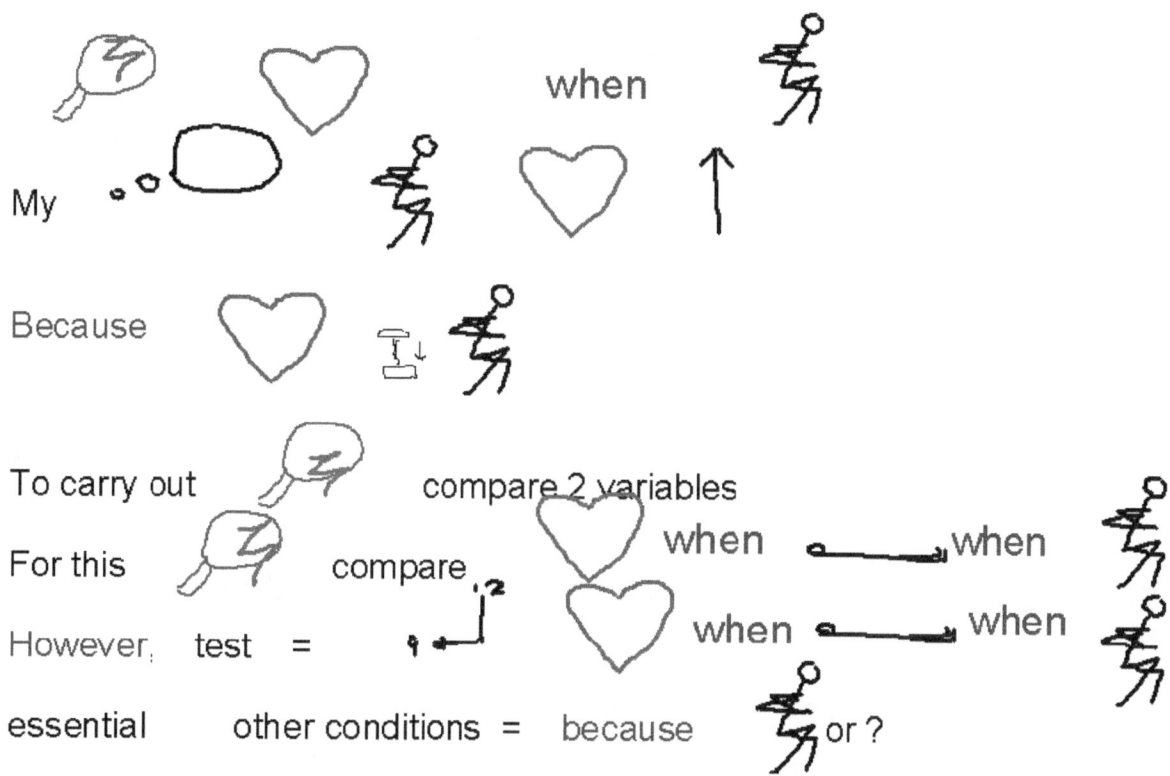

Investigation into the effect of exercise on heart rate

- Ask the students to stand up and then 'perform' the text for them with actions building the text up line by line so that they repeat the words and actions after you (as illustrated online). Slowly build up the whole text so that all the students are engaged in talking the text. Make certain they are using the right intonation and, as they get more secure in imitating the text, back off and become quieter and quieter so that it is the student voice that dominates the talking of the text.

- Next, get the students to perform the text in groups and finally in pairs.

Analysing the text

Once they have internalised the pattern of the text in this manner, which will not take long, show them the text exemplar on the whiteboard. (See **Handout 31e** online for a copy of this text.)

Exemplar text for the opening section of an investigation into the effect of exercise on heart rate

I am investigating what happens to my **heart** when I take exercise.

My **hypothesis**, what I think will happen, is that exercise will make my heart beat faster because the heart has to pump blood faster to enable me to do the exercise.

To carry out an investigation, you must compare two variables: two things which change or vary. For this investigation, I will compare my heart rate when I am resting and when I am taking exercise.

However, it is important to make the test fair. To make this test fair, I must record my heart rate for exactly the same amount of time when I am resting as when I am exercising. It is essential that all the other conditions remain the same because, otherwise, I wouldn't know if it was the exercise or something else that was making the difference.

● Now, using a flip chart alongside the text on the whiteboard, work with the class to box it up (plan it as a simple two-column grid) so they can see how it is structured and can start to understand the ingredients that go into making the text work. This boxed-up plan for the first stage of science investigations can then be displayed on the washing line.

Boxed-up planning for a science investigation: does exercise affect heart rate?

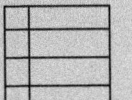

Headings for any science investigation	
Introduction: State what is being investigated	Effect of exercise on heart rate
Prediction: State what you think will happen	Exercise makes the heart beat faster because it has to pump blood faster
Variables: Explain that you have to compare two variables	Compare heart rate when resting and when exercising
Fairness: Explain why the test must be fair and how to make it fair	Time heart rate for exactly same amount of time when resting and exercising Everything else must be the same, otherwise wouldn't know what was making the difference

● Discuss with the students why planning what you are going to write by boxing it up in this manner can be useful. Discuss with them how to make this into an ingredient for a toolkit for science investigations. You might end up with:

- o Plan it: Box up your investigation so that you guide the reader through each stage logically.

- Next, lead the students through the basic analysis of each paragraph so that they have identified:

    - o topic sentences

    - o any useful connectives or sentence starters that help link the explanation together

    - o the phrases that can be used for any investigation

    - o any technical vocabulary.

Consolidate their understanding by working with the class to colour code the text so that they can easily see how what they have learnt about explanation text in one curriculum area is relevant to another.

Turn the key phrases they have identified into posters as in the examples below and display them so that when they write similar text, they have the useful phrases to support them. These posters can be added to as more useful general phrases emerge from similar text, including the best of the students' answers for these types of questions. Encouraging the students to recognise phrases that could be useful will build up their familiarity with the target language of science.

Poster C

Useful sentence signposts for investigations

- *I am investigating what happens to*
- *My hypothesis*
- *To carry out an investigation*
- *For this investigation, I will compare*
- *it is important to make the test fair.*
- *To make this test fair*
- *It is essential that all the other conditions remain the same because*

Poster D

Useful linking phrases for investigations

- *when . . .*
- *because . . .*
- *However, . . .*
- *Otherwise, . . .*

Poster E

Useful expressions for investigations

- *what I think will happen*
- *you must compare two variables: two things which change or vary.*
- *However, . . .*
- *Otherwise, . . .*
- *I must record*
- *for exactly the same amount of time*
- *I wouldn't know if it was the_____ or something else that was making the difference.*

It is useful, Blue Peter style, to have a completed fully analysed version like the one below to show the class once they have been involved in thinking about how to analyse it themselves.

Boxed up, colour-coded exemplar investigation text to show how it works

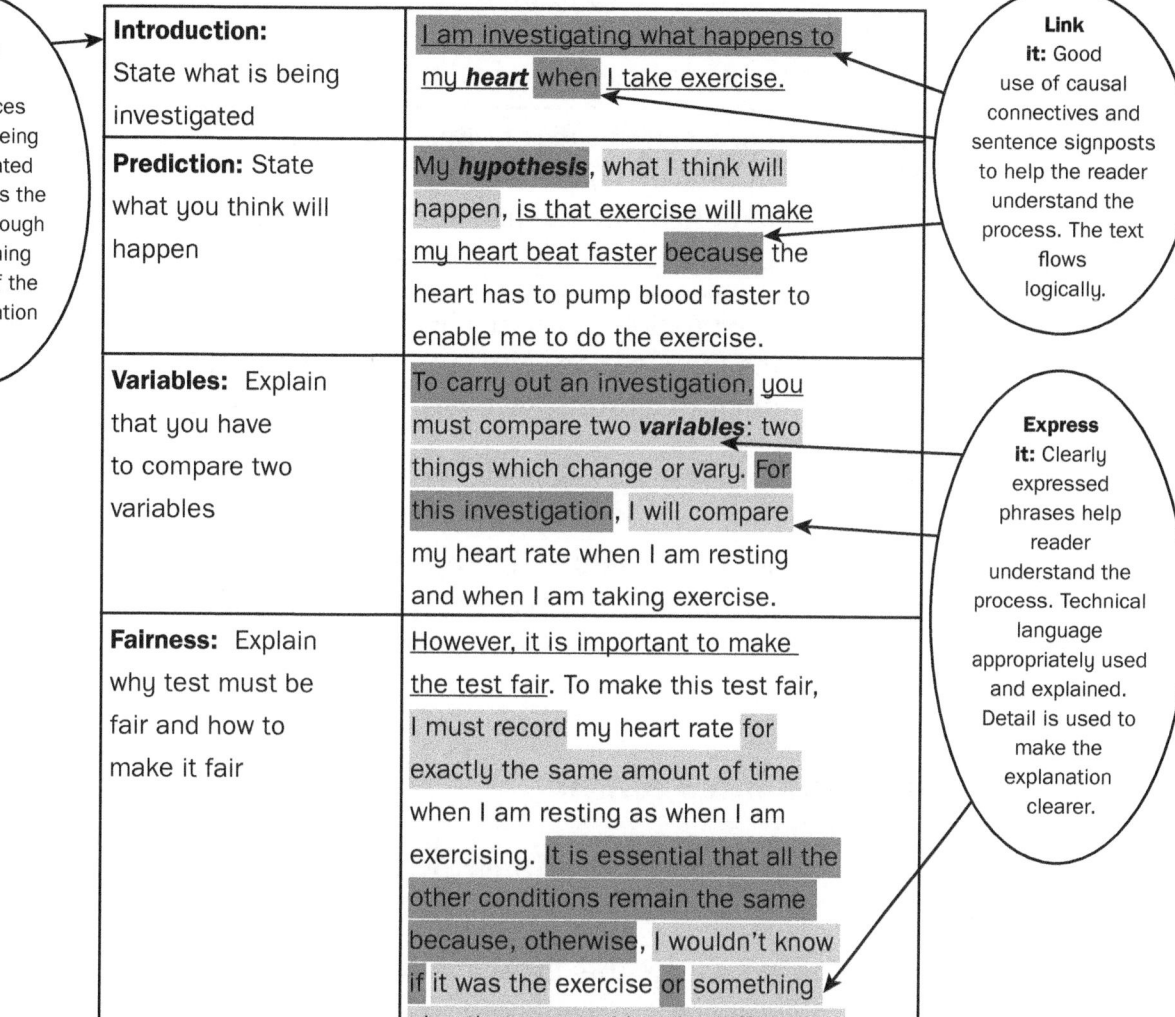

Plan it: Introduces what is being investigated and guides the reader through the opening stages of the investigation

Introduction: State what is being investigated	I am investigating what happens to my **heart** when I take exercise.
Prediction: State what you think will happen	My **hypothesis**, what I think will happen, is that exercise will make my heart beat faster because the heart has to pump blood faster to enable me to do the exercise.
Variables: Explain that you have to compare two variables	To carry out an investigation, you must compare two **variables**: two things which change or vary. For this investigation, I will compare my heart rate when I am resting and when I am taking exercise.
Fairness: Explain why test must be fair and how to make it fair	However, it is important to make the test fair. To make this test fair, I must record my heart rate for exactly the same amount of time when I am resting as when I am exercising. It is essential that all the other conditions remain the same because, otherwise, I wouldn't know if it was the exercise or something else that was making the difference.

Link it: Good use of causal connectives and sentence signposts to help the reader understand the process. The text flows logically.

Express it: Clearly expressed phrases help reader understand the process. Technical language appropriately used and explained. Detail is used to make the explanation clearer.

Co-constructing the toolkit

Use this version to help construct the toolkit. If the Talk-for-Writing approach is being used throughout the school, the students will already be familiar with the Plan it, Link it, Express it, Check it stages of the toolkit. Discuss the ingredients for the toolkit with the class so that they understand what they all mean. The more the toolkit has been co-constructed, the more use it will be.

At the end of the process, your toolkit might end up looking like this:

The scientific investigation toolkit

Plan it:	• Box up your investigation to guide the reader through each stage logically (see boxed-up plan for investigations) • Introduce what is being investigated clearly

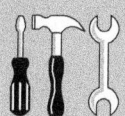

Link it:	• Use sentence signposts to clearly introduce each stage of the investigation (see **Poster C**) • Use causal connectives to help the reader understand how the process is linked together (see **Poster D**) • Check that the text flows logically
Express it:	• Use well-expressed phrases to help the reader understand the process (see **Poster E**) • Use detail to help make the investigation clear • Use technical language appropriately and explain it if necessary
Check it:	• Read the investigation through, checking it for accuracy (spelling, grammar and punctuation) and improve it if it doesn't sound right • Make certain it explains how the investigation was set up clearly

Displaying these 'writing ingredients' is important because they will be central to the shared and independent writing as well as informing self/peer evaluation and feedback from the teacher. They are a key element in embedding learning.

Applying what they have learnt

● Ask the students to quickly create their own text map (as it is easier to recall the text from your own symbols).

● Now ask them to write up the investigation from memory. Leave the boxed-up planning and posters displayed to help them but remove the text. They should have internalised the text, so they should be able to write a good version of the text they have recently talked.

Encouraging self-assessment and using assessment to establish the next steps

● Ask each student to write a short comment at the end of their investigation stating how well they think they have written up the investigation and any improvements they think could be made.

● Now ask them to share their version with a partner so that, using the investigation toolkit to help them, they can discuss what's good about it, how it could be improved, and make any necessary improvements. The chances are that it will be very similar to the one that was internalised at the start of the lesson – that's the whole idea at this stage! If it is different but scientifically correct and coherent, then that is even better as it shows the students have internalised the ideas and started to express them in their own way.

- It is a good homework for them to teach the text to a member of their family. The more they have internalised the text, the easier it will be to build on this the next time they do an investigation.

- When you mark the work, you will be able to see if any aspects of writing up the investigation need more attention and can then spend some time helping them get this right immediately the work is handed back so they learn from the process.

The innovation and independent application stages

The next investigation might perhaps not be until the following term, for example, photosynthesis. Again you will have framed the learning, introduced the technical language perhaps with a never-heard-the-word grid and integrated the key language and phrases into the unit by warming up the words and phrases. Now you have reached the stage where you want them to write up the investigation. Challenge them to recall the words of the investigation into the effect of exercise on the heart. Provide them with the text map to help recall it.

Display the boxed-up planning for the earlier investigation and the investigation toolkit to help them remember the type of text that is needed. Using the flip chart, now innovate on the initial planning so they can see how to adapt it to suit the photosynthesis investigation and understand that the overall structure of the writing is the same.

Then display the text for the earlier investigation on the screen and highlight the sentence starters and connectives and the expressions that are generally useful for investigations, as illustrated below.

I am investigating what happens to my heart when I take exercise. My hypothesis, what I think will happen, is that exercise will make my heart beat faster because the heart has to pump blood faster to enable me to do the exercise.

To carry out an investigation, you must compare two variables: two things which change or vary. For this investigation, I will compare my heart rate when I am resting and when I am taking exercise.

However, it is important to make the test fair. To make this test fair, I must record my heart rate for exactly the same amount of time when I am resting as when I am exercising. It is essential that all the other conditions remain the same because, otherwise, I wouldn't know if it was the exercise or something else that was making the difference.

Through shared writing, model for the students how to turn it into the photosynthesis investigation. Below are a few useful phrases the teacher might

like to use to involve the students in the activity. (For a full list of such phrases, see **Handout 3** in the online resources.)

- Turn to your partner and . . . /finish that sentence off.

- In your pairs – quick . . . /add a little more information.

- What's this paragraph all about?

- We've got _____. What else do we need? What could follow? You tell me.

- Does it all fit together logically?

- What would make it flow better?

- Let's read it through and see if it makes sense.

The more students can be involved in seeing how the writing 'works', the more they will be able to write independently. Without this sort of shared writing, all that students tend to learn is that they can't do it, and this understandable lack of confidence is a big barrier to trying at all.

You may want to add to the useful word and phrase lists as a result of your work on this latest investigation.

Explaining to others – talking the text before you write

Now model for the students being the visiting professor who has come to tell the class how to investigate photosynthesis. In pairs, the class can practise being visiting professor. The more they have to talk the text before they write it, in a variety of forms, the easier it will be for them to write as the words will just flow.

Applying what they have learnt

Now ask them to write up their own investigation on photosynthesis. Display the original boxed-up planning, the earlier investigation text, the investigation toolkit and the posters but remove the shared writing, otherwise they will just copy it. (*Note*: With creative writing, it is best to leave the shared writing on display and encourage the class to express ideas in different ways. With this sort of factual writing there is often not so much flexibility.) Hopefully now they will have internalised the pattern of language sufficiently to be able to write the investigation themselves.

Encouraging self-assessment and using assessment to establish the next steps

- When they have completed it, again ask them to share their text with their response partners and, using the investigation toolkit to help them, discuss what has worked well and any improvements that could be made. Allow time for the students to make these improvements.

- Ask each student to write a short comment at the end of their investigation stating how well they think they have written up the investigation and any further improvements they think could be made.

- When you mark the work, apart from noting if there were any flaws in their scientific understanding, you will be able to see which aspects of writing up an investigation need more attention and can then spend a little time helping them get this right immediately the work is handed back so they learn from the process.

- Revisit these aspects when next you do an investigation so the next steps the students need to make to improve their work are very clear.

When they do another investigation, say the following term, they should be in a position to recall the pattern of investigation, look at the investigation toolkit to support them, as well as the boxed-up planning and the posters, and then write up their own investigation coherently. This is the *independent application stage*. Again, if possible, the students should be given the opportunity to act as response partners as well as having the time to act on any suggested improvements before the work is handed in for marking. The more the students are put in teacher role, and learn how to comment on work effectively, the more independent they will become because having to comment on someone else's work helps you reflect on your own work.

If, by this third investigation, they are still unsure of the patterns of sentences to use, then a little more shared writing followed by more opportunities to be visiting professor may be necessary to help set them off in the right direction. If this method is built on throughout KS3, they should be independent writers of investigations by the end of that stage because they have the tune in their heads and they could teach another student how to write up a science investigation.

Why internalising the text has proved popular with secondary teachers

The word-for-word internalising of text, supported by text maps and actions, has proved both popular and effective in secondary schools with students of a wide range of ages because it engages the students and helps them understand and see how they could succeed.

Subia Shahir, a science teacher from Belle Vue Boys School, Bradford, who was part of the Bradford pilot of the approach, summed up the benefits of using signs and symbols to recall text as follows:

- Inclusive

- Helped students organise and plan what to say

- Improved recall

- Improved word retrieval

- Helped students process sequences, sounds and words quickly

- Helped students retain a sequence of information

Two of her students made the following comments:

> *In science, I know the whole process of photosynthesis as Miss Shabir modelled it to us . . . In my exam I am going use this to help me to revise.*

> *Using actions to demonstrate acid rain has helped me to learn the effects it has on the environment.*

Teachers from a wide range of subjects have said to me how the approach has really engaged students from Year 7 through to sixth formers. A deputy head teaching PE commented that the approach was just perfect for engaging GCSE PE students in internalising the complex vocabulary required. And it engages the teachers too, as you can see from the picture below of teachers learning how to teach in talk-for-writing style. When you've been sitting down for quite some time on a training day, it's good to get up and do something physical – which is exactly how the students feel.

Teachers talking the text

Top tips for creating and presenting your own talking-the-text activity

- It's important to select/write an exemplar text that is at the right level, i.e. challenging for the class but not so challenging as to be unrealistic. Make certain it contains all the language features you want to focus on; for example, connectives and sentence signposts plus phrases that will be generally useful for the sort of writing you are trying to encourage. Ask yourself, 'What would I be able to put on sentence signpost/useful phrases posters from this passage?' as a good guide as to whether the text is worth internalising or not. Even if you don't write the passage yourself, you will probably need to adapt a passage to suit your purposes.

- When performing the text for the class, stress the triggers that are key to coherence and strengthen recollection through movements*.

- Don't create too many movements, as this can make it too complicated.

- Say the lines expressively – if the students are dull, then you were dull. If they start to chant the words rather than express them, demonstrate the right tone again.

- Begin as a performance, then back off and increasingly hand over to the class and get the students to do the telling.

- Get the students to sketch their own version of the text map, as it is much easier to remember from your own squiggles than those of someone else. Ban clip art, as it is the hand–brain connection that is important here.

- Once the students have learnt the text as a whole class, get them to try in groups and then in pairs.

- Concurrently reinforce the key language features and technical spelling through the rest of the unit.

*Deciding on the actions to illustrate the text can be an excellent whole-class activity. It's probably best to have an idea of what actions will work best and then allow the students to suggest alternative approaches. Many primary schools have adopted fixed movements for a few key connectives like first, next and unfortunately. If you want to use the often-used actions for these connectives, see the resources page of the talk4writing website (www.talk4writing.com/id42.html). If you click on 'download key actions', you will get a poster of Pie illustrating these. Many schools create their own posters with the students doing the actions.

Step D continued: More sophisticated approaches to internalising the tune of exemplar text

(This chapter is supported online by **Handouts 32–39, Slides 42–43**, plus the video clips from **Part 2: Step D**.)

There is a wide range of alternative, more sophisticated ways that teachers can use exemplar text to provide a model for students to imitate so that they can internalise the patterns of language required to enable them to produce similar writing independently. A range of these approaches is illustrated below, beginning with those that take the exemplar text as their starting point, followed by examples that build up to the exemplar.

Section 1: Approaches beginning with exemplar text:

Although each example has been linked to a particular subject in order to illustrate it, each approach can easily be adapted to suit the needs of a range of subjects. All of these imitation approaches take some time to teach effectively, but this is time well spent because it lays the foundations on which the students will be able to base their independent writing skills so that by the time they reach KS4 they are confident communicators in the subject. Not only will this save time in the long run but also raise the quality of the students' understanding alongside their ability to communicate coherently. If a subject is only taught from KS4, it is still a very useful way to establish the key pattern of text for the subject in Year 10.

SECTION 1: APPROACHES BEGINNING WITH EXEMPLAR TEXT

Step Di: Establishing 'what = good' by comparing short texts

A simple, useful way of providing students with a good example to imitate is to let them compare several different versions of the same text and establish 'what = good' and use this to construct their own toolkit for this type of text. This is particularly useful when the text focused on is short so, for example, it is suited to showing how to write instructions. It is also a good way of helping students focus on writing an effective single paragraph analysis for music, or effective introductions to discursive essays in English, history, geography or RE. It is best to do this activity on an issue that students have studied, as it helps to have knowledge about what you are about to write about, whether that's musical analysis, an introduction, instructions or anything else! Introductions are a particularly good thing to focus on because this method helps you to bring out the fact that you can't decide on your introduction until you have some idea about how you want to answer the question. In effect, you have to plan the middle and what you are going to say before you can plan how to introduce it.

To set up a comparing-text activity, create three or four versions of the same text. Make one version an exemplar, containing all the features you would want. Make one or two of the others contain some of these features but be flawed in some way. If possible, make these flaws typical of the sorts of errors students in the class you are teaching tend to make when they attempt this type of writing. Do not include spelling mistakes in any of the versions, as the focus should not be on surface errors but on the style, clarity and purpose of the writing. It is useful to include one piece of writing that is rather good but is entirely the wrong sort of writing given the task. Students have to recognise that 'good' depends on the purpose of the writing. Insecure writers tend to fall back on recount writing, thus as long as the purpose is not recount writing, you might want to make the version that has lost the plot a recount.

Below is an example of this approach for writing instructions. On page 179 you can find an example for introductions as part of a larger unit of work.

Writing effective short paragraphs

Ask the students in pairs to:

- Select which of the four examples is the best given the task. (In this example, the task is to write clear instructions for an experiment to show how water affects the growth of cress seeds.)

- Decide what key ingredients help make it good.

- Discuss what lets the other versions down.

Handout 32: Establishing 'what = good' for instruction text (science)

Example 1: To find out how water affects the growth of cress seeds

Instructions

Get four petri dishes and put some cotton wool and cress seeds into each of them. Then you have to put no water into one of the petri dishes. Using a measuring cylinder you have to measure 10 ml of water and put this into the next petri dish. Again, using a measuring cylinder you have to measure 15 ml of water and put this into the last petri dish. All these petri dishes have to be left in the light for one week and then using a ruler we can measure how much the cress grew.

Example 2: To find out how water affects the growth of cress seeds

Equipment:

four petri dishes

cress seeds

measuring cylinder

water

cotton wool

ruler

Diagram:

cotton wool

seed

lid

petri dish

1. Put the same amount of cotton wool into four petri dishes.
2. Press the same amount of cress seed into each dish.
3. Do not put any water in the first petri dish.
4. Put 5 ml of water into the 2nd dish, using a measuring cylinder.
5. Put 10 ml of water into the 3rd and 15 ml into the fourth petri dish.
6. Leave the dishes for one week in the light.
7. After one week, measure the length of the cress seeds using a ruler.

Example 3: Cress seed experiment

Smiling smugly, I had pictured myself growing the best cress seeds in the class – mine all tall, green and healthy looking while all the others were wilted, thin and mangy. Sadly, this turned out not exactly to be the case. Apparently, we were supposed to set up four different dishes and treat the little blighters differently to illustrate some point or other. As usual, I wasn't really listening and just set up one dish.

Enthusiastically, I overwatered this and somewhat drowned the seeds. Perhaps I should cross 'Follow in Einstein's footsteps' off my career list.

Example 4: To find out how water affects the growth of cress seeds

Equipment:

Four petri dishes; water; measuring cylinder; cotton wool; cress seeds

Diagram:

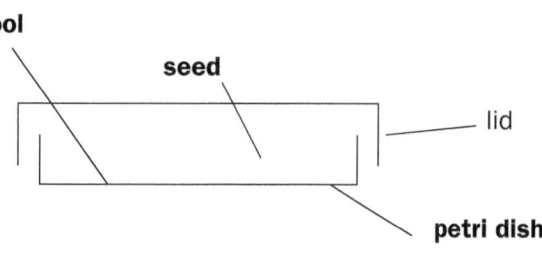

cotton wool

seed

lid

petri dish

I will set up four sets of the equipment as shown in the diagram, placing cotton wool and cress seeds in each of the petri dishes. I'll leave one dry, put 5 ml of water in another, 10 ml in a third one and finally 15 ml in the fourth. Then I will put the petri dishes in the sun for one week. I'll measure the length on the plants at the end of that week.

- Once they have done this, ask them to check their findings with another pair.

- Then get the groups to feedback on their toolkit ingredients and build up a class version, which may end up looking something like the one below. It is important that the class is involved in this process rather than just being given the toolkit. If they are just presented with the criteria, they will not have understood or internalised them.

The instruction writing toolkit – consider including the following

Plan it: order the information chronologically	• Introduce your instructions stating clearly what they are about • List any equipment needed • Make certain that everything is listed in the order in which it is used
Link it: put the steps in order	• List the steps in order. Link them by time connectives, numbers, letters of the alphabet or bullet points
Express it: make the instructions clear	• Keep the instructions as clear, simple and short as possible • Keep your instructions in the imperative – (bossy verbs): e.g. 'Put', 'Press', 'Do not' • Use descriptive language only when it is needed to make the instructions clear e.g. 'red button', 'turn right' • Use diagrams where they will help • Use technical language if necessary, preferably illustrated by a diagram
Check it: make certain your spelling and grammar are correct	• Read your instructions through, checking for accuracy • Check they tell the reader clearly what to do

- Then ask the students to use this toolkit to complete a similar writing task.

- Once they have completed their work, ask them to share their instructions with a partner so that they can discuss whether they have followed the class's instructions for writing clear instructions. Allow time for them to revise their work in the light of the discussions.

- Before handing in their work, they should write a short comment on how well they think they have completed the task.

- Again, when you mark the work, check to see if they are all applying the ingredients of the toolkit appropriately and, if not, devise some activities to help them understand. Then allow time to remedy errors when the work is handed back so the students are not only aware of the steps they need to take to improve their work, but have had a go at putting them into practice. In this way, formative assessment of the students' work drives the next stage of our teaching and the student's learning.

Step Dii: Using exemplar text to help students understand 'what = good' for any text type

This can be easily applied right across the curriculum. All that is needed is a good exemplar text of whatever writing is required and then adapt the following approach to suit the type of text desired. The example here focuses on short explanation text.

When first introducing the students to writing explanation text for your subject, prepare some exemplar text that is similar in structure to the sort of text you want them to be able to write. Give the students a copy of this text to analyse in pairs. (See **Handout 33** online for a plain version of the text on page 132.)

Read the exemplar text to the class so they have heard the text read well and then ask the students to do the following, modelling the stages as necessary; that is, if they don't know what boxing up is, then model it for them (see page 14). Equally, if the students are not familiar with highlighting useful phrases, then this will need to be demonstrated. Ask the students to follow these instructions:

- In pairs, analyse the structure of the text by boxing it up.

- Now highlight the text identifying any linking phrases that could be useful for explanation writing.

- Next, highlight the text identifying any other general phrases that could be useful for explanation writing.

- Annotate the text drawing out the features you have identified.

- Check with another pair whether their analysis is similar.

Now ask the students to feed back their ideas so that the class co-constructs an analysis of the text. The annotated text will probably look something like this:

Exemplar explanation text boxed up to show how it is structured

Why do we change the clocks twice a year?

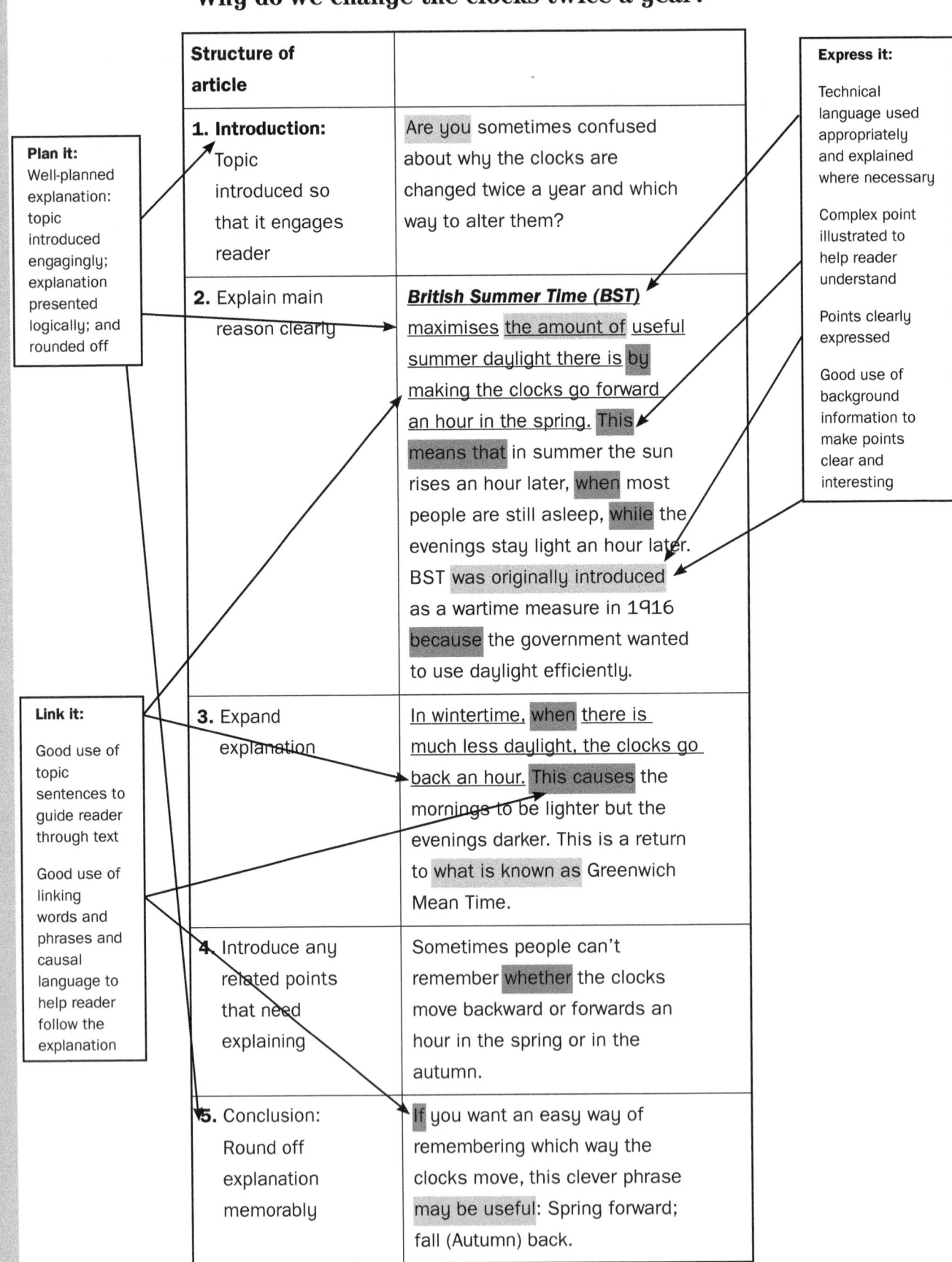

Plan it:
Well-planned explanation: topic introduced engagingly; explanation presented logically; and rounded off

Link it:
Good use of topic sentences to guide reader through text

Good use of linking words and phrases and causal language to help reader follow the explanation

Structure of article	
1. Introduction: Topic introduced so that it engages reader	Are you sometimes confused about why the clocks are changed twice a year and which way to alter them?
2. Explain main reason clearly	*British Summer Time (BST)* maximises the amount of useful summer daylight there is by making the clocks go forward an hour in the spring. This means that in summer the sun rises an hour later, when most people are still asleep, while the evenings stay light an hour later. BST was originally introduced as a wartime measure in 1916 because the government wanted to use daylight efficiently.
3. Expand explanation	In wintertime, when there is much less daylight, the clocks go back an hour. This causes the mornings to be lighter but the evenings darker. This is a return to what is known as Greenwich Mean Time.
4. Introduce any related points that need explaining	Sometimes people can't remember whether the clocks move backward or forwards an hour in the spring or in the autumn.
5. Conclusion: Round off explanation memorably	If you want an easy way of remembering which way the clocks move, this clever phrase may be useful: Spring forward; fall (Autumn) back.

Express it:

Technical language used appropriately and explained where necessary

Complex point illustrated to help reader understand

Points clearly expressed

Good use of background information to make points clear and interesting

Use this to draw out all the features for your explanation writing toolkit and the related posters that illustrate the features. This should be co-constructed with the class so they understand all the elements. You will probably end up with something like this:

The explanation writing toolkit – use the following guidelines to help you

Plan it: order the information logically	• Box up your explanation, ordering your points logically • Introduce your explanation with a hook to interest your reader (remember your audience) • Round off the explanation effectively
Link it: make your explanation fit together	• Link your points clearly with one argument building on another using causal connectives and sentence signposts (see **Poster A**) • Read your article through to check that it flows
Express it: make your explanation clear and interesting	• Use well-chosen points to explain clearly to the reader (see **Poster B**) • Use detail to help make pointsclearer • Use background information to engage the reader • Use technical language appropriately and explain it if necessary
Check it: make certain your spelling and grammar is correct	• Read your explanation through checking it for accuracy and improve it if it doesn't sound right. Check it is well punctuated and all words are spelt correctly • Make certain your writing explains clearly in a coherent and engaging way

Poster A

Useful linking and signposting phrases for explaining something

- *Are you . . . .?*
- *This means that*
- *when*
- *while*
- *because*
- *this causes*
- *whether*
- *if*

Poster B

Useful general phrases for explaining something

- *the amount of*
- *was originally introduced*
- *what is known as*
- *may be useful*

Innovating on the exemplar text

Display the exemplar text and use it to demonstrate to the class, through shared writing, how they can innovate on it to explain something else related to the topic they are studying. Again, the list of shared writing phrases in **Handout 3** may be useful here. The more students can be involved in seeing how the writing 'works', the more they will be able to write independently.

Once they have seen how to use the model to write an alternative explanation, ask the students to have a go at writing their own explanation.

When they have finished, get them to share their explanations with a partner and, using the toolkit to help them, decide on any improvements that could be made.

When you take the work in to mark it, use the categories from the toolkit to help you decide which aspects need further work.

When you hand the work back, devise activities to go over these points and give the students time to polish their work in the light of this, so that they immediately act on the feedback and are aware of the next steps they need to make to improve their work. Add useful phrases that have come out of the students' writing to the posters so they can see how to build up the range of phrases they can use.

Step Diii: Using icons and exemplar text to help students talk the text in their own words

(Watch the video clip **Part 2: Step D: Using icons to recall key points** to illustrate this activity.)

Having experienced the power of using symbols to help students internalise exemplar text, Jo Tyrrell-Baldwin, a technology teacher from Portslade Aldridge Community Academy, Brighton, decided to adapt the approach to suit the needs of product analysis in technology. The following approach could be adapted to suit any subject where students have to evaluate something.

She decided to experiment with the idea of the students, for their first product analysis, developing their understanding of the concept by focusing on the underlying elements and not having to worry about the actual product. So she made the ludicrous product pictured on the next page to allow someone suffering from a cold to always have paper to wipe their nose.

The students had already experienced warming-up-the-word activities, so they knew what the key terms of product analysis meant. The instructions for the task were as follows:

First, ask the students to come up with symbols to represent the nine headings for product analysis.

Manufacturing	Materials	How is it used?
Mechanisms	Ergonomics	Environmental impact
Maintenance	Marketing	Improvements

Ask a few students who have come up with good ideas to draw their symbols for the class. Ergonomics is a particularly useful one to demonstrate. Students can choose to hijack ideas, or stick with their own. This process will help them remember the headings and their meaning.

Then ask the students to put their symbols in a sensible order – there is no fixed order for this but it is more logical to begin with manufacturing and end with improvements.

The students are then shown the joke product that they are to analyse and are provided with brief exemplar paragraphs showing how to write product analysis using the headings. See pages 138–139 and see **Handout 34a** online for a non-annotated version of this text.

Now model for the students how to turn a paragraph into a series of symbols and then present the paragraph using only the symbols to support your delivery.

Text map for 1. Manufacturing

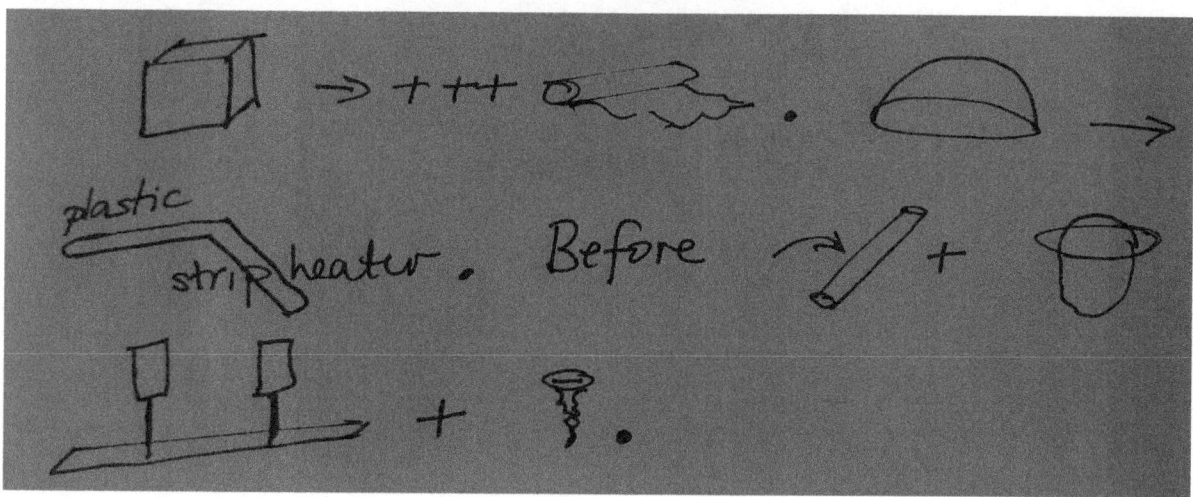

(A flip chart is ideal for this, as the students can see the paragraph on screen and the images that represent it on the flip chart. Then blank out the screen (press B) and present the paragraph.) It is not the intention to get the paragraph word-for-word perfect but what is important is to be able to coherently express all the points linking them appropriately.

Divide the students into fours and give each student two paragraphs to turn into symbols. Student A does paragraphs two and three, student B paragraphs four and five, student C paragraphs six and seven and student D the final two paragraphs. Once they have had time to rehearse individually, see if they can present the gist of their text coherently to their group just by looking at their text map. Ask one or two students to present their paragraphs to the class. This process will help internalise the language of product analysis.

Given the ridiculous nature of the project, you may wish to help develop their confidence in manipulating language by now telling them that they are in role as a health and safety inspector and ask them to present their information again. Soon they should be able to present the information powerfully in a variety of ways without needing to look at the icons, since the process will have fixed the images in their brain. The picture below shows science teacher

Matt Renshaw from Pendle School, Lancashire in role presenting the *Improvements* paragraph.

Then ask the students in pairs to highlight any linking phrases in one colour and any other phrases that may be useful for any product analysis in general in a different colour. Do the first paragraph for them so they have a model to follow. Some of the phrases could be highlighted in either colour, so the colour is not crucial. What matters is that the students can recognise generally useful phrases including linking phrases.

You will probably end up with a text that looks a bit like this:

---

1. Manufacturing

This product is made from a range of materials. The framework would have been made by line bending the plastic on a strip heater. Before it is attached to the tube and elastic head band, the metal straps are drilled and screwed to the plastic.

---

2. Materials

The product is made from plastic tubing and has a head strap which is made from material, probably elastic, to fit around the head. The paper roll is held in place by a framework that is also made of plastic.

---

3. How is it used?

The roll of paper, which is like a toilet roll, unravels and you blow your nose on it. When you tear off what you have used, you have a fresh sheet for next time. You don't need to carry tissues in your pocket, as it is on your head!

4. Mechanisms

There are very few mechanisms used on the product, though there is rotary motion when the roll of paper rotates.

5. Ergonomics

The product is made to fit on a human head by use of elastic and a round plastic tube. It does fit, so at a basic level it is ergonomically sound, although it is uncomfortable.

6. Environmental impact

This product would have some impact on the environment. It is designed to be made from metal and plastic, which are recyclable. However, the elastic is not and it and the paper would have to be thrown away. It would also use a lot of energy to produce each part and transport it.

7. Maintenance

There are very few moving parts to this product, so it would not need much repair or maintenance. However, it would need to have the roll of paper replaced when it ran out.

8. Marketing

To advertise and sell this product you would have to make it more attractive, otherwise it will be unmarketable. If it was made less bulky and offered in a range of colours to suit different types of people, it would be easier to sell.

9. Improvements

This product is very impractical and therefore a number of major improvements need to be made. The roll of paper gets in the eyes so it needs to be held out of the way. Moreover, if you wore it out in the rain, the paper would become soggy and thus would have to be protected from the elements. Finally, it looks both uncomfortable and unattractive so a significant redesign is needed.

(Adapted by Julia Strong from work done by Jo Tyrrell-Baldwin from Portslade Aldridge Community Academy, Brighton)

Pull out all the useful connectives and phrases that could be used for any product analysis so you build a bank of useful phrases posters. These can be displayed on your washing line.

Poster C

Useful linking phrases and sentence starters for product analysis

- *The/this product is made from*
- *Before it is attached to . . .*
- *which is made from/of . . .*
- *which is like a . . .*
- *When you . . .*
- *though there is . . .*
- *This product would have . . .*
- *which are recyclable.*
- *However, . . .*
- *so it would not need . . .*
- *otherwise . . .*
- *There are very few . . .*
- *It is designed to be . . .*
- *To advertise and sell this product . . .*
- *It would also use . . .*
- *If it was made of _____ it would be . . .*
- *therefore, . . .*
- *Moreover, . . .*
- *Finally,*

Useful general expressions for product analysis

Poster D

- *a range of materials.*
- *would have been made by . . .*
- *is held in place by . . .*
- *very few mechanisms used on the product . . .*
- *some impact on . . .*
- *would have to be thrown away.*
- *a lot of energy to produce . . .*
- *moving parts to this product . . .*
- *it would need to have . . .*
- *you would have to . . .*
- *. . . need to be made.*
- *a significant redesign is needed.*

Many teachers in different schools have recognised that this engaging 'start with fiction' approach is an effective way of helping students focus on the language of expression unhindered by the need to also focus on the facts of a real product. This is illustrated by the exemplar text below for an imaginary product to help Year 10 technology students focus on the language of product evaluation and the following plenary session feedback from a business studies department.

Evaluating my Mega Bubble Blowing Machine (MBBM)

(See **Handout 34b** online.)

For my controlled assessment, I designed and made an MBBM for children and men of all ages. My machine provides essential bubble blowing in a mega way, using SMART materials to provide structure and support for the bubbles.

It has been designed to ergonomically fit into the user's hand, with a soft-grip palm support for added comfort and user safety. It is lightweight and easy to carry and can easily be folded away for storage. In addition, the appearance of the MBBM is modern in shape but has a contemporary feel and touch.

The product can be used both indoors and outside due to hardwearing and robust materials that were chosen as a result of extensive testing of a range of possible materials.

To keep costs low, I would use computer-aided design and manufacture, possibly a 3D printer and ABS plastic. The cost for each product will be between £10 and £15, which, through my survey of users, is a price that consumers felt was reasonable.

The prototype I made was thoroughly tested by a range of possible users. From their feedback, I made a number of modifications including thickening the handle and including a non-slip surface to the handle.

In conclusion, I believe I have fulfilled the needs of my clients as specified in the design brief.

(Adapted from the work of the technology department, Graham School, Scarborough)

Step D approach iv. Analysing advanced exemplar text to raise the quality of written expression

Once students are reasonably skilled writers, a very good way of helping them move to a higher level for any significant writing task is to help them internalise sophisticated appropriate exemplar text and involve them in analysing how it works. In effect, it is advanced raiding the reading and can be adapted to suit the needs of any curriculum area that requires students to craft a series of well constructed paragraphs.

The example here from English Literature was developed by Andy Breckenridge, an English teacher at Blatchington Mill School, Brighton. It is so powerful that I would recommend it to anyone who was wanting to demonstrate to a department or a whole school staff why using exemplar text is effective.

To understand and illustrate the power of this approach first look at the 'before' text on page 144 (Handout 35) written by a year 9 boy, and then look at the 'after' text on the facing page (145), written by the same boy. When I first saw the original work, I spent some time analysing that the handwriting was the same for both pieces of work– it was so hard to believe the same writer had written them.

This impressive improvement in the student's quality of writing was achieved through using Philip Ardagh's review of the **"The Book Magpie"** by Markus Zusak, as the exemplar text – from the Guardian Book Reviews (www.guardian.co.uk/books/2007/jan/06/featuresreviews.guardianreview26). If you download this as your exemplar text, you might want to ask teachers to identify where they can spot the influence of the exemplar text in the style of the student's second piece of writing.

A good additional question to ask if you were running a workshop session on this example would be to see if groups of teachers could suggest how the teacher used the exemplar text to achieve the progress illustrated by the after text. Ask for feedback and flip chart up the suggestions. The more teachers are asked to think about how they can use text as an exemplar imaginatively, the easier they will find devising their own exemplar text-based activities to suit their subject.

The techniques the teacher actually used are listed on page 146. Again it is worth going over each of these and involving your audience in the processes to help them understand how exemplar text can be used.

The next stage, of course, is for people to try the approach themselves using powerful exemplar text related to whatever they are teaching. The example starting on page 152 shows how this approach can be adapted for science.

Handout 35: 'Before' and 'after' texts for staff training (English and general)

Before: Social worker report on Christopher (main character in 'The Curious Incident of the Dog in the Night-Time') before the Talk-for-Writing approach – no exemplar text used)

Christopher is a very intelligent and logical young man. He is also extremely bright. Because of his disability, he finds it hard to communicate or chat. But he is quite clever so he will be able to learn, like he already has.

Christopher's relationship with his father is quite unique. They are very understanding of each other. Father has grown used to Christopher and never gets too angry, unless Christopher steps out of line. However, father has quite a short temper.

Christopher's relationship with his mother is quite different to that of his father's. Christopher doesn't really feel any emotion and he talks about her quite a lot. I don't think he knows what he feels about his mum.

I think Christopher should stay at his dad's but he should be told that his mum isn't actually dead so that he can visit her and stay with her sometimes. If he stays with her he will get told by her why she left and if he gets shown the letters and given an explanation then I think it will do him some good. However, I think his mother should take some responsibility and maybe get some training on how to care for Christopher.
– Year 9 Student A

After: Book review on 'The Curious Incident of the Dog in the Night-Time' after the Talk-for-Writing approach – using an exemplar text to support writing

In modern day Britain, the harsh reality of life is often shielded from young people with disabilities. This is mostly the case in this wonderful book. This book acts not only as a pleasurable read but as a sort of campaign. It opens your eyes as to how dismissive and ignorant one can be in everyday situations. A wonderful insight into the human mind, Haddon keeps you flying high right to the end.

Haddon's novel tells of a fifteen-year-old boy named Christopher, who suffers from Asperger's Syndrome. He lives in the bubble of a well-organised life until he finds the dog of one of his neighbours in their front garden. Christopher's bubble is instantly popped and his life is thrown into many twists and turns. Shocks for the reader come in their dozens and hit the reader straight on. The ups and downs in Christopher's life throughout the course of this book play a main role in the plot.

Haddon's choice to have the story narrated by Christopher may not seem an appropriate choice but it is truly effective and engaging. If the story was told from a third person point of view, then the reader wouldn't be able to develop a sort of understanding of Christopher. His innocence, and knowledge of maths, the outside world and minutiae of everyday life is portrayed in an extremely insightful and personal account.

As well as Christopher, characters who are vital to the story are Ed Boone, Christopher's dad and boiler maintenance worker; Mrs Shears, neighbour of the Boones, whose dog is murdered; and Judy Boone, Christopher's mum, who comes as a shock to both the reader and Christopher.

Haddon has worked with children who suffer from Autism and Asperger's throughout his life. This experience shows in his writing. Without this experience or inspiration, we wouldn't have been given such a fine read.

The winner of the Whitbread Book of the Year, the Guardian Children's Fiction Prize and the South Bank Show Book Award, 'The Curious Incident of the Dog in the Night-Time' is a great achievement. To say that this book is a great page turner would be an understatement. – **Year 9 Student A.**

The teacher achieved this progress by thoroughly familiarising the students with the pattern of the text they needed to write by using the following steps:

1. Select an excellent exemplar text. In this case the teacher was teaching how to review a novel that includes serious comment about the nature of humanity, so he selected a top quality review about another novel with a similarly serious but very different focus.

2. Read the exemplar text to the class so they hear the text read well and then ask the pairs to read the text to each other, changing reader when the punctuation changes. (The text was displayed on screen with punctuation clearly visible in red.) This activity makes the students more aware of how the sentences are constructed in clauses to build up the meaning.

3. Model for the students how to create a text map like the D&T example on page 137 for the opening paragraph of the text using no words, or as few words as possible.

4. Give a copy of the text to every pair, allocating different paragraphs of the text to different pairs, and ask each pair to create their own text map for their paragraph and see if they can recall the gist of their paragraph just by looking at the text map.

   a. Ask them to hide the original, and see if they can relate their piece of text back to each other using their text map. Again, they are not trying to get the text word for word the same as the original – what matters is that the student can express the information coherently.

   b. Select some of the best performers to present their paragraph to the class so that all the class hears some of the text again.

5. Give the students a copy of the full text and ask the students, in pairs, to highlight the exemplar text – underlining topic sentences, and identifying general phrases that could be useful for writing any book review.

6. Turn the key phrases they have identified into posters and display them so that when they write they have the useful phrases to support them. The phrases below are typical of the sorts of phrases that will emerge from a quality review and can be added to as more useful general phrases emerge from similar text. Co-construct with the class what these phrases are useful for and include this ingredient in your toolkit for writing book reviews.

Useful sentence signposts and linking phrases for book reviews

Poster E

- *At the beginning of . . .*
- *One of the reasons why . ..*
- *The emerging relationship between . . .*
- *The story is told by . . .*
- *This narrative device is . . .*
- *We are introduced to . . .*
- *This atmosphere develops throughout . . .*
- *This is a cleverly shaped piece of storytelling . . .*
- *In addition to . . .*
- *However, the way in which . . .*
- *but also . . .*
- *It is a significant work because . . .*
- *This book is so impressive because . . .*
- *I can enthusiastically recommend . . .*
- *The novel provides an insight into . . .*

Link it

Link the review together clearly using linking phrases and sentence signposts effectively

---

Poster F

Useful general expressions for book reviews

- *the central character of the story is . . .*
- *may well conjure up images of . . .*
- *the narrator's voice enables the reader to . . .*
- *_____'s totally engaging story . . .*
- *. . . introduces the reader to . . .*
- *the significance of the title . . .*
- *Memorable characters are . . .*
- *who is obsessed by . . .*
- *provides a startling insight into . . .*
- *are central to the plot.*
- *hints at what may happen.*
- *The book was inspired by . . .*
- *a great page-turner . . .*
- *includes such . . .*
- *An award-winning . . .*

Express it

Use well-chosen phrases to help the reader understand what the book is about

The teacher then displayed a fully annotated version of the text for the class to consider (similar to that illustrated on page 150) which focused on its structure and illustrated how the boxing up technique helps you see how the article has been structured.

Such an approach can then be used to draw out all the features for your book review toolkit. This should be co-constructed with the class so they understand all the elements. You will probably end up with something like this:

The book review writing toolkit – consider including the following

Plan it: order the information chronologically	• Box up the review in paragraphs, remembering your audience, presenting the information in a logical order • Include the central theme of the novel, how the story is narrated, central characters and what inspired the writer to write it, using brief detail to engage the reader • Introduce the review in an engaging way to hook your reader • Conclude your review with a recommendation
Link it: make your article fit together well	• Link your ideas clearly using sentence signposts and connectives appropriately (see **Poster E**) • Read your review through to check that it flows
Express it: make your article clear and interesting	• Use well-chosen phrases to interest the reader in the review (see **Poster F**) • Sum up key points effectively • Use detail to help make key points clearer and more interesting • Vary the length of your sentences to help engage the reader • Explain any technical points if appropriate
Check it: make certain your spelling and grammar are correct	• Read your review through, checking it for accuracy and improve it if it doesn't sound right • Make certain it informs the reader in an interesting and engaging way

The teacher then modelled for the class how to box up a plan for a review based on the structure of the exemplar text and pitched at an adult audience. The class then completed their planning for homework.

The following lesson they drafted their review. Ideally, allow time for them to complete the writing in class time and then share their writing with a partner to discuss what has worked and what could be improved. Allow time for the students to undertake the improvements that they choose to make. Encourage students to then write a comment on their work reflecting on how well they think they have completed the task. This is an excellent way of getting a dialogue going about the next steps the student needs to take to improve their writing.

When you take the work in to mark it, use the categories from the toolkit to help you decide which aspects need further work. When you hand the work back, devise activities to go over these points and give the students time to polish their work in the light of these activities so that they immediately act on the feedback and are aware of the steps they need to take to improve their work.

One good way of embedding what has been taught is to display an excellent piece of work from one of the students and ask the class to discuss what makes it good and then collectively box it up and annotate it to bring out its features as illustrated below by Student A's text. This embeds learning, providing a good way of adding useful phrases to the posters and helping students recognise that their work can be exemplary too.

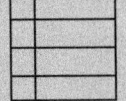

Boxing up and annotating a book review to show how it works

Structure of article	
Beginning: Introduce central theme of novel including detail to interest the reader	*In modern day Britain, the harsh reality of life is often shielded from young people with disabilities. This is mostly the case in this wonderful book. This book acts not only as a pleasurable read but as a sort of campaign. It opens your eyes as to how dismissive and ignorant one can be in everyday situations. A wonderful insight into the human mind, Haddon keeps you flying high right to the end.*
Middle: • Key plot details	*Haddon's novel tells of a fifteen-year-old boy named Christopher, who suffers from Asperger's Syndrome. He lives in the bubble of a well-organized life until he finds the dog of one of his neighbours in their front garden. Christopher's bubble is instantly popped and his life is thrown into many twists and turns. Shocks for the reader come in their dozens and hit the reader straight on. The ups and downs in Christopher's life throughout the course of this book play a main role in the plot.*

Plan it: Well-structured article in 6 paragraphs presenting information clearly, logically, briefly and engagingly

Express it: Engaging phrases used to interest reader

Sum up key points effectively

• How story is narrated	*Haddon's choice to have the story narrated by Christopher may not seem an appropriate choice but it is truly effective and engaging. If the story was told from a third person point of view, then the reader wouldn't be able to develop a sort of understanding of Christopher. His innocence, and knowledge of maths, the outside world and minutiae of everyday life is portrayed in an extremely insightful and personal account.*
• Key characters and small details to whet appetite	*As well as Christopher, characters who are vital to the story are Ed Boone, Christopher's dad and boiler maintenance worker; Mrs Shears, neighbour of the Boones, whose dog is murdered; and Judy Boone, Christopher's mum, who comes as a shock to both the reader and Christopher.*
• Brief information on what inspired the novel and comment on this	*Haddon has worked with children who suffer from Autism and Asperger's throughout his life. This experience shows in his writing. Without this experience or inspiration, we wouldn't have been given such a fine read.*
End: Draw review to an end with general comments on its effectiveness. Include recommendation if want to recommend it. Do not give away end of story.	*The winner of the Whitbread Book of the Year, the Guardian Children's Fiction Prize and the South Bank Show Book Award, 'The Curious Incident of the Dog in the Night-Time' is a great achievement. To say that this book is a great page-turner would be an understatement.* – **Year 9 student**

Link it:
The focus of each paragraph is clearly introduced by sentence signposts or connectives

Express it:
Sum up key points effectively

Detail selected to help reader picture what is being explained

Sentence structure varied keeping the reader engaged

Step Dv: Analysing A* exemplar examination answers to raise the quality of written expression

At Key Stage 4, the above approach can easily be adapted to help students cope successfully with the complex demands of exam questions that require extendedwriting. By using A* exemplar examination answers interactively, students can be helped to understand 'what = good' and learn how to replicate it. Because the approach enables students to internalise the structure and tune of top-quality answers, and involves them in analysing the answers, it helps students move to a higher level when answering the real examination questions. In effect, this is advanced raiding the reading. If you just present them with the answers and the examination guidance on 'what = good', they are much less likely to understand and remember the key points because they need to be actively involved in developing the points themselves.

The approach will be most effective if, after analysing the exemplar text and establishing the toolkit for this type of question, the students then have to write a similar sort of text themselves. Therefore, if your exemplar text is explaining the advantages and disadvantages of something, it would be good to teach it just before asking them to write a similar explanation for a different topic they have studied. This is illustrated in this example, which moves through the following logical stages:

- Stage 1. Analysing the question

- Stage 2. Using the information provided to help answer the question

- Stage 3. Internalising the pattern of language of the exemplar text

- Stage 4. Analysing the exemplar text

- Stage 6. Explaining to others

- Stage 7. Applying what they have learnt

- Stage 8. Encouraging self- assessment

- Stage 9. Using assessment to establish the next steps

First, analyse the type of question that requires an answer of a paragraph or more that is typical of exams for your subject. For example, if you analyse science exam questions, most are a form of explanation even if that word doesn't appear in the question, so it is most logical to help the students know how to answer the various types of explanation questions asked. The toolkit ingredients for successful answers (based on the examiner's guidance) will be very similar for all the different command terms, with the key differences often being how to structure the answers to suit the demands of each question – so it is this feature that is focused on in particular at the beginning of the science example below.

Science example: Using exemplar text to help students understand 'what = good' when answering 'advantages/disadvantages' type explanation questions

Stage 1. Analysing the question

- First, present the students in pairs with an advantages/disadvantages type of question, in this case from physics.

Handout 36a: Advantages and disadvantages of solar energy for heating water

The picture shows one type of solar water heater. Water from the tank is slowly pumped through copper pipes inside the solar panel where the water is heated by energy from the Sun.

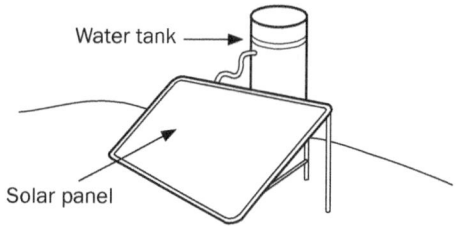

Each day the average European family uses 100 kg of hot water. It takes 16 800 000 J of energy to heat this mass of water to the correct temperature.

The bar chart shows how the amount of solar energy transferred to the water heater varies throughout the year.

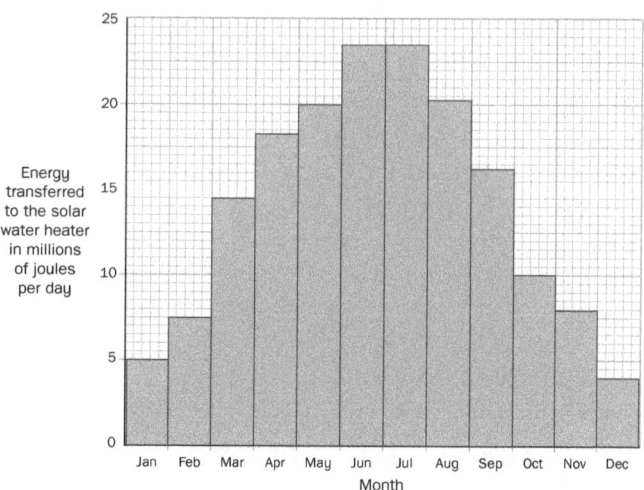

In this question you will be assessed on using good English, organising information clearly and using specialist terms where appropriate.

The water in the tank could be heated by using an electric immersion heater. Outline the advantages and disadvantages of using solar energy to heat the water rather than using an electric immersion heater.

(From AQA's *Guidance on Quality of Written Communication (science)* document)

Ask the students in pairs to underline the actual question and then check with another pair to see if they have come to the same conclusion.

Stage 2. Using the information provided to help answer the question

- Given the question, ask them first to discuss how the information provided is going to help them answer it.

- Next ask them to box up a plan showing how the answer should be structured. (If they have not done boxing up before, then model how to do it.)

- Ask them to check their plans with another pair to see if they are similar.

- Get the groups to feed back, including establishing that the chart will help them to understand the limitations of solar panels, and box up the resulting plan on the flip chart. They can then adjust their planning if necessary.

The plan will probably look something like this:

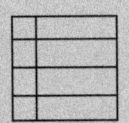

Boxed-up planning for advantages and disadvantages of using solar energy for heating water

Advantages	• Renewable energy source • No pollutants – carbon dioxide/sulphur dioxide • Greenhouse effect/acid rain • Contrast with immersion heater – fossil fuels, pollution
Disadvantages	• Only works in daytime • Affected by cloud • Graph shows only effective April to September • Therefore needs to be supplemented

Stage 3. Internalising the pattern of language of the exemplar text

- Give each pair of students a copy of an exemplar answer with the punctuation in bold and underlined so it is easy to identify. Ask them to read the text to each other, changing reader when the punctuation changes. Model the first few sentences for them, using a good reader as your partner, if they have not done this before. This activity will make them more aware of the content by helping them see how the sentences are constructed in chunks – clauses and phrases – to build up the meaning.

Handout 36b: Exemplar answer for advantages and disadvantages of solar energy for heating water

The main advantage of using a solar panel to heat water is that it uses a renewable energy source rather than fossil fuels. This means that no pollutants, such as carbon dioxide and sulphur dioxide, are released by the combustion of fuels. Carbon dioxide contributes to the greenhouse effect and sulphur dioxide contributes to the formation of acid rain. In contrast, if water is heated by an electric immersion heater, the electricity will most probably have been produced by power stations that burn fossil fuels.

The main disadvantage of the solar heater is that it only heats the water when daylight is available. On cloudy days, the solar heater might not produce sufficient hot water for the family. The graph shows that the solar heater will only heat sufficient water between April and September. This means that it must be supplemented by another source of heat, such as an immersion heater, during the rest of the year.

(Adapted from AQA's *Guidance on Quality of Written Communication (science)* document)

● Now model for the students how to create a text map like the example below for the beginning of the opening paragraph of the text using no words, or as few words as possible.

Text map for the opening line of advantages and disadvantages of solar energy

● Next, ask each pair to create their own text map for one paragraph (one person doing the advantages, the other the disadvantages). Ask them to hide the original and see if they can recall the gist of their paragraph just by looking at the text map.

- Now ask them to relate their piece of text back to each other using their text maps. They are not trying to get the text word for word the same as the original – what matters is that the student can express the correct information coherently. By talking the text in this manner, they will internalise useful phrases in their heads.

- Select some of the best performers to present their paragraph to the class so that all the class hears the text again.

They should now be very familiar with the pattern of the text and should, therefore, be able to start analysing it effectively.

Stage 4. Analysing the exemplar text

- Ask the students, in pairs, to highlight any general phrases, including sentence signposts and connectives, that could be useful for explaining the advantages and disadvantages of any scientific scenario, and to highlight in a different colour specialist vocabulary. (If this is the first time they have done something like this, then model how to do it for the beginning of the first paragraph.)

They will probably end up with something like the following:

Highlighted exemplar text to show generally useful phrases for advantages/disadvantages explanations and specialist vocabulary

The main advantage of using a **solar panel** to heat water is that it uses a **renewable energy source** rather than **fossil fuels**. This means that no **pollutants** such as **carbon dioxide** and **sulphur dioxide** are released by the **combustion of fuels**. **Carbon dioxide** contributes to the **greenhouse effect** and **sulphur dioxide** contributes to the formation of **acid rain**. In contrast, if water is heated by an **electric immersion heater,** the **electricity** will most probably have been produced by power stations that burn **fossil fuels**.

However, the main disadvantage of the **solar heater** is that it only heats the water when daylight is available. On cloudy days, the **solar heater** might not produce sufficient hot water for the family. The **graph** shows that the solar heater will only heat sufficient water between April and September. This means that it must be supplemented by another source of heat, such as an **immersion heater**, during the rest of the year.

It's a good idea to turn the key phrases they have identified into posters and display them so that when they write similar texts, they have the useful phrases to support them. Here the sentence signposts and connectives have been separated from the other general phrases. These posters should be added to as more useful general phrases emerge from similar text, including the best of the students' answers for these type of questions. Encouraging the students to recognise phrases that could be useful will build up their familiarity with the target language.

Poster G

Useful sentence starters for advantage/disadvantage explanations

- *The main advantage of*
- *This means that*
- *In contrast,*
- *However,*
- *The main disadvantage of*
- *The graph shows that*

Poster H

Useful general phrases for explanations

- *will most probably have been*
- *such as*
- *are released by*
- *contributes to the formation of*
- *might not produce sufficient*
- *supplemented by another source of*
- *contributes to*
- *during the rest of the*

- Now ask the class in pairs to annotate the text to bring out all the features that have contributed to it getting full marks.

- Then ask them to discuss their findings with another pair and adapt their annotations in the light of the discussion.

- Ask the groups to feed back their annotations and use the best of these to build up a class version. If the students have omitted key points, then ask questions (for them to discuss in pairs initially) to draw out the missing points.

Your final version will probably look something like this:

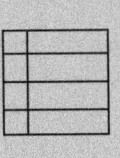

Annotated version of 'Advantages and disadvantages of solar energy for heating water' to show why it is an excellent answer

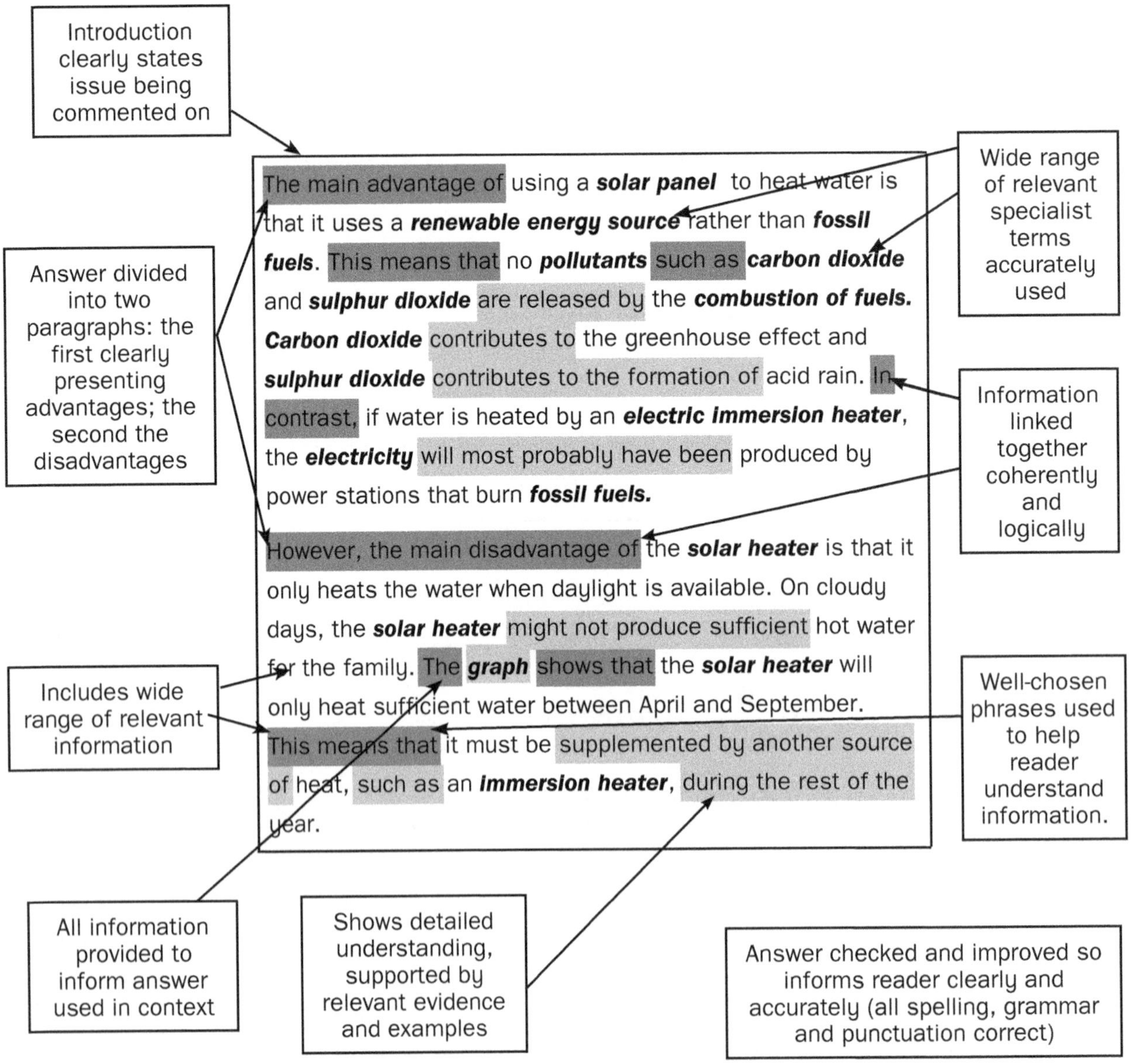

Introduction clearly states issue being commented on

Answer divided into two paragraphs: the first clearly presenting advantages; the second the disadvantages

Wide range of relevant specialist terms accurately used

Information linked together coherently and logically

Includes wide range of relevant information

Well-chosen phrases used to help reader understand information.

The main advantage of using a **solar panel** to heat water is that it uses a **renewable energy source** rather than **fossil fuels**. This means that no **pollutants** such as **carbon dioxide** and **sulphur dioxide** are released by the **combustion of fuels**. **Carbon dioxide** contributes to the greenhouse effect and **sulphur dioxide** contributes to the formation of acid rain. In contrast, if water is heated by an **electric immersion heater**, the **electricity** will most probably have been produced by power stations that burn **fossil fuels.**

However, the main disadvantage of the **solar heater** is that it only heats the water when daylight is available. On cloudy days, the **solar heater** might not produce sufficient hot water for the family. The **graph** shows that the **solar heater** will only heat sufficient water between April and September. This means that it must be supplemented by another source of heat, such as an **immersion heater**, during the rest of the year.

All information provided to inform answer used in context

Shows detailed understanding, supported by relevant evidence and examples

Answer checked and improved so informs reader clearly and accurately (all spelling, grammar and punctuation correct)

Stage 5. Using the analysis to co-construct the toolkit

- Using these annotations, co-construct with the class the toolkit for answering any advantages/disadvantages question in science. Your toolkit will probably look something like this:

The explaining advantages and disadvantages toolkit for science – use the following suggestions to help you

Plan it: decide what information to include and how to organise it	• Divide your answer into two paragraphs, clearly presenting:
	  1. the advantages;
	  2. the disadvantages
	• Use all information given to inform answer appropriately
	• Include relevant information you know about topic
	• Use intro to state issue being commented on

Link it: make your answer fit together well	• Link information together coherently and logically using causal and other connectives as appropriate (see **Poster G**)
Express it: make your answer clear	• Use well-chosen phrases to help reader understand information (see **Poster H**) • Show detailed understanding, supported by relevant evidence and examples • Include as many relevant specialist terms as possible, used accurately
Check it: make certain your spelling, grammar and punctuation are correct	• Read your answer through, checking that it flows coherently • Check it for accuracy and improve it if it doesn't sound right • Make certain it informs reader clearly and accurately

Stage 6. Explaining to others – an expert calls

- Now model for the class how to be the expert from the examination board who has come to tell the class how to get full marks when answering advantages/ disadvantages type questions, using the solar panel question to illustrate the points. In pairs the students take turns in being the expert.

- Select budding experts to present their sxplinations to the class. (The more the class has to explain the process, the more they will remember how to approach such questions and know 'what = good'.)

Stage 7. Applying what they have learnt

Now present the students with a similar style of advantages/disadvantages explanation question for a topic they have just studied. To support them, display the annotated exemplar text on screen, as well as the toolkit and related posters for this sort of text.

- Ask them, in pairs, to underline the actual question and then check with another pair to see if they have come to the same conclusion.

- Given the question, ask them first to discuss how the information provided is going to help them answer it and then to box up a plan showing how the answer should be structured.

- Again, ask them to check their plans with another pair to see if they are similar. Get the groups to feed back and box up the resulting plan on the flip chart. They can then adjust their planning if necessary.

- You may want them then to use symbols to represent the key points they want to make. Ask them to present their answer to their partner in talking-the-text style so they can practise making their ideas flow. The more practice students have at talking the text, the easier they will find writing this sort of text.

- Each student then writes up their own answer, using the exemplar text and related posters to help them. Make certain they read their answer through, correcting it where necessary.

Stage 8. Encouraging self-assessment

- The pairs then share their answers and, referring to the toolkit to support them, discuss what's good about them, how they could be improved, and make any necessary improvements.

- Ask each student to write a short comment at the end of their answer stating how well they think they have answered the question and any improvements they think could be made.

Stage 9. Using assessment to establish the next steps

- When you mark the work, apart from noting any deficiencies in their understanding of the particular issue being explained, establish, using the toolkit as a useful guide, what needs to be focused on next to help the students answer these sorts of questions.

- Use the student's self-assessment comments to begin a dialogue on what is good about their work and how it could be improved. (The more the inner judge within the student's mind can be trained to assess their own work, the more progress they will be able to make.)

- When the work is handed back is the best time to do work on rectifying any deficiencies in their knowledge or their ability to express this knowledge coherently.

- Allow time for the students to amend their work in the light of the activities so they immediately learn what they need to do to improve.

By the time a class has gone through this process, they should have begun to internalize the general approach. This means that it should be possible, for any type of question they need to be able to answer, to move swiftly to the toolkit stage with the students in role as visiting examination expert. The more a similar approach is used, the more likely the students are to internalise the pattern of how to tackle questions effectively.

Step Dvi: Using the boxing up approach to help unpick tricky questions and plan your answer

For subjects that require sophisticated discursive writing skills, the following approach may be useful. A key problem with sophisticated discursive essay questions is that you can get lured in the wrong direction by the question. For example, consider the tricky question 'The outbreak of World War One was caused by the alliance system. Discuss.'

The unwary may think that this means you spend all your time focusing on the alliance system's contribution to the outbreak of the war.

Again the boxing up planning method can provide a handy solution to analysing the question and planning your answer appropriately but this time add a question analysis box at the beginning that includes the fail-safe check, since there is always the danger that you lose sight of the actual question.

Boxed-up planning for complex questions

Stage 1: Question analysis – establish the underlying question	
Jot down the question	What is this actually asking?
'The outbreak of World War One was caused by the alliance system. Discuss.'	What caused the outbreak of WW1? Was the alliance system the key factor?
Fail safe	Look back at the original question and check that you haven't misinterpreted it

Stage 2	
Insert underlying question here: What caused the outbreak of WW1? Was the alliance system the key factor?	In introduction briefly state how significant the role of the alliance system was to the outbreak of the war
List the key factors that contributed to the outbreak of WW1 in order of importance	Factor 1 Factor 2 Factor 3 Factor 4 etc.

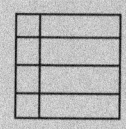

How significant was the alliance system to the outbreak of the war?	
Conclusion: Which factor or factors contributed most?	

(Adapted from the work of Craig Thomas, Tupton Hall School, Derbyshire)

Once the class has worked through one such question, you can work with the class to create generic boxed-up planning for the 'Was X caused by Y? Discuss' type of question and create similar generic plans for other frequently recurring types of questions.

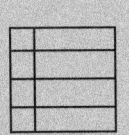

Generic boxed-up planning for 'Was X caused by Y? Discuss' type of questions

The underlying question hiding within the question: Why did X happen? How significant a factor was Y?	In introduction briefly state how significant the role of Y was in causing X
List the key factors that contributed to X in order of importance	Factor 1 Factor 2 Factor 3 Factor 4 etc.
How significant was Y in causing X?	
Conclusion: Which factor or factors contributed most to X?	State key factor/s and if these do not include Y briefly refer to Y's role in relation to the others

You may want to use the icon process here (see page 135) to help the students decide on the order they want to put the factors in and how they would express that order.

SECTION 2: APPROACHES BUILDING UP TO EXEMPLAR TEXT

In the last section, all the examples started with the exemplar text, and then worked backwards through analysis to build up the skills required. In this section, the process is reversed. The following examples all illustrate ways of building up to exemplar text.

Step Dvii: Sorting activities to help students write coherent chronological text

Effective clumping and explaining the clumps and how they relate to one another is a useful skill for students to acquire in a wide range of subjects. This can best be taught initially with any topic that fundamentally requires recount because the basic order of such text is chronological. However, there is still the question of how best to clump these chronological events in some logical way, rather than leaving them as an endless list. There is then the question of how to link these clumps so that their significance is clear.

The example below is based on the evacuation in Britain during the Second World War, a topic much focused on in primary school from the perspective of what it felt like to be packed off to an unknown family carrying a small case and wearing an identity label. In secondary schools, the focus will be more analytical, for example, on the different stages of the evacuation, like the activity here.

This example assumes that the teacher introduced some of the key vocabulary and concepts alongside the key facts of the situation. The teacher now wants the students to tackle this relatively straightforward question pitched at an adult audience.

What were the different stages of evacuation during the Second World War and what triggered each stage?

Task 1: Sorting the information

The students are asked to arrange the information cards into chronological order, turning over any information they think is not relevant given the question but saving anything to one side that might be useful for a good introduction, conclusion or explanation.

Handout 37a: Card sort for the different stages of evacuation during the Second World War

January 1940: Almost 60% evacuees returned home	**7 September 1940**: Blitz began. Children evacuated/re-evacuated
1–4 September 1939: 'Operation Pied Piper' began. Three million evacuated, many of them children	**13–18 June 1940**: Following German occupation of France, approximately 100,000 children evacuated/re-evacuated
Approximately 14 million Russian civilians died in the Second World War	Children were labelled like pieces of luggage, separated from their parents and accompanied by an army of teachers
June 1944: German V1 rocket attacks on Britain began. One million evacuated from London	**11.07 am on Thursday 31 August 1939**: 'Evacuate forthwith!' announcement broadcast
2009: First national memorial commemorating evacuation planned	**By May 1941**: 43,000 killed across Britain and 1.4 million homeless

Before war started, four million civilian casualties predicted in London alone	**Sunday 3 September 1939**: Britain declared war on Germany
May 1945: Second World War ended – V1 rocket attacks cease	**End of 1941**: City centres, especially London, became safer

Once the groups have had time to do their own version, the teacher may want to display the information in chronological order and discuss why they have discarded the card on the overall number of civilian deaths in Russia but kept the undated information about being labelled like luggage just in case it came in handy as a powerful image.

At the end of this process, the teacher can discuss with the class what they have just been doing and flag it up as part of the toolkit for writing this sort of text.

Plan it

Organise your information into chronological order

Task 2: Boxing up the information
The teacher now displays the outline grid for a boxed-up plan below to support the following activity.

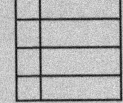

Outline plan for deciding how to box up information

Beginning: Introduction	
Middle:	• ...
	• ...
	• ...etc.
End: Conclusion	

The students are then given the following instructions:

- Start by deciding how many stages of the evacuation you think there were and place these in order in the middle section. These boxes (clumps of information) will form your main paragraphs. Ignore the introduction and conclusion at this point (since these will be dependent on how you have chosen to clump the information).

- Now decide on a good piece of information to provide the hook for your introduction and another to make the conclusion powerful and put these in the right-hand column. (Point out that when the students actually come to write/talk the text, they might want to alter these as it's only when you start expressing your points that you really know what works.)

- Think of a good heading for each of the middle clumps and write them on the left-hand side of the box.

Again, once the students have had time to make their own decisions, the teacher may want to display a version of how the information could be boxed up.

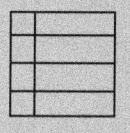

Handout 37b: Boxing up the information – What were the different stages of the evacuation during the Second World War and what triggered each stage?

Key stages and causes	Key information
Introduction with hook	• Before war started, 4 million civilian casualties predicted in London alone
Middle: Stage 1: war is declared	• **11.07 am on Thursday 31 August 1939**: 'Evacuate forthwith!' • **1–4 September 1939**: 'Operation Pied Piper' began – evacuation of nearly three million people, many of them children • Children were labelled like pieces of luggage, separated from their parents and accompanied by an army of teachers • **Sunday 3 September 1939**: Britain declared war on Germany • **January 1940**: Almost 60% evacuees returned home
Stage 2: the invasion of France	• **13–18 June 1940**: Following German occupation of France, one million children evacuated/re-evacuated
Stage 3: the blitz	• **7 September 1940**: Blitz began. Children evacuated/re-evacuated • **By May 1941**: 43,000 killed across Britain and 1.4 million homeless • **End of 1941**: City centres, especially London, became safer

Stage 4: V1 rocket attacks	• **June 1944**: German V1 rocket attacks on Britain began. One million people evacuated from London • **May 1945**: Second World War ended – V1 rocket attacks cease
Conclusion	• **2009**: first national memorial commemorating evacuation planned

Plan it

Decide how to box your information into significant sections

Task 3: Planning a good introduction

The teacher then reminds the students that it is important that an introduction is relevant and hooks the reader. (If the teacher has done a 'what = good activity' with the class on introductions (see page 179), then this could also be referred to and the co- constructed introduction toolkit could be displayed.)

The students are then asked to think up a good way to introduce their explanation. The teacher hears a few of the suggestions and, using shared writing techniques, models how to write an introduction so the students see how to do this. Again the shared writing sentence starters may be useful (see **Handout 3** online) to support the teacher in doing this. It's important that the shared writing is regularly read aloud to the class so everyone can hear if it works. Students need to see this demonstrated, as often they don't read their writing through and do not see this as part of the process. The students can now have a go at writing their own introduction. Once they have written their introduction, ask them to discuss it with a partner to determine what works and if there is anything that needs improving.

Task 4: Crafting good sentence starters

Endless lists of precise dates to introduce facts can be very confusing and dull. Now they have sorted the information into chronological order and boxed it up, the teacher could provide the class with some possible good sentence starters, like the examples below, and ask them in pairs to decide which dates they could replace with the alternatives to make the writing clearer and more interesting. Students could then discuss their ideas with another pair. The more they can start talking the phrases, the more likely they are to add such phrases to their writing repertoire.

Useful sentence signposts for signalling change of time

Poster I

- *Interestingly, x days before . . .*
- *In the first x days of . . .*
- *However, just x months later . . .*
- *Unfortunately, by the middle of x, the situation rapidly deteriorated because . . .*
- *However, by the end of a further x months . . .*
- *After x years of . . .*

Link it

Introduce your sections with engaging sentence signposts signalling the order of events

Task 5. Talking the text type

The more the students can be supported in talking the text type before they actually write it, the more the writing will flow when they do write it. Given that this text is chronological, it lends itself to being mimed (alternatively, you could use the symbols approach but mime probably works better here). Mime is an extremely powerful way of fixing a series of events in your mind, as you have to focus intently to mime something.

The teacher could ask the students in groups of four to devise a way of miming the different stages of the evacuations and their causes. If one or two groups are particularly good at this, they could present their mime to the whole class.

The miming process should have fixed the order of events in their heads so that they are now in a position to be able to 'talk the text type'. Ask them in pairs to present their account orally to their partner as if they were explaining the evacuations to the whole class. In turn, each pair should comment on what was good and discuss how the presentations could be improved.

Now model for the students how to be the visiting TV history professor who's come to tell the class all about the different stages of the evacuation of sections

of the population in the Second World War. They can then practise being visiting professor and a budding professor could present to the whole class.

If you pull together all the toolkit ingredients you have developed throughout the unit, you will probably end up with something like this:

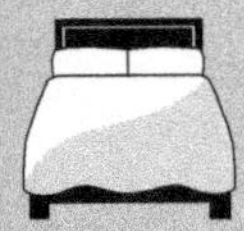

The account writing toolkit

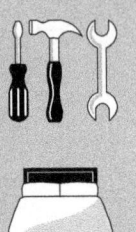

Plan it: order the information chronologically	• Analyse the question, work out what it includes • Box up your information into chronological order and decide how to clump it into logical sections, remembering the audience • Answer the question introducing what is being explained clearly • Use an interesting point as a hook to engage your reader • End with a relevant and interesting conclusion
Link it: make your article fit together well	• Introduce your sections with engaging sentence signposts and time connectives signalling the order of events (see **Poster I**) • Use causal sentence signposts and connectives to explain the events to your reader • Read your account through to check that it flows
Express it: make your article clear and interesting	• Use well-chosen phrases to help readers understand the information and keep them interested • Use detail to help make points clearer • Use technical language appropriately and explain it if necessary
Check it: make certain your spelling and grammar are correct	• Read your account through, checking it for accuracy and improve it if it doesn't sound right • Make certain it informs the reader in an interesting and engaging way

Now when they come to the write, the words should flow with relative ease so they can confidently write interesting, well-expressed accounts. The teacher should keep the boxed-up version of the text on the screen to help them, alongside the toolkit for writing accounts plus the poster of useful phrases.

The students then write their own version, and share it with a partner to discuss and make improvements. Finally, the students write a comment stating how well they think they have completed the task. The teacher then marks the work using this as a key formative assessment opportunity both to continue the individual dialogue with students about the next steps they need to take to improve their work, and to decide on the next aspects to focus on with the class as a whole to help them progress.

One good way forward is to select the best piece of work and display it on screen and ask the students in pairs to discuss how they would annotate the exemplar version, seeing if they can identify all the ingredients from the toolkit and selecting how to highlight all the sentence starters and phrases that could be used in similar types of writing.

You may then want to pull all their ideas together on screen for them like the annotated example below. (See **Handout 37c** online for a non-annotated version of the text.) They could then reread their work and make immediate improvements.

Annotated exemplar version: 'What were the different stages of the evacuation during the Second World War and what triggered each stage?'

Plan it: Well-structured account presenting the four stages clearly and logically. Text opens with good intro that interests reader and ends with clear statement answering the question and keeping reader engaged	**Introduction with hook**	Many people think that the mass population evacuation in the Second World War was one big event but in fact there were four separate mass evacuations, often of the same people as, understandably, they kept returning home. These evacuations were triggered by different threats throughout the war.	
	The first stage: war is declared	The initial evacuation was carried out because of the fear of massive civilian casualties. Before the war started, four million civilian casualties were predicted in London alone. Thus, at 11.07 am on Thursday 31 August 1939, the chilling words 'Evacuate forthwith!' were broadcast throughout Britain. And so began 'Operation Pied Piper', the four-day evacuation of nearly three million people, many of whom, as the name suggests, were children. So by the time Britain officially declared war on Germany on Sunday 3 September 1939, the evacuation was almost complete. However, just four months later, by the beginning of 1940, almost 60% of evacuees had voted with their feet and returned home.	**Link it:** Good use of range of interesting time and causal connectives to link information together clearly
	The second stage: the invasion of France	Unfortunately, by the middle of that year, the situation rapidly deteriorated because, in June 1940, Germany had occupied France. As a result, one million children in Britain were evacuated, some for the first time and others re-evacuated.	
	The third stage: the Blitz	However, by the end of a further three months, the situation had deteriorated even further with the coming of the Blitz, when London and other major cities were repeatedly bombed night after night. This led to the third evacuation or re-evacuation of children. By the end of May 1941, 43,000 civilians had been killed across Britain and 1.4 million were homeless. These are chilling numbers but far short of the initial predictions. Encouragingly, by the end of that year city centres, especially London, became safer.	

		Express it:
The fourth Stage. V1 rocket attacks	However, after two and a half years of relative calm in the cities, in June 1944 the Germans began the V1 attacks on Britain with devastating casualties. This triggered the f nal phase of the evacuations. Only with the ending of the war, a year later in May 1945, did the rocket attacks cease.	Well-chosen phrases help reader understand and remain interested in information. Technical language appropriately used
Conclusion	If you visit the Imperial War Museum and listen to the moving memories of those who were evacuated, you get some insight into the trauma that this massive and repeated movement of people caused. It is therefore perhaps surprising that it wasn't until nearly 65 years later, in 2009, when most of the evacuated were old or had died, that the f rst national memorial commemorating the evacuation was planned.	

Pull out all the useful connectives and sentence signposts that could be used for other pieces of history work so you are building a bank of useful phrases posters. These can be displayed on your washing line.

Poster J

Useful linking phrases for historical recount and explanation

Time connectives and sentence signposts
• Before the x started
• And so began
• So by the time
• However, just x short months later,
• by the middle of that year,
• It is therefore, perhaps, surprising that it wasn't until nearly
• However, by the end of a further x months,
• However, after two and a half years of
• Only with the ending of
• A year later

- *By the end of*
- *Encouragingly, by the end of that year*

Causal Connectives and Siznposts

- *The initial x was carried out because*
- *were triggered by*
- *This triggered*
- *This led to*
- *As a result,*
- *the situation rapidly deteriorated because*
- *when most of the*
- *Thus,*

Link it

Link the explanation together clearly using time and causal connectives as well as sentence signposts effectively

Useful expressions to describe and explain what happened

Poster K

- *voted with their feet*
- *as the name suggests*
- *you get some insight into*
- *the situation had deteriorated even further*
- *but far short of*

Express it

Use well-chosen phrases to help the reader understand the information

Step Dviii: Sorting activities to help students structure and express points clearly

One of the most powerful ways of helping students structure and express discursive essays is to use advanced sorting techniques combined with focused talk to help students learn:

- how to structure information to meet the demands of the question

- how to link this information effectively.

This technique is illustrated below by adapting Christine Counsell's excellent 'Fire of London' activity.

This approach can be easily adapted to meet the needs of any subject that requires discursive writing and can also be adapted to support any analytic work including focused paragraphs. It assumes that a topic has been thoroughly taught and you are now at the stage when you want the students to answer a discursive/ analytic question. Obviously, this will take some teaching time, but the more thoroughly this is taught early on (or early in the exam years if your subject is not taught lower down the school), the better the students will be at expressing their ideas and the more progress they will make. Ideally this approach could be developed in the first three years to help students think about how to structure and express their work and then could be refined further to meet the specific requirements of formal exams as exemplified in the geography example that follows this history example.

Objective: To be able to write powerful discursive/analytical text

The specific question the students are required to answer in this example is 'Why did the Great Fire of London get out of control and destroy so much of London?'

The first time you ask a class to tackle a discursive/analytical question, you may want to begin with a how-to-start-planning-your-answer activity that helps students think about the logical steps they need to follow if they are to answer such questions effectively. The following cards can easily be adapted to suit any discursive/analytical question.

How-to-start-planning-your-answer activity

Provide the students in pairs with the following set of cards. Ask them to discard any cards that are not relevant, given the question 'Why did the Great Fire of

London get out of control and destroy so much of London?', and then to place the remaining cards in logical order. Ask them to check their order with another pair and discuss any differences.

Handout 38a: How-to-start-planning-your-answer activity

• Sort the information into key points	• Read your essay throughand improve it
• End with an interesting conclusion summing up your argument	• Include all the information you know about the Fire of London
• Select relevant information	• Decide on the most logical order for your key points
• Decide how to introduce your essay so that it answers the question and engages the reader	• Make your ideas flow so one point follows on logically from another
• Support your ideas with evidence andcomment	• Present each key point in a new paragraph and introduce it with a topic sentence
• Include interesting information about any fires you have experienced	• Choose effective words and phrases to express your ideas clearly and interestingly

Ask the class to feed back their ideas and build up a plan of action in chronological order. It will probably look like that below. This list can then be displayed whenever they are attempting discursive work. As you can see, this list is the basis of the discursive writing toolkit. Stress the point that you can't work out how to introduce your answer until you have planned how you are going to answer the question.

The planning and writing discursive text toolkit

Plan it*:	1. Select relevant information
	2. Sort the information into key points
	3. Decide on the most logical order for your key points
	4. Decide how to introduce your essay so that it answers the question and engages the reader
Link it:	5. Present each key point in a new paragraph and introduce it with a topic sentence
	6. Make your ideas flow so one point follows on logically from another

Express it:	7. Support your ideas with evidence and comment
	8. Choose effective words and phrases to express your ideas clearly and interestingly
	9. *End with an interesting conclusion summing up your argument
Check it:	10. Read your essay through and improve it

*End with an interesting conclusion summing up your argument is part of the planning process but chronologically it is the final thing that is written, hence it has been placed chronologically for the purposes of this activity.

This activity lays the foundations for going through each of the stages showing the students how to tackle them as exemplified below.

Stage 1. Selecting the relevant information

This first stage of selecting relevant information is absolutely crucial. If faced with questions we don't really know how to answer, most of us fall back on some form of rambling recount, telling everything we know about the topic in an unstructured way. Professor David Wray aptly refers to this as the 'the bed-to-bed style of writing'.

To help students avoid this trap, present each pair with some key information about the topic on cards but include at least one piece of information that is relevant to the topic but not to the question. Then ask the pairs to select which of the statements is the *least relevant* to the question, 'Why did the Great Fire of London get out of control and destroy so much of London?'

Handout 38b: Selecting relevant information cards for the Great Fire of London question

Water supplies were unusually low in 1666	Officials did not believe it was going to spread and took no action when it started
Houses in London were built very close together	Someone started a fire in Pudding Lane
Throughout London, heating and lighting were provided by fire	House fires were common and often extinguished by demolishing surrounding property
The mayor allegedly said: 'Pish! A woman might piss it out,' and refused to order the surrounding property to be demolished	The wind on the day of the fire was very strong
Most buildings were made of wood	Fire-fighting equipment was not good enough to cope with a large fire

Ask the students to discuss their conclusion with another pair. Hopefully, groups will have selected *Someone started a fire in Pudding Lane*. Discuss why this is not relevant to the question and how it encourages you to recount everything you know about the fire rather than focus on the question asked.

After each set of activities, co-construct with the class the ingredients to add to the toolkit for discursive writing so that when they come to write the answer they will be familiar with the toolkit and have started to internalise it so that effective planning becomes automatic.

Following discussion of this activity, the class will probably come up with an ingredient like this:

'Analyse the question and decide what key information you need to include'

Stage 1a. Identifying short- and long-term causes

Now ask the students to sort the remaining statements into short-term and long-term causes. This will be key to their understanding of how to answer the question, so ask them to think up arguments for and against why each short-term cause could be the deciding factor and discuss these with another pair. Get groups to feed back their conclusions.

Stage 2. Clumping the information into key points

Now ask the students in pairs to clump the information into key points, give each clump a heading and then compare their conclusions with another pair. Stress that there are different ways of clumping the information. Get feedback from the groups and establish the most common key clumps, which will probably look like the clumps below.

Built environment	Weather	Equipment for fire-fighting	Human error
Most buildings were made of wood	Water supplies were unusually low in 1666	Fire-fighting equipment was not good enough to cope with a large fire	The mayor allegedly said: 'Pish! A woman might piss it out'
Houses in London were built very closely together	The wind on the day of the fire was very strong	House fires were common and often extinguished by demolishing surrounding property	Officials did not believe it was going to spread and took no action when it started
Throughout London, heating and lighting were provided by fire			

Stage 3. Turning your headings into effective topic sentences

Being able to write good topic sentences is key to effective communication. You have to know the point you are trying to make and devise a sentence that introduces it clearly. The more skilled the students become at this, the more coherent their writing will be; so they need to have this skill modelled for them and then practise it.

You might want to take the first key point, the **built environment**, and model for them how to write a sentence that would introduce the paragraph about the built environment. For example,

'A key factor in the spread of the fire was that the streets of London in 1666 were a serious fire hazard.'

Discuss with the class how the paragraph could then be built up from this point by evidence and comment to make a strong paragraph.

The students could then in pairs draft a topic sentence to introduce why the weather conditions were key and several pairs could feed back their ideas so that the class becomes more confident about how to write the sentence that introduces a point.

Stage 4. Using icons to rehearse your ideas orally and decide the order of your key points

The way that you organise your key points is central to building up a coherent argument. We have probably all experienced that feeling in an exam, that by the time you have finished answering the question you know how to answer it, but by then it is too late to start again. The more we can encourage students to plan their ideas before they launch into writing, the more they will be able to write a coherent discursive argument. Before they actually write, it is useful if the students can have attempted to express their ideas orally in the language in which they should be writing them. This will help them to write with confidence, as they will have adjusted their ideas as a result of trying to present their points coherently.

One of the best ways of deciding on the key order of points is to use symbols to represent each key point and then try to orally link the points together. Model for the students how to create symbols/icons to represent the key points, as illustrated here, and then ask them to devise their own symbols and to decide on the order in which they want to present the information and use the symbols to represent this order.

Fire of London icons

Fire of London icons in order

Show them how to do this, for instance by starting with the housing image, then human error, then equipment and finishing with the wind as the short-term killer factor. This, in effect, is your *boxed-up planning*. Now model for the students how to use your images to help them present the arguments coherently in a logical order.

Ask each pair to jot down their key symbols in the order in which they want to present their points – supported by any other symbols that will help them to remember the information that they want to include and give them a short time to think about what they are going to say.

Next, ask them to take it in turns to talk their presentation to their partners as if they were the visiting professor come to tell everyone why the Great Fire of London destroyed so much of London. The pairs can then discuss how the presentations could be improved and they might find that they want to alter the order in which they presented their key points so as to make their argument flow logically.

You may want to select some budding professors to stand up and present to the whole class. This will provide an excellent opportunity for students to magpie good ideas, words and phrases from these budding professors, which they can then use in their own work.

A more challenging activity, if you want to stretch the students further, is to then encourage them to be tentative when presenting their points. After all, they are only presenting an interpretation of the facts, not absolute truths. Model for them a range of tentative phrases, for example 'It would appear that', 'It is probable that', 'One possible explanation is that', and then ask the students to present their ideas again but this time more tentatively. (For more detailed work on being tentative, see page 75.)

In any situation where students have to make oral presentations, ban anything being written down and only allow them to have symbols for the key points. If it's written down they will just read it out. Only having the symbols to remind you of the order frees up your mind to be able to express what you are trying to say and leads to coherence. Try it, it works! This will not only greatly improve the quality of their presentation but also of the writing that follows it because, as you try to talk your text, you become aware if one section does not lead to another and you may decide to alter the order in which you are going to present the information so that it flows more logically.

Now return to your toolkit and amend the ingredients in the light of these activities. The class will probably come up with additional points, such as:

- Analyse the question and then decide what points you are going to make and the logical order in which you will make them.

- Present each key point in a new paragraph and introduce it with a topic sentence.

- Link your ideas together so they flow logically.

Stage 5. Writing effective introductions

Now is the moment to focus on how to write a powerful introduction because it illustrates the fact that you can't decide on your introduction until you have some idea about how you want to answer the question. In effect, you have to plan the middle before you can plan the introduction. Now the students have established how they want to answer the question, use the 'what = good' technique for writing powerful paragraphs, as illustrated on page 127. Ask them in pairs to:

- Select which of the four introductions is the best given the question.

- Establish what key ingredients help make it good.

- Decide what lets the other versions down.

Handout 38c: Comparison activity to select the best introduction to the question, 'Why did the Great Fire of London get out of control and destroy so much of London?'

Introduction 1	Introduction 3
The Great Fire of London destroyed a lot of London. I think the mayor was very silly and it was all his fault because he didn't listen to what anyone said and if he had done something about it earlier on then it wouldn't have burnt so many houses and then London would have been all right.	Have you ever wondered why the Great Fire of London got out of control and destroyed so much of London. Today in history we have been discussing this and there are lots of reasons and I am going to tell you what we have decided.
Introduction 2	**Introduction 4**
House fires in 17th century London were an everyday occurrence and yet one such fire destroyed so much of London that it has become known as the Great Fire of London. Perhaps the explanation for why this particular fire got out of control is that such destruction was inevitable, given the way London was built, and was just waiting for the right weather conditions to happen.	Someone started a fire in Pudding Lane. The flames swiftly set the wooden beams alight and the wind spread the flames from one wooden house to another, lighting up the night sky. House after house, street after street, quickly went up in flames and in a very short time most of London was alight like a forest fire. Officials tried to pull down houses to extinguish the flames but it was out of control. They just had to flee and watch London burn.

Once they have done this, ask the students to check their findings with another pair and then get the groups to feed back on their toolkit ingredients for good introductions and build up a class version that may end up looking something like the one below. It is important that the class is involved in this process rather than just being given the toolkit. If they are simply presented with the criteria, they will not have understood or internalized them and therefore will probably not be able to apply them.

The discursive introduction writing toolkit

Plan it: order your introduction logically	• Analyse question, work out what it includes and decide how to answer it, remembering audience • Introduce response clearly, making certain answering question asked • Include hook to engage the reader • Don't try to put all points into introduction • Don't bore audience by repeating question and saying how going to answer it • Check that intro flows coherently

Then ask the students to use this toolkit to write their own introduction. Once they have completed their work, ask them to share their introduction with a partner so that they can discuss whether they have followed the class's instructions for writing good introductions. Allow time for them to revise their work in the light of the discussions. Again, when you mark the work, check to see if they are all applying the ingredients of the toolkit appropriately and begin the next lesson with activities to secure these features, allowing time for the students to remedy errors when the work is handed back so they are not only aware of the steps they need to take to improve their work, but have had a go at putting them into practice. If this is not done, then all that time spent marking may have been wasted.

Stage 6. Using shared writing to show them how to do it

The teacher can now use the best of the students' introductions and the earlier presentations as a basis to model shared writing, as the class should now have plenty of ideas about how to write this essay. If this is the first time the class has attempted this sort of writing, you will need to model how to write the whole essay so they understand how important it is to make ideas flow. Display your boxed-up icons so they can see your planning and then, with the help of the class, craft the answer to the question involving the students with phrases like:

- Which do you think would work best?

- Let's just read that and see how it sounds

- We've got _____, what else do we need? What could follow? You tell me.

- Which bits don't seem to fit?

- What would make it flow better?

For more examples of useful phrases to use for shared writing, see **Handout 3** online.

Throughout the process, the teacher will regularly read the writing out to the class so they can hear it and decide if it works. All the time, the teacher will model what a good writer does. This may include slightly moving away from your plan, as often in the actual process of writing you refine your initial thoughts.

You will end up with a shared writing example somewhat like the one below, which can then be displayed when the students are writing their own essay to support them. See **Handout 38d** online for a copy of this exemplar text.

'Why did the Great Fire of London get out of control and destroy so much of London?'

House fires in 17th century London were an everyday occurrence and yet one such fire destroyed so much of London that it has become known as the Great Fire of London. Perhaps the explanation for why this particular fire got out of control is that such destruction was inevitable, given the way London was built, and was just waiting for the right weather conditions to happen.

A key long-term cause of the fire was that in 1666, London was a mass of narrow streets lined by closely packed wooden houses heated by fire. In such circumstances, it was inevitable that fire would often break out and, when it did, it would spread rapidly from house to house.

Because firefighting equipment was not very effective, the main method of preventing the fires from getting out of control was demolishing neighbouring buildings to prevent the fire from taking hold. Such preventative action could, perhaps, have limited the fire to a few buildings but the mayor rejected such action, allegedly saying, 'Pish, a woman might piss it out!' One probable explanation for what, in hindsight, appears to be serious human error, is the fact that the authorities would have to recompense property owners whose buildings were demolished and so the powers that be were often reluctant to select this solution. This contributed to the conditions for the Great Fire.

However, it would appear that the weather was the deciding factor. Unfortunately, when the fire broke out, the wind was very strong, so it rapidly spread from street to street with the wind fanning the flames. To make matters worse, there had been much less rainfall than usual that year so water levels were low, which made accessing water to douse the flames more difficult. Significantly, the fire was not extinguished until the wind subsided some two days later.

In conclusion, it would appear that at some point it was inevitable that London would burn to the ground because of the closeness of the wooden houses. Human error alone, although a contributory factor, is not liable to be the main cause, as it is reasonable to assume that the officials behaved similarly when other fires occurred. There is, however, much evidence to suggest that it was the strong wind that happened to be blowing at that time that was the deciding factor.

Throughout the shared writing process, ask a student to act as teaching assistant and jot down all the useful phrases on a flip chart that emerge from the discussion about how best to express the points. These can then be displayed as posters when the class is writing to support them. Below, some possible useful phrases that might have arisen from the shared writing have been divided into sentence starters and connectives, general useful phrases and tentative phrases. These posters can be added to as more useful phrases emerge from later discursive text, including the best of the students' work.

Poster L

Useful sentence starters and connectives for discursive writing

- *A key long-term cause of*
- *In such circumstances,*
- *because*
- *However,*
- *The main reason*
- *The main method of*
- *Such preventative action*
- *To make matters worse*
- *It is therefore reasonable to conclude*

Useful phrases for discursive writing

Poster M

- an everyday occurrence
- has become known as
- just waiting for the right conditions to happen
- such destruction was inevitable
- helped create the conditions for
- was bound to happen
- the fact that
- the deciding factor

Useful tentative sentence starters and phrases

Poster N

- Perhaps the explanation for why
- could perhaps have
- One probable explanation
- allegedly saying
- It is worth considering
- for what, in hindsight, appears to be
- probably would not have
- It would appear that
- There is much evidence to suggest that

Stage 7. Co-constructing the toolkit for discursive writing

Throughout, the students should have the guide to planning and writing discursive text displayed to support them. Now use the shared writing to finalise the toolkit for discursive writing. The toolkit you construct with the class may end up looking something like this.

The discursive writing toolkit

Plan it: order points logically building up to a reasoned conclusion	• Analyse question then decide what points to make and logical order in which to make them • Introduce answer clearly, making certain it answers question asked, and include hook to engage reader • End essay with a clear conclusion giving coherent reasons supporting viewpoint
Link it: make points flow so reader can follow argument	• Present each key point in new paragraph and introduce with topic sentence • Link ideas together so flow logically using effective causal connectives or sentence signposts (see Posters L) • Read through to check that writing flows logically
Express it: make information clear	• Select good phrases to help reader understand and keep interested so want to read on (see Posters M/N) • Express key points clearly and support by appropriate evidence and comment • Use powerful words and phrases to suit purpose and interest reader
Check it: make certain your spelling and grammar are correct	• Read essay through, checking for accuracy. Are the sentences correctly punctuated and words properly spelt? • Improve it if it doesn't sound right.

This toolkit should be displayed the next time the class does discursive writing.

Stage 8. Writing and improving your discursive essay

Each student then writes their own answer to the question, using the toolkit, the shared writing text and the related posters to help them. Once they have finished their first draft they should read it through correcting and improving it if necessary. Hopefully the shared writing process will have illustrated that good writers amend their work.

The pairs should then share their work and discuss what's good about each essay and how it could be improved, and then make any necessary improvements.

When the teacher marks the work, in addition to noting any deficiencies in the class's understanding of the particular issue being discussed, they can establish, using the toolkit as a useful guide, what needs to be focused on next to help the students answer these sort of questions. When the work is handed back is the best time to do work on rectifying any deficiencies. If time is not set aside for this, then what was the point of doing all the marking?

Stage 9. Consolidate learning by providing an exemplar version of the writing task set

One good way of consolidating learning is to select the best of the essays written by the students and to display this using a visualiser. Read the essay out to the class so they can hear how the text flows and then ask the students in pairs to act in teacher role and pretend they were explaining to a class why this work was good. Encourage them to use the toolkit to help them. For example, they might use phrases like the following:

- Good topic sentences have been used to introduce each point, for example . . .

- All the key points are ordered logically so the argument is coherent, beginning with . . . and ending with . . .

- The essay begins with an interesting, relevant introduction that hooks the reader.

- Each of the points is clearly explained and backed up with evidence, for example . . .

- Each paragraph is introduced by a clear signpost to guide the reader, for example . . .

Go round the class listening to the pairs as they act in teacher role and ask one or two budding teachers to present their explanation to the whole class. The more the students become used to talking about what makes writing effective, the more they will be able to help themselves make their own writing effective because this process helps develop their inner judgement about what works.

At the end of this activity, allow time for the students to amend their work so they immediately put into practice what they need to do to improve.

Step Dix: Building up the exemplar text through phrase-building blocks – an MFL example

Many aspects of the Talk-for-Writing approach will be familiar to teachers of languages. Since language teaching is oral based, it's all about establishing the tune and pattern of the target language. The material below, developed by the modern foreign languages department at Ipswich High School, could be adapted to support students in evaluating their progress with any topic if you change the categories to suit the appropriate subject.

First, they adapted the learning frame on page 35 to help develop the range of phrases students had at their command when writing a formal letter in French, a task suited for more advanced learners of French. Only the first column is filled in at the beginning of the unit; the second and final columns are filled in at the end of the unit to indicate the additional phrases the students now know and additional phrases they still need.

Handout 39a: Formal letter writing (and speaking)

Appropriate for a formal letter	**What I know to begin with** (jot the appropriate phrases here in French)	**What I now know** (jot any additional appropriate phrases here in French)	**What more do I need to know?** (jot down in English the formal phrases you think you might need that you don't know how to express in French)
Starting			
Thanking			
Ordering			
Sending			
Asking information			
Complaining			
Finishing			

Having filled in the first column above, the students in pairs match the two halves of the sentences below, which are presented as cards to be sorted, and then arrange them into a coherent letter. Finally, they read the letter to each other sentence by sentence to check that they have made the right selections and to hear the pattern of the language.

Handout 39b: Sorting activity

Je vous remercie	de votre brochure que nous avons reçue la semaine dernière et que vous avez élaborée pour différents clients.
Mon patron m'a demandé	de vous écrire pour vous dire qu'il apprécie la qualité de vos produits.
Pourriez-vous	nous envoyer des échantillons et des prix pour les articles ménagers dans votre dépliant.
Nous aimerions aussi	savoir quel est le délai de livraison de vos marchandises.
Y-aura-t-il	une remise si nous achetons plus de cinquante articles.

Then, using Worksheet 3 (**Handout 39c**), they try to complete the phrases orally, when they no longer have access to the full text.

Handout 39c: Completez les phrases

(a)   Je vous remercie de . . .

(b)   Mon patron m'a demandé de . . .

(c)   Pourriez-vous

(d)   Nous aimerions aussi savoir . . .

(e)   Y a-t-il . . .

(f)   Je vous prie . . .

Next, to help the students internalise the correct language, they first construct the letter again, this time using the dominoes below, and then write it out being careful to select only one option where there is a choice. For the complete handout, see the resources online.

Handout 39d: Reconstructing the letter

Madame	Je te/tu/vous remercie	de votre brochure que/ qui	nous avons reçue

la semaine dernier/ prochaine/ dernière	et que vous avez élaborée	pour vos/ vous/votre différents clients.	Mon patron

m'a demandé	de vous écrire	pour vous dire qu'il apprécie/ appreciera/	la qualité de vos produits.

Students are then asked to work in groups comparing their versions and justifying their choices.

To reinforce their understanding of formal and informal phrases, the students in pairs are then asked to sort the following phrases:

Handout 39e: Sorting the formal from the informal

Appropriate for a formal letter	Not appropriate for a formal letter
Je vous remercie de	Mercie de ta lettre
Monsieur	Cher monsieur
Nous voudrions commander	Je veux avoir
Je vous prie d'agréer monsieur l'assurance de mes	Grosses bises
Nous vous prions de trouver ci-joint	Un grand merci pour
Suite à votre demande	Je t'envoie
Ne hésitez pas à	
Veuillez trouver ci-joint	
Nous vous serions reconnaissants de	Je veux recevoir

The students are then asked to write a formal letter using the phrases they have been focusing on. They share their letter with their partner and together check if it is appropriate and correct.

To help them in this checking, they could be provided with an exemplar letter like that below:

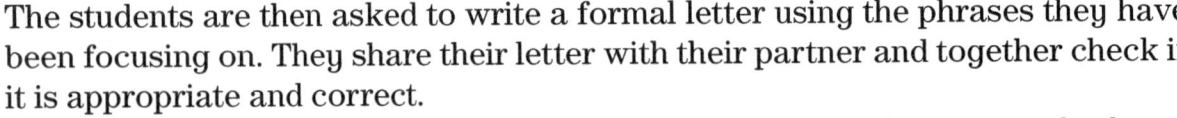

Handout 39f: Exemplar letter

Madame,

Je vous remercie de votre brochure que nous avons reçue la semaine dernière et que vous avez élaborée pour différents clients.

Mon patron m'a demandé de vous écrire pour vous dire qu'il apprécie la qualité de vos produits.

Pourriez-vous nous envoyer des échantillons et des prix pour les articles ménagers dans votre dépliant.

Nous aimerions aussi savoir quel est le délai de livraison de vos marchandises.

Y-aura-t-il une remise si nous achetons plus de cinquante articles?

Dans l'attente de votre lettre,

Salutations distinguées.

Finally, they return to the first worksheet (**Handout 39a**) and fill in the middle and end columns.

Step Dx: Using focused discussion to support students: case studies from geography and art

Case study 1: Geography KS4 case study on improving students' ability to answer analytical questions

The geography department at Longhill High School, Brighton, analysed what aspects of the GCSE exam were causing students the greatest problems. As a result, they decided to use the Talk-for-Writing approach to put more focus on helping students consider a variety of options and justify their final choices orally before attempting to write. In particular, they wanted to support the students by devising sorting activities that supported the students in discussing the key issues and explaining to others. Such an approach helps students internalise how to approach answering a similar question in the real exam, as well as the sorts of phrases such a question requires.

In the exam, students are asked to make links between the options proposed in the question and various related issues from a resource booklet. They need to express these links coherently, presenting a balanced view and justifying their choices. The class referred to here had initially experienced trying to write such essays without the level of support suggested below, as the student feedback at the end of this section reflects.

The exam board's Level Four descriptor for this activity is as follows:
The candidate presents a report that deals with some range of viewpoints and 'view holders', both positive and negative, in detail. They are clearly linked to the issues concerned with development. The issues will be at a range of scales and address both sustainability and the problems of the people in Mauritania. An overall view of the situation is discussed, which includes a detailed comparison of the options, leading to a clear justification of their choice. The candidate conveys a real understanding of sustainability and development. Reasoning is sophisticated/elaborated using accurate and geographical language. (12–14 marks)

The following stages outline how the teachers supported the students in understanding how to tackle such challenging questions:

Stage 1: Warming up the phrases they will need to justify their decisions

To warm up the sort of sentence signposts and connectives the students would need to use if they were to justify their choices effectively and link their points coherently, the teachers developed warming-up-the-phrase activities like those outlined on pages 38–69. This helped the students became more familiar with introducing points and justifying their arguments using phrases like:

- The three options all have advantages and disadvantages . . .

- All the alternatives offer . . .

- The most important factor is . . .
- X is a good option because . . .
- In the longer term, . . .
- In the short term, . . .
- The most useful option is . . .
- However, . . .
- In contrast to this, . . .
- On the other hand, . . .
- In addition to this, . . .
- Although . . .
- Whereas . . .

Stage 2: Understanding the question

Below is the WJEC GCSE geography question that was focused on:

> The government of Mauritania is keen to develop the country. How they choose to do so must be sustainable and improve the quality of life for the people of Mauritania.
>
> Write a report for the government of Mauritania. You may also use information from other parts of the paper, from your studies and ideas of your own.
>
> You should advise them on which of these options they should use to develop Mauritania.
>
> - selling fishing rights
> - increasing steel production
> - promoting tourism
>
> You must **explore all three options** and refer to their potential **positive and negative** effects in order to recommend which option(s) will be **best for the people and for the sustainability of Mauritania's economy.**
>
> You may recommend one option or a combination of options.

Students in pairs were asked to analyse the question and explain clearly what they had to do to another pair of students.

Feedback from this activity helped to establish that they had to write a report for the Government of Mauritania advising them which of the three options bullet pointed above would best help achieve a sustainable economy and quality of life for the people of Mauritania. They would need to provide the pros and cons of all three options and justify their final recommendations.

Stage 3: Identifying the relevant information

Sections A and B of the paper provided the students with background information to help answer the question. The key information relating to the three options acquired from these sections was given to the students on hexagons, some of which are displayed below. The hexagons (from the Triptico website: http://www. triptico.co.uk/thinklink. html) are useful because their shape allows a range of links to be made to each option.

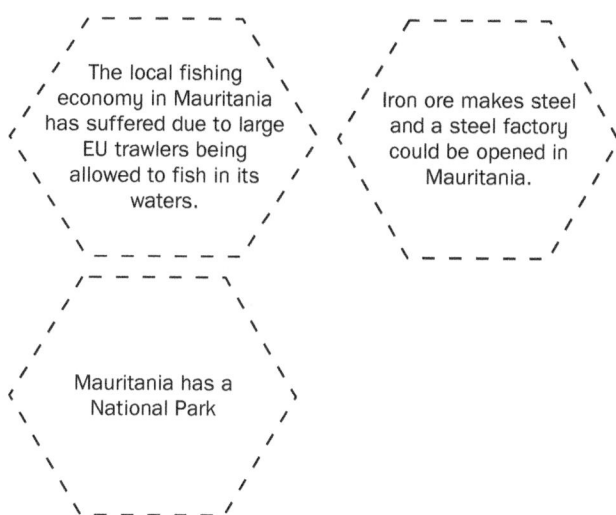

The students were then provided with blank hexagons and asked to discuss in pairs if they could think of any additional useful information from sections A and B that would be useful for each option and to write this information on the blanks. They had to be able to justify why this information would be useful. They came up with a wide range of additional points, some of which are illustrated below:

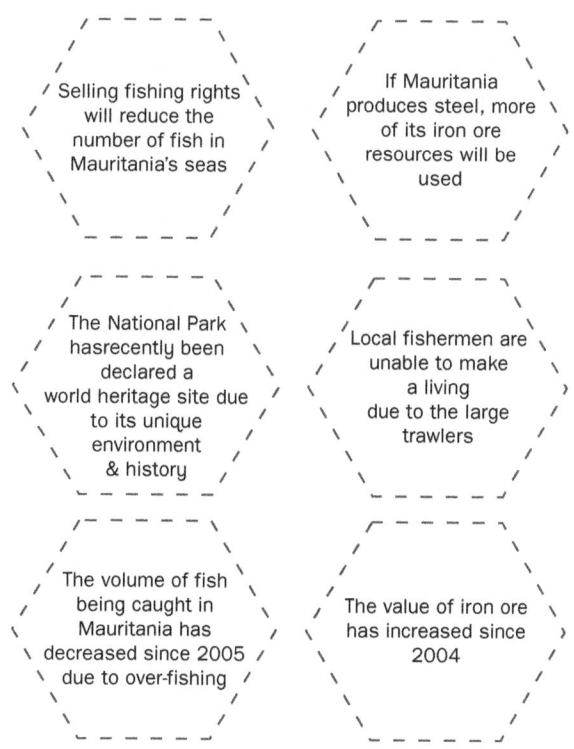

Stage 4: Helping the students clump the information and present their ideas coherently

The class was divided into groups of six so that each pair on a table would initially focus on one of the three development options.

Each pair was asked to link the relevant information to their option and to be able to explain this link and how it could affect development in Mauritania.

The pairs then had to swap places on their table and explain to their new partner, in teacher role, why they had made the links they had made and how these factors could affect development.

Typically, a pair focusing on the tourism option would have linked the following points and would have had to justify their choice:

Stage 5: Helping students explore the links between the options, and their advantages and disadvantages

The students in pairs were then asked to make links between the three options, as well as to consider the pros and cons of each option in helping Mauritania achieve both sustainable economic development and quality of life for its people. They had to be able to justify any links they had made, as well as being able to explain the advantages and disadvantages coherently.

Below is an example of how one group linked the points about tourism.

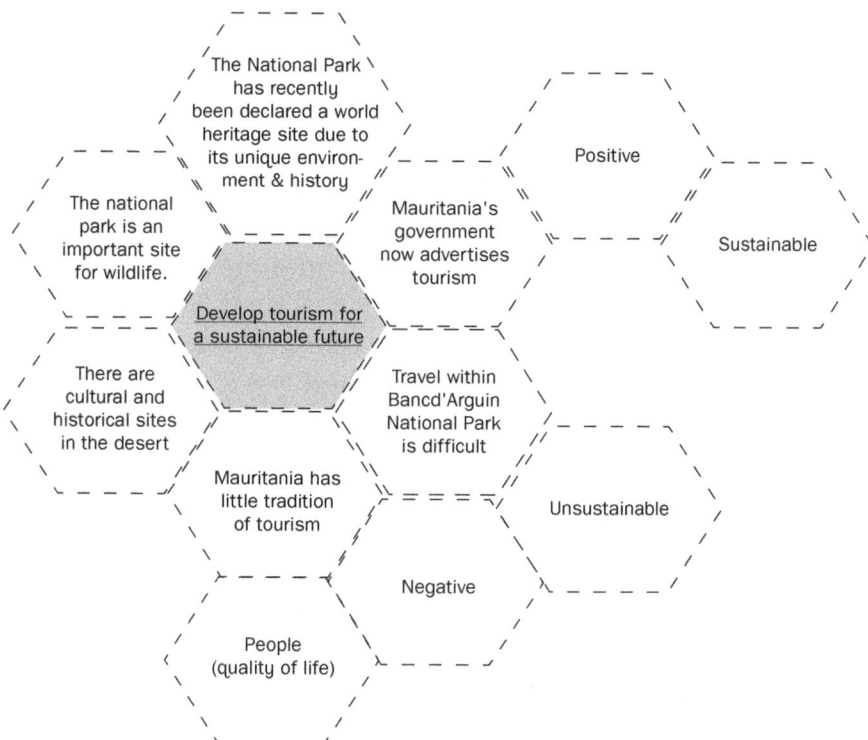

Following this support, the students found it much easier to write a coherent essay that met the requirements of the question. Feedback from the students confirmed that they had found that it helped them understand what to do:

> *I enjoyed talking about the options and telling the class why some were good and some were bad. It helped me write a detailed answer that argued my choice well.*

> *Using the hexagons was useful because they helped me visualise each of the options and their impacts. In the exam, I found it hard to organise all of the information but I now understand how I can do this.*

> *In the exam, I didn't know how to include sustainability and the environment into my answer but the hexagons helped me make sure that these were included and explained.*

(Thanks to Hannah Rei, Jo Cassidy and Tony Salmon, geography teachers at Longhill High School, Brighton, for providing the material for this case study)

Case study 2: Helping students evaluate art through focused discussion

This is how Simon Farrell from the art department at Cardinal Newman School, Hove, developed the Talk-for-Writing approach to suit the requirements of art.

Art is not a text-based subject but it is important for the students to have the vocabulary to enable them to evaluate and appreciate art both for its own sake and to develop their own understanding and practice. The art department found that if Year 10 students were given some research work into an artist for homework (e.g. *Find out about the work of* **William Nicholson** *and his still life paintings, including what he painted and why and how did he paint it, and describe the techniques used – stippling, impasto etc.*), a typical result would be:

William Nicholson

William Nicholson (1872–1949) who is known by many for his early woodcuts and the radical posters of the Beggar staff Brothers in the 1890's, has become recognised as one of the leading English artists of his time for the whole range of his work. His haunting downland landscapes, his remarkable still lifes, which capture light and colour in an entirely fresh way, and the varied portraits by which he mainly earned his living . . .

A glance tells you that this is courtesy of Google and has not involved the student in personal visual analysis. The teacher rectified the problem in the following way.

The class spent a lesson looking at images by the artist. The students, working in small groups, were then asked to focus on one aspect of their image: subject, composition, mood/meaning or process. Word banks were available on each table. The students' ideas were then transferred onto mind maps like the one below.

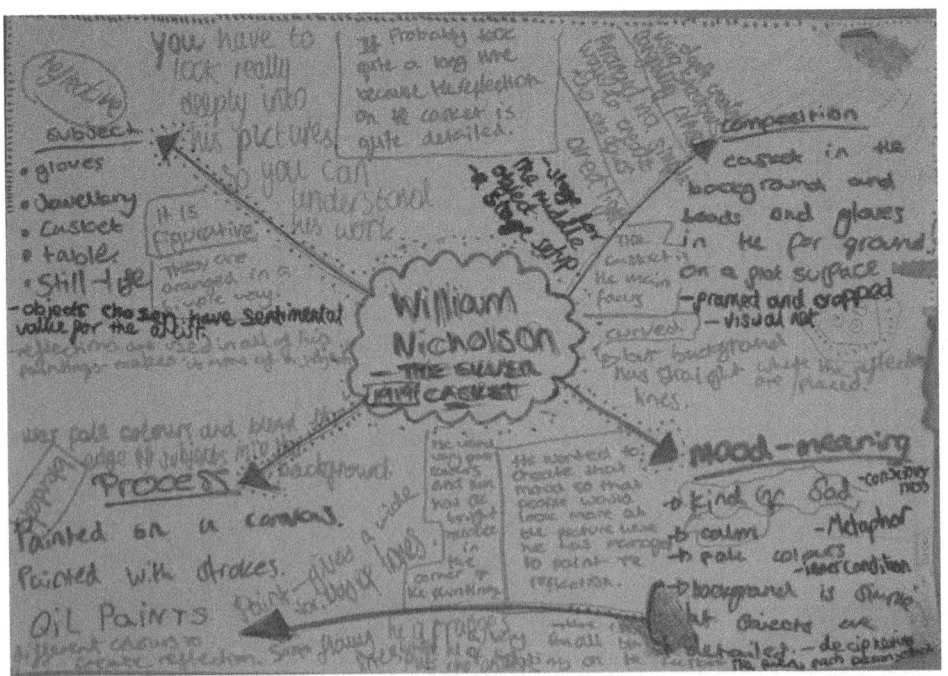

Each group developed their own ideas to contribute to the discussion. For example, group 2 focused on mood and had jotted down the following reactions to the mood of the image they were looking at:

- Moody.

- It looks lifeless and depressing because of the black colour used. It looks dull and gives the viewer a sad portrayal of the picture.

- Sad because of the dull limited colours used.

- A little light in the picture could be symbolic of hope if the painter, William Nicholson, felt he was in a dark place emotionally, and could represent light at the end of the tunnel.

The groups then fed back to the whole class and ideas were written on the board. They were then asked to write about their image using the prompts from the board.

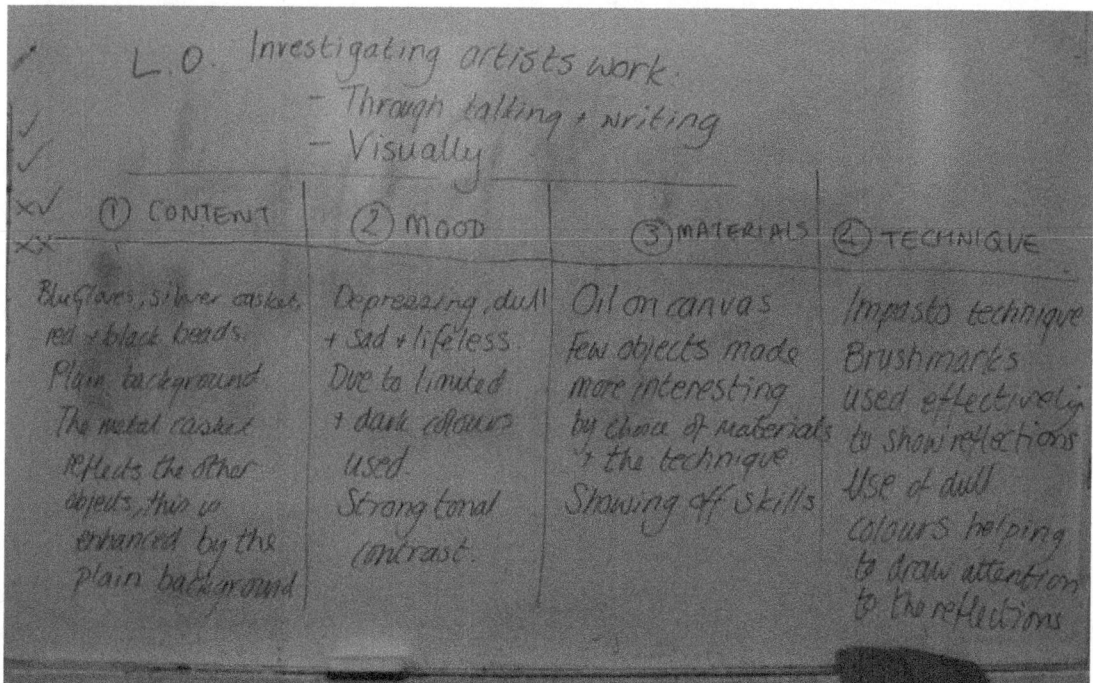

As a result of the approach, the students were able to effectively analyse elements of the artist's work independently, as illustrated by one student's work:

> This picture contains a main silver tall pewter jug. It contains bright reflections and a plain background of orange. This is made to enhance the jug in the centre. A white newspaper is shown at the bottom of the image.
>
> This picture has a strong contrast of colours; the illuminating, in comparison to the silver, dark orange. It is also evident between both silver and the dark orange and the white newspaper. In some areas (the background) it can be seen as dull and the silver jug can be plain. The white paper lightens the mood.
>
> The materials used are oil on canvas. He used this because the few objects that there is, it makes it more interesting. He might have been best at this and used this material to show off his artistic skills.
>
> The lines are rough and aren't smooth. The use of dull colours are used to bring attention to the reflections on the silver jug.

If such an approach were used in KS3 to familiarise students with the language of art evaluation orally (not to write it down but to be able to talk about it), then students opting for art GCSE would have already internalised some of the key language of art evaluation and would be in a very good position to develop their art communication skills. Those only taking art until the end of KS3 would have enhanced their understanding and appreciation of art as well as extended their vocabulary.

A similar approach could be adopted by all the practical subjects. It is important that the focus on literacy enhances the quality of learning in subjects like PE, D&T, art and music by raising the level of the student's understanding by appropriate talk activities rather than by trying to force these departments to focus excessively on writing when this is not what the subject is about.

A useful way of taking this group forward now would be to write your own exemplar piece based on the best of their work (or to put one or two of the best pieces on screen) and get the students to highlight any phrases they think could be useful for future art evaluation. The class could then co-construct the art evaluation toolkit.

The art evaluation toolkit – some useful approaches

Plan it: order the information logically	• Introduce the art/artist being evaluated
	• Box up four paragraphs commenting on the key art evaluation focuses:
	  ○ content
	  ○ mood
	  ○ materials
	  ○ technique

Link it: make your ideas fit together well	• Link ideas together so they flow logically using effective causal connectives or sentence signposts • Read evaluation through as you write to check that it flows
Express it: make your points clear and interesting	• Use well-chosen phrases to interest reader and explain points clearly to help reader picture what you are describing. (Look at suggestions drawn up by class) • Use detail to make key points clear and interesting • Use technical language if necessary, explaining if appropriate
Check it: make certain your spelling and grammar are correct	• Read your evaluation through, checking it for accuracy and improve it if it doesn't sound right • Make certain it informs the reader in an interesting and engaging way

Step E: Consolidating learning to build in progress

(This chapter is supported online by **Handouts 40–41, Slide 44**, plus the video clip from **Part 2: Step E.** Suggestions for how to present this step on a training day are on page 217.)

Research has shown that the most effective ingredients for helping students retain learning are explaining to others, practice by doing, and discussion (see page 211). These ingredients underpin the Talk-for-Writing approach and are reinforced by its imitation, innovation, independent application structure. Therefore, if the approach is followed systematically, it will automatically consolidate learning within and at the end of lessons as well as within and at the end of a unit. Throughout, the key formative assessment practices below, which contribute to consolidating learning have been emphasised and highlighted by the embedding learning icon:

- involve the students in explaining to others;

- co-construct key learning points;

- once students have completed a piece of written work, get them to

  - share it with a partner, discuss how it could be improved and make improvements,

  - write their own comment on how well they have completed the task;

- mark work, decide on what elements need strengthening; focus on these when handing back work and get students to amend their work in light of feedback and activities;

- devise language activities that revisit the target language of the unit;

- involve the students in summing up what they have learnt.

Moreover, if the approach is used consistently across the curriculum, students will be able to transfer learning much more coherently from one subject to another, which should significantly enhance their ability to consolidate learning.

Below are a few suggestions for embedding learning at the end of units.

Step Ei: Revisit the framing learning grids

The framing learning grids introduced on pages 35–37 are an excellent way of consolidating learning as well as building on prior learning.

What do I know?	What I will find out?	What have I learnt?

Not only do they provide a useful way of consolidating learning throughout the unit by summarising what is discovered as the unit develops, but they can also provide the information for a sorting activity to consolidate learning at the very end of the unit as illustrated below.

Co-constructing the key learning points

A good way of establishing the final version of the *What have I learnt?* column is to first get the students in pairs to finalise their version, then ask them to discuss their version with another pair and establish a best version. Then, through feedback from the groups, co-construct the class's version and display it.

Using a completed learning frame as a sorting activity

Using the final co-constructed learning frame, provide the students in pairs with the cards to sort. This is illustrated by the science example below, which is in brief note form. (Remember to rearrange the cards before cutting them up so that they cannot be reassembled by matching the cut lines.)

Handout 40: Summing up key points sorting activity for photosynthesis (science)

1. What is photosynthesis?	The process by which a green plant uses sunlight to build up carbohydrate reserves
2. When does photosynthesis occur?	daytime
3. What are the two raw materials needed for photosynthesis?	– carbon dioxide – water
4. What are the two products of photosynthesis?	– sugar – oxygen
5. Where, exactly, does photosynthesis occur in a plant cell?	– chloroplast
6. How could you prove that plants 'breathe out' CO_2?	It makes limewater go milky

7. How are roots adapted to absorb as much water as possible?	hairs (increase surface area)
8. What special features do leaves have to allow gases to enter and leave?	holes (stoma)

Once the students have sorted the cards, if the 'answers' are in note form, as in this example, ask them to turn them into full sentences. Then ask them to be the visiting professor who has come to tell the class all about the topic. Let them practise in pairs and then select some leading professors to explain to the whole class.

Alternatively, instead of visiting professor, try 'mobile phone'. The students place their chairs back to back (this aids focus) and pretend to be talking on a mobile, taking it in turns to explain the topic to each other. The more the students have to vocalise what they have learnt, the more they will understand and remember it.

Using framing learning grids to reflect on learning

Another useful method is to adapt framing learning grids to help students reflect on their learning and the next steps they need to take to make progress, using grid headings like these:

What I can already do and can explain how I do it	What I think I can do but I am not sure about explaining	What I get confused by and need to understand better

At the end of a unit, ask each student to fill in the grid in relation to whatever topic is being taught. The maths example below (see **Handout 41** online) focuses on what students now understand about addition. The teacher has used the grid as a way of making students reflect on their understanding. The students were provided with additional tasks, which they have to try to do and then decide which column they are placing them in and explain why. The teacher modelled for them how to explain.

For example, the following addition tasks were provided:

a. $3 + 6 =$

b. $4 + 8 =$

c. 47

   $+\underline{18}$

d. 124 +

   187

   296

   $\underline{383}$

e. There are 47 people on a bus. 26 get off but 19 more get on. How many people are on the bus now?

The completed Year 7's addition learning frame might look like this:

What I can already do and can explain how I do it	What I think I can do but I am not sure about explaining	What I get confused by and need to understand better
(a) $3 + 6 = 9$ I use counting on. I sometimes swap the numbers around to make it easier. (b) $4 + 8 =$ I still use counting on but sometimes I use friendly pairs to 10 then think what else needs to be added on.	(c) $\begin{array}{r} 47 \\ +18 \\ \hline 65 \end{array}$ Not certain if I can use friendly pairs to help here. Get confused when I have to carry one to the next column (d) $\begin{array}{r} 124\, + \\ 187 \\ 296 \\ \hline 383 \end{array}$ I often make mistakes when I have to add up a lot of numbers	(e) The bus problem I panic as soon as I see these. I don't know if I'm supposed to add or subtract here.

Again this is potentially an excellent formative assessment and embedding learning activity. Students could share their grids and see if they could help each other with any of the stages they are still unsure of. The more the students are put in teacher role, the more they will understand what they have learnt and retain their learning.

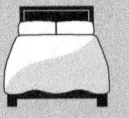

Step Eii Revisit the never-heard-the-word grid

At the end of a unit revisit the never-heard-the-word grid (see pages 39–46) to consolidate learning and check that the students have internalised the technical language of the unit. And, of course, the technical word dominoes (see pages 61–65) are an excellent way not just of consolidating the technical vocabulary but also overall understanding of the topic, since the different concepts have to be interrelated.

Step Eiii: Creating living sentences to sum up key learning points

You may want to consolidate whatever the students have just learnt by devising living sentences to sum up the key learning points. For example, if you present the three clauses below on separate strips of card, and get three students to hold up the cards (or use the washing line), the students can see how these clauses can be placed in any order to achieve a complex sentence summing up what they have learnt about the effect of exercise on the heart. Not only are these great for classroom display but they also help students to see how they can spin the clauses in sentences in a variety of ways.

| during vigorous exercise | the heart must pump blood faster to the cells |

| in order to replenish oxygen supplies |

Sadly, not all complex sentences are so obliging, but you can normally devise a two-clause summative sentence that can be spun round in such a manner.

Step Eiv: Annotate another exemplar and present findings in role as teacher

Provide a different exemplar version of the writing task set (an excellent piece of work completed by one of the class would be good – as illustrated on page 50). Students, working in pairs, annotate the text, using the text toolkit to help them, before presenting their findings to another pair in teacher role.

Step Ev: The visiting professor TV challenge

Challenge the students in small groups to come up with an engaging five- minute TV slot pitched at an adult audience explaining whatever they have just learnt.

Step Evi: The in-teacher-role challenge

At the end of a unit, set your class in pairs the challenge of teaching the same topic to a class a year younger than themselves. They can use or amend any of the material they have used in class or devise their own materials. They should be prepared to present their ideas to another pair.

The more we provide students with opportunities to explain to others, the more they will retain what they have learnt; the more coherently they are able to express their learning, the more they will be able to learn and the more confident they will become in expressing their learning. They will also be able to read around the topic more easily which in turn will strengthen their understanding.

One school timetable in Manchester was such that the Year 11s were timetabled in maths at the same time as Year 10s. This enabled the maths department to have Year 11 teach aspects of the syllabus to Year 10, providing not only one-to-one support for Year 10s but also putting Year 11s in teacher role.

Back in the 1960s, my excellent A-level economics teacher asked me to try to help one fellow student who was having great difficulties with the subject. Suddenly being put in the role of having to explain things that perhaps I had only half understood was very useful, as it made me aware of which areas I needed to work on. Unfortunately, my teaching skills couldn't have been up to much as I don't think I helped my colleague particularly but I learnt a lot; my ability to express economic concepts improved in leaps and bounds.

The consolidating learning video clip (see online video resources **Part 2: Step E**) is particularly interesting because it both illustrates consolidating learning from the students' perspective and from the teachers as learners' perspective.

Part 3

Achieving an effective whole-school approach

The first steps to establishing a whole-school approach

Perhaps one of the key reasons why most attempts at achieving an effective approach to literacy across the curriculum have failed is that, under extreme pressure from above to get something done in order to impress a passing inspector, some poor soul has burnt the midnight oil creating a policy that bears remarkably little relation to practice. This then rots on some shelf and every now and again is dusted down and everyone is told that next week is extended writing week, etc. As I write, I picture the monster posters of the correct versions of the most regularly misspelled words that mushroomed on the walls of every classroom of the school I taught in back in the mid-1970s, following the Bullock Report. Everyone taught beneath them as usual ignoring their existence. It has to be practice, theory, practice, and that practice has to be actively supported and developed by the majority of teachers – otherwise, there is no policy.

So the first stage for the coordinator is to internalise the approach yourself by trying it out on classes. Use **Handout 1**, available from the online resources, which provides an overview of the approach and **Handout 1a**, the accompanying toolkit, which includes a range of possible activities to help you adapt units. This will mean that you will be able to speak with confidence when you introduce others to the approach.

Here are some of the email messages I have received from teachers who have gone away and done just that; the response of the classes obviously firing them on to move forward.

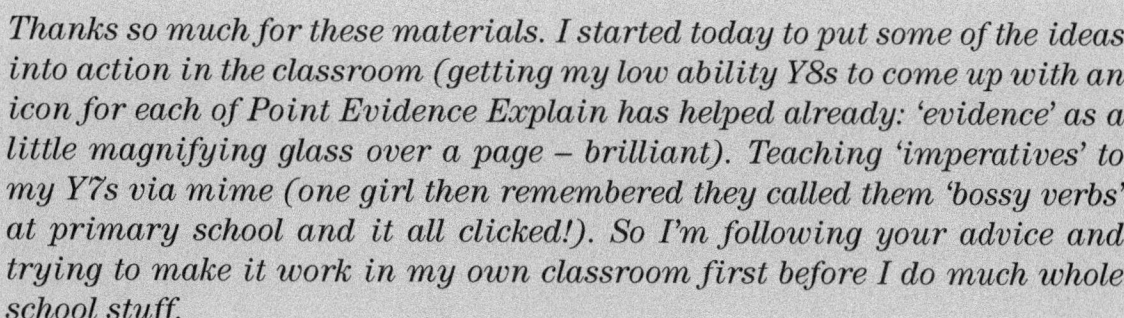

Thanks so much for these materials. I started today to put some of the ideas into action in the classroom (getting my low ability Y8s to come up with an icon for each of Point Evidence Explain has helped already: 'evidence' as a little magnifying glass over a page – brilliant). Teaching 'imperatives' to my Y7s via mime (one girl then remembered they called them 'bossy verbs' at primary school and it all clicked!). So I'm following your advice and trying to make it work in my own classroom first before I do much whole school stuff.

(Literacy coordinator from a school in North Yorkshire)

"Thanks for an incredibly powerful and engaging workshop today – I took a lot from it and will be spearheading literacy renewal at my school in Feltham. I look forward to letting you know how it goes."
(Literacy coordinator – Feltham)

I attended your Talk-for-Writing conference in London last Friday (you may remember me, I was the Professor of Dragonology). I found the entire day truly inspirational! It is now my job to inspire others in my school.
(Reading Assistant Head – and Professor of Dragonology)

I think this was dynamite and is THE issue we should focus on as it encompasses much of the AFL and behaviour sessions.
(Teacher following school training day in Coventry)

Once you have tried out the approach yourself, there are then two ways forward. One is to hold a whole-staff training day and train everyone, but I would recommend the second approach, as follows. Begin with a group of enthusiasts and develop the approach alongside them before tackling the whole staff. Having critical mass on your side is crucial. Avoid being pressurised into diving into the whole-day approach because of the need to be seen to be doing something. The second approach is much more likely to succeed in the long run.

However, if you do decide to begin with the whole-school training day approach, I would suggest setting up a group of enthusiasts afterwards to help you develop and embed the approach. The material below is relevant to both approaches.

Setting up a small group of enthusiasts to develop the approach

The immediate 'To do' list looks like this:

1. Develop your own examples using the approach

2. Build up the school's focus on developing a reading culture

3. Create a small engaged working party including an SMT heavy hitter

4. Develop the approach within each of the areas represented

5. Build from this base to reach out to the whole staff through a training day and follow-up sessions with examples from across the curriculum from your school

6. Embed through whole-school policy approach (see Chapter 11 on page 219)

Stage 1. Develop your own examples using the approach – as explained in part 2

Stage 2. Build up the school's focus on developing a reading culture

As explained on page 20, a reading culture is key to the success of this approach because it is from reading that the students will be able to further develop the range of vocabulary and sentence patterns that they are familiar with and are thus able to use themselves. All the guidance for doing this is available online from Reading Connects so I am not attempting to repeat any of the guidance here. However, literacy coordinators may find **Handout 42** (see online) on creating a school community that reads very useful as an overview. In addition, the Talk-for-Writing emphasis on exemplar text and raiding the reading will raise the profile of reading, while the focus on the pattern of language will increase students' ability to read text since familiarity with the pattern of language underpins fluent reading.

Stage 3. Create a small working party of enthusiasts

The Talk-for-Writing approach to building a whole-school literacy strategy is inspiring and rewarding but it is still hard work and you need other people to spin ideas off, to try out ideas in different circumstances and to help you devise ways round obstacles. Together you can create something really powerful.

The key thing, when setting up your working party, is to ensure that you are only involving enthusiasts who are willing to experiment and try the approach out. If possible, include someone from each of the different types of subjects (i.e. the practical subjects as well as humanities, English, science and maths). Don't let anyone in management make you include, for example, the disillusioned head of a department that is not doing very well. You need a dream team to get the ideas off the ground and then you can reach out to help others from a position of strength. If you are forced to include dragooned members, you will waste time trying to make them smile and look involved and this they will not do; in effect, this is guerilla war! There will be a lot of people out there who just want to carry on teaching as they have always taught and resist any change. The most effective way of making them change their practice is to make them want to change their practice because they can see that the ideas could really make a difference. Instructing people doesn't really work because it's easy to retreat to your classroom and carry on as before cunningly adapting your teaching with whatever elements management want only when you know someone is going to come and observe you.

The final ingredient for your group is at least one senior management heavy hitter. However good a group of teachers may be, if there is no one to bend the ear of management successfully, you will not be able to move forward very effectively.

Stage 4. Develop the approach within each of the areas represented

Work with this group to enhance understanding of the Talk-for-Writing approach. Begin by providing training for them in the approach, as outlined on pages 215–217, preferably using some examples you have developed as well as material from this handbook. Make the training as interactive as possible (see guidance below) as everyone learns best by doing. If you have a very small group, don't be tempted just to sit and discuss. It's essential for people to be actively involved in the approach by experiencing what the activities are like in practice. It's actually far harder to provide interactive training for five people than for a hundred, as you feel more self-conscious, but go for it – it works.

Once people are in a position to start trialling the approach themselves, you might want to include sessions on how to develop exemplar text and an understanding of the key language patterns underpinning each subject. Another area in which you might want to offer specific training is shared writing, as involving the students actively in the process is a real skill. Support each other in developing case studies showing how the approach can be used and, where relevant, include exemplar text and shared writing so that teachers become aware of the potential of these aspects to help students learn. The more the group members can involve their departments in the approach via show- and-tell sessions within department meetings, the larger a critical mass of potential supporters ou will have achieved by the time you reach out to the whole staff.

There will probably be some exemplary Talk-for-Writing primary schools in your area. A great way to strengthen understanding of the process would be to arrange for the group to observe some primary lessons taught in this style.

Stage 5. Build out from this base to reach out to the whole staff

You will now be in a good position to hold a very effective whole-school training day on the approach full of examples from across the curriculum from your school. Before focusing on the content of this training, it might be useful to think about how to express that content first. Here are a few training tips that have worked well for me in the 500 or so whole-school training sessions on literacy across the curriculum that I have presented.

Some tips on providing whole-school training

1. **Remember your audience.** Always think audience and purpose to help you decide the form that the training will take, just as you have to think audience and purpose before you start writing anything.

2. **Don't worry about the hard-core reactionaries.** There will always be a few people who don't want to know. Don't let them put you off. Before you begin, picture their body language as you begin the day, and use this as a source of private entertainment as they react in the manner expected (and

occasionally you'll even be surprised by someone who is more positive than you had imagined). Keep smiling and focus on those who want to be involved, which will be the majority. If someone is really irritating you, try not to look at them or get someone to send them on an errand.

3. **Keep it interactive.** Remember that human beings don't listen attentively for very long, so you need to present all the material as interactively as possible to involve the audience and provide a model of good teaching. We all know what being bored silly on training days feels like. So rather than telling people things you think they need to know, devise engaging ways of turning key information into interactive activities so people learn through doing. Begin with an engaging activity rather than the Literacy-Strategy-style lecture on how we're all not doing well enough (an approach guaranteed to turn your audience off).

For example, in groups, ask the staff to decide quickly which are the two most/least effective approaches for helping pupils retain information (see **Slide 3** on the online resources):

- audio- visual

- reading

- discussion

- explaining to others

- listening

- demonstration

- practice by doing

When the groups have had a short time to discuss the question, ask a couple of groups what they have decided – the chances are they will have come up with the 'right' answers. Then show them the results of the research (see **Slide 4** on the online resources).

Retention rates in order of effectiveness

- explaining to others   90%
- practice by doing   75%
- discussion   50%
- demonstration: 30%
- audio-visual   20%
- reading   10%
- listening   5%

(Research: National Training Laboratories, Bethel, MA, USA)

Now ask them whether they think most secondary teaching focuses on the top or the bottom half of the list. The chances are they will answer the bottom half. This is a useful discussion point and leads nicely into introducing the Talk-for- Writing approach.

All information that you may want to give can be spun round to become interactive like this – not only does it engage the audience more but they are also more likely to reflect on the significance of the information. Intersperse information giving with interactive learning so the audience never has to listen for more than a few minutes.

4. **Keep it as simple and non-technical as possible.** Many secondary teachers (apart from English teachers) will not be familiar with the text-type approach to teaching non-fiction anymore than they will be familiar with the technical language of English grammar, unless they teach modern languages. I have tried to keep this handbook as simple as possible and used technical grammatical terms as sparingly as possible.

5. **Celebrate the different structure and tunes of the languages in your school.** Put up a slide with 'The cat sat on the mat' in a range of languages spoken by students in your school beginning with the languages that you know (see below and **Slide 8** on the online resources). The idea is that teachers, preferably tutors, do this activity with their groups, so they start by putting 'The cat sat on the mat' on the whiteboard with 'the cat' in one colour, underlining the verb and putting the rest of the sentence in a different colour, as illustrated below. The class is then asked if they can write this sentence in any other language. In some schools, you will end up with a very long list and it is nearly always longer than you would have expected.

Celebrate and be aware of the different structure and tunes of the languages in your school

- The cat <u>sat</u> *on the mat.*   (English)
- Kedi *kilimin üstünde* <u>oturdu</u>.   (Turkish)
- Le chat <u>s'est assis</u> *sur le tapis.*   (French)
- Die Katze <u>saß</u> *auf der Matte.*   (German)
- El gato <u>se sentó</u> *en la estera.*   (Spanish)
- <u>Eisteddodd</u> y gath *ar y mat.*   (Welsh)
- Η γάτα <u>που κάθεται</u> *στο χαλί*   (Greek)
- <u>坐</u>*席子*的猫   (Chinese)
- Кот <u>сидел</u> *на циновке*   (Russian)

This activity has two purposes: the first is to celebrate the wealth of languages you may have in a class and to allow everyone to feel proud of the languages that they know; the second is to see visually how some languages have a very different pattern to English. If a student is regularly putting all their clauses in a 'strange' order, this probably reflects the typical order of the key language they think in – so they have not yet got the tune of English. The Talk-for-Writing approach is an excellent method for helping students learn that tune as the collective retelling of text supports everyone. Feedback from schools where the majority of students do not speak English at home has been extremely positive. The whole-class approach to presenting text is particularly powerful, as students get the opportunity to hear their voices speaking the tune of English.

6. **Involve the audience in the activities that the students would be doing.** For each of the steps of the Talk-for-Writing approach, include activities where the staff are actually doing an activity that the students would do: for example, make them stand up and learn a text with actions in Talk-for-Writing style; involve them in a dominoes activity and a phrases-sorting activity by making sets of the activity and getting the teachers to complete the activity in groups. This demonstrates the power of sorting activities to achieving focused engaging discussion. Also make them have a go at presenting the gist of the text from icons because doing is believing. And, of course, involve them in being visiting professor.

7. **Provide examples from a wide range of subject areas but avoid English examples as much as possible.** This handbook provides over 70 handouts from 14 subject areas, so you will have no shortage of choice. It's essential that subjects see that the approach could work for them. Examples from English lessons just reinforce the belief that this is not the concern of other subjects.

8. **Keep it pacy.** There's a lot of material to cover, given the range of needs of the different subject areas combined. If the presentation moves fairly quickly, and remains practical, the audience is more likely to stay engaged.

9. **Make certain there is a narrative to what you are presenting.** Check that there is coherence between one section of your presentation and the next so there is flow – you may find it useful to use icons here to help you see the big picture of the order in which you are presenting things. Practise so you know what that flow is. Very quickly you will internalise what you want to say and how one part links to the next. This gives you confidence, which is essential because providing whole-school training is no easy task.

Suggestions for how to use the online video clips and related slides to support training

The video clips were filmed at a training session in Brighton, at Varndean School, in November 2012. This handbook plus the online resources, combined hopefully

with the examples of the process that you and your group develop, will provide excellent material for several training days and workshop sessions.

The online resources includes a set of slides to adapt plus a range of video clips to use, either to support your understanding or to show to your audience at a training session. (Please note, if a slide has a purple star on it, it is for the presenter only and is not to be given to the audience within the presentation handout as it provides answers.)

For whole-staff training, it is probably best to begin with a whole-school training day, followed up by a range of other training days and workshop sessions over at least a year. I would suggest that the morning of the first training day is used to present the approach interactively, while the afternoon session is a workshop for departments to start adapting a unit of work. (If your school has opted for the magnificently named 'twilight sessions', I'm tempted to say 'you're doomed' because no one, after a full day's teaching, will be in the appropriate mental state to start focusing on training.)

For the morning input, you may want to devise a range of interactive activities following the structure of this handbook, tailored to meet the needs of your school. The more you can showcase examples that have worked with students in your school, the better. You may want to use the slides available within the online resources as a template, supported by video clips. These online clips and the related slides both follow the same structure as the book – that is, an introduction followed by the five steps to adapting units of work to integrate the approach. **Handouts 1** and **1a** provide a useful overview of these five steps, including practical suggestions for how to adapt units.

Introduction

To help introduce the day, you may want to use the opening of the **Part 1: Introduction** clip, since it helps to establish how important the pattern of language is to understanding.

It will then be useful to establish the following three fundamental things:

1. **Interactivity matters.** You may want to use **Slides 4** and **5** to establish this (how to do this interactively is explained on page 210).

2. **The layout of any teaching space should facilitate interactivity.** First, try and ensure that the layout of the room in which you are presenting is as suited to interactivity as possible (i.e. groups seated at tables, preferably two tables together to form an L-shape, with everyone being able to see the whiteboard, the flip chart and the washing line clearly). A visualiser will also be useful (see pages 22–24 and **Slide 6**). Use this set-up to illustrate this point explicitly and try to illustrate making learning visible throughout your presentation. You may want to use the short clip from the end of the introduction to the video here to help establish this.

3. **Formative assessment, which is dependent on interactivity, underpins all effective learning** (see **Slide 7**).

Ingredients of different text types

Since text type will probably still underpin how text is taught across the curriculum in primary schools and throughout English in the secondary curriculum, although it does not feature in the new curriculum, you may want to include this within your introduction. **Slides 9–11** are relevant here. **Slide 10** is a useful activity following which it's helpful to provide people with **Handout 2a**: The key typical ingredients of non- fiction text types, which provides a useful overview.

If you want to provide more help here, **Handout 2b: Non-fiction text type ingredients game** works well. Provide each group (two–four people) with a copy of the sheet cut up into cards. Then name a non-fiction text type, for example explanation, and see if they can divide the cards into *typical* or *not typical* for this type of text. The question mark is for terms where there is no agreement – or somewhere to place the terms that you don't understand! This activity is also good for KS3 English students.

Introducing the Talk-for-Writing approach

I would then suggest adapting **Slides 12–21** and presenting them as interactively as possible to make your audience aware of the potential progress that Talk-for-Writing style teaching can achieve and how to teach in this manner. You may find it useful to watch **Part 1i: *Understanding the process behind the progress – how Talk for Writing works*** and **Part 1ii: *How to teach in Talk-for-Writing style*** from the video yourself to establish how to do this. In addition, you may want to show some of these clips to your audience and also give them **Handout 4b**, which sums the process up. The online video clips illustrate the *Imitation stage*, including *imitating the text, boxing up the text and analysing it*, and *co-constructing the toolkit*; followed by the *Innovation stage*, which is introduced by *shared writing*. However, the more your audience experiences first hand analysing the progress the child has made between writing about bats and hedgehogs, the more they are liable to begin to understand the process that the teacher went through to achieve such progress. This section should take them interactively through these stages and then allow you to refer back to these stages as subsequent parts of the presentation help the audience understand the process.

The five steps for amending units

Now that you have established the overall process, introduce the five steps that help you plan such units of work. For each step, select the material that you want to illustrate from the related chapters from the book and the handouts from online.

Step A: Creating exemplar text that builds in progression

(See Chapter 3, pages **33–37**, **Slides 22–8**, and the video clip from **Part 2: Step A**)

Ask everyone in the audience to bring some exemplar text relating to GCSE in their subject to the training session. The more they have a concrete example in front of them that they can start to relate the ideas to, the more likely they are to grasp why the process may be useful to them.

Understanding why exemplar text is so useful and being able to analyse it is key – only then will you be able to help the students analyse the text and co-construct the ingredients. So you may want to begin this section with **Slide 25** – the colour-coded music text. Display the slide and ask your audience to discuss in pairs what the blue equals, etc. Look at the **Part 2: Step A** video clip for an example of how to present this.

Draw out each feature in turn. You may then want to use **Handout 4c** – exemplar text from various departments. Perhaps cut this down to text from four departments (or even better replace it with text provided by teachers in your school) and ask the staff to select one text, preferably related to their subject. Ask them to see if they can highlight all the features. **Handout 4d** provides you with examples of all the exemplar extracts 'colour coded'.

Suggest the idea of a whole-school approach to colour coding text (as outlined on pages 27–9) and then, following the training day, actually establish it, including an exemplar text working party using your enthusiasts group to help you. The last section of the **Part 2: Step A** video clip would be useful to show here.

Step B: Warming up the words

(See Chapter 4, pages 38–69, **Slides 29–35** and the video clips from **Part 2: Step B**)

This section, with its focus on technical vocabulary, is the easiest for anyone to get their head round and a useful introduction to putting the emphasis on oral activities. The online video clip that begins this section (**Part 2: Step B**) introduces this point and may be useful to show here. I would suggest you definitely include never-heard-the-word grids (see page 39 and related handouts) – preferably custom made by departments in your school – and then create a set of dominoes (see page 61 and related handouts) for teachers to try out in small groups of two to four, so that they can actively experience the power of this approach. Dominoes for the technical language of literacy are a good idea here (see **Handout 14b** online). The video clip about dominoes is probably most useful for the trainer to look at to decide how they want to present the approach, but you may find it useful to show on a training session.

Step C: Warming up the phrases

(See Chapter 5, pages 70–103, **Slides 36–9** and the video clip from **Part 2: Step C**)

As stressed before, nothing will be more powerful than warming-up-the-phrase material developed across the curriculum in your own school, but there is a range of approaches illustrated on the online resources that you might find useful either to help you understand how to develop the approach or to show extracts from on training days. Demonstrate how to use a cloze passage to draw out particular language features – for example, connectives – and then develop a poster to display on the washing line. The video clips include useful examples of *Highlighting, Sorting* and *Sequencing*, which you may want to show as well as providing opportunities for your audience to try out these approaches themselves.

Step D: Internalising text

(See Chapters 6 and 7, pages 104–197, **Slides 40–3**, plus the video clip from **Part 2: Step D**)

I would love to have been able to provide the excellent examples of classes imitating the text in science and maths that I have but unfortunately it has proved impossible to gain permission to make these available. If you go to www.talk4writing.com/id6 you will find some useful examples of children talking text and teachers being taught how to do it. These are all primary examples but the approach works equally well in secondary schools – it's just that the exemplar text is more advanced. Hopefully, you will have been able to develop your own video clips from imitating text activities developed in your school. However, as suggested above, you might want to use **Part 1ii: Imitating the text** to help you see how to train teachers in helping classes to imitate text. It also might be useful to show this section to staff. Chapter 7 includes a range of more sophisticated ways of helping students internalise text. See page 143 for an over-view of how to present one of these activities on a training day.

There are two clips on the video within Step D that you may find useful. The first is *Visiting professor*. As illustrated here, the technique is used to help warm up the phrases before trying to write a text but, as explained in the book, this technique is also an excellent way of consolidating learning at the end of a unit, as it is a fun way of involving students in explaining to others. The second useful video clip is *Using icons to recall key points*, which illustrates how to talk the gist of text using icons. This is a particularly useful clip because it illustrates powerfully how the approach can build the presenter's confidence. I would advise doing the activity with the staff but perhaps using the first half of the clip to set the activity up, if you don't want to illustrate how to do it yourself, and have the second half available to illustrate the power of the approach.

There are also two short clips from Year 11 science students from Pendle Vale College, Lancashine, explaining now the approach has both helped them understand what to write and improved the quality of their writing. Many thanks to science teacher Matthew Renshew for supplying these.

Step E: Consolidating learning to build in progress

(See Chapter 8, pages 198–204, **Slide 44**, plus the video clip from **Part 2: Step E**)

It is important to bring out in the training that, as explained in Chapter 8, if the approach is followed systematically, it will automatically consolidate learning within and at the end of lessons as well as at the end of a unit, because consolidating learning is built in throughout (see **Slide 44**).

It is therefore important to have threaded these features into the earlier steps where appropriate and then pull everything together in this section. You may wish to select some of the activities suggested in Chapter 8 but hopefully you will be able to supplement these with examples from your school. You may find the Step E video clip very useful to show here, as it illustrates embedding learning both from the students' and the teachers' perspectives. It would sum up a morning's training session rather well.

The final video clip (**Part 3: Maths appendix**) would also be useful here as it shows maths teachers Zeb and Ed explaining how the whole approach applies to maths and emphasises how your understanding of its usefulness develops over time. Alternately, you might want to show this clip much earlier, especially if you were doing a session that particularly focused on boxing up and analysing text.

Applying the training immediately through a workshop and plenary session – see Slide 45

Any training will only be effective if it is followed up. If possible, it is good to have an hour-long workshop and a 30-minute plenary session as the afternoon of the initial training day. In this way, the audience immediately gets to apply what they have heard to their subject area. A useful focus for the workshop is to ask them to apply the 5 steps to a unit/or units of work for their subject. It's a good idea to allow departments a short amount of time to discuss what they are going to do as a group and then divide into working pairs/groups as suits each area.

My advice here is to keep everyone in the same space. This keeps the session focused. If everyone escapes to their various departmental lairs, the chances of every group staying on task is slim and it makes it so much harder for you to go round and support each group.

Finish the day with a plenary session where every department feeds back briefly on what they have focused on. Then provide some clear next steps with a timetable. For example, in one term's time, everyone is expected to have developed at least one unit of work in Talk-for-Writing style. Some of these can then be showcased at the next training session and more workshop time given to departments to further develop their approach. You will then be in a position to embed the approach as explained in the next chapter.

10 Embedding the approach through co-constructing your policy

A whole-school training day is obviously only an early stage in achieving a whole-school approach. It will take at least a year from this point to really start to embed the approach and, more likely, two or more. This requires senior management support, as this needs to be the focus of a number of training days, and departmental meeting time needs to be given over to focusing on the approach not for a term or two but for every meeting if it is to succeed. What works in the classroom has to become the focus of what we discuss. Many primary schools that have succeeded in changing the learning culture in their schools through Talk for Writing recognise that it is always on the agenda. A toolkit for literacy coordinators may be useful here.

The literacy coordinator's toolkit for effectively embedding a whole-school approach to literacy

1. Provide ongoing training

2. Develop exemplar text across the curriculum

3. Establish a means of ensuring the students make progress year on year

4. Establish a learning culture among staff to develop the approach

5. Develop a consistent approach to formative assessment

6. Establish your whole-school policy plus a mechanism to review it

1. Train all staff in the Talk-for-Writing approach and embed the concept of ongoing training

A training day as outlined in the previous chapter covers all the staff who attend on that day but this training will serve little purpose unless staff can see that it is just the beginning of the process and that a structure is in place to develop the approach as outlined here. There is also the question of ensuring all new staff and any staff who were absent are inducted into the approach. The most logical way is to get all departments to include it within their training programme for staff. This, of course, assumes that all heads of department can see the power of the approach and want to adapt it to suit the needs of their subject. A good way of achieving this is to have a development programme set up within the school so that every department knows that they are trialling the approach and that there will be opportunities to feed back and refine it before it becomes policy.

It is essential that developing the approach features on subsequent training days with, perhaps, more focused workshop time. Adapting units of work takes time and this should be recognised within the school training programme. Focus is important. The National Literacy Strategy would have been far more successful if more time had been devoted to embedding what worked and listening to and adapting what didn't, rather than endlessly coming up with something new to focus on – especially when the new was often the old disguised in the latest lingo.

2. Develop exemplar text across the curriculum

All staff will need support in developing exemplar text and ensuring that this text reflects appropriate progress from year to year. As suggested earlier in this handbook, we all need help in developing exemplar text. It shouldn't be seen as a weakness to seek support but a strength – a sign that you are determined to ensure that what the students are offered is as good as it can be. The more your working party has an overview of the type of text that is required by different departments, the more you will be able to hone your approach to suit different departmental needs and help the students transfer knowledge about communication skills from one subject to another.

I would suggest that every department sets up its own exemplar text working group and that these groups are supported by the project working party who, by this time, will have developed expertise in this area through their own practice and through sharing ideas within the working party. (See the end section of the **Step A: Creating the right exemplar text** video clip.)

This working group could also be used to establish the colour coding for exemplar text to be applied consistently across the curriculum as demonstrated throughout this book. When deciding on your colour coding, it's useful to look at whatever IT system your school uses and check what the colours look like on that. In addition, you need to get someone who is colour-blind to check that they can distinguish the colours. Obviously you have to avoid red. As pointed out earlier, see page 28 departments can use any additional colours they choose to highlight specific additional features that are relevant to their subjects.

Consider providing surgeries to develop skills. In addition, if you are aware that many teachers in your school haven't grasped the difference between 'it's' and 'its' and other commonly seen errors, you may want to consider holding grammar and punctuation surgeries for staff and devise entertaining ways of teaching main clauses and subordinate clauses, etc.

When working at the National Literacy Trust surrounded by young people with firsts from Oxford, I was interested to see how poor some of the punctuation and grammar was and found people extremely receptive to attending voluntary lunchtime training sessions to help them understand these things. As one person put it, 'I wish someone had taught me this years ago.' By the time this book is published, hopefully *Jumpstart Grammar* by Pie Corbett and myself will also have been published. This should be a very useful book to help train staff as well as teach children.

You could also hold shared writing surgeries to help everyone to improve their ability to demonstrate interactively how to write. This is a real skill and needs support. It is also at the heart of helping students learn how to write effectively in the tune of each subject.

3. Establish a means of ensuring the students make progress year on year

Your working party will also be invaluable for developing and monitoring how the school ensures that the students are being challenged to make progress every year as the exemplar text is key to this. As the approach progresses, teachers will become ever more skilful at seeing how to provide step-by-step progress to achieving powerful communicators in their subject; the students will benefit greatly, teachers will find teaching more rewarding and any visiting inspector will leave impressed. Moreover, being a member of the working party will provide invaluable experience for those seeking leading management positions in schools.

4. Establish a learning culture among staff to develop the approach

The approach can only be developed through practice and reflection. In effect, all staff members need to become engaged in how applying this approach to their subject can really make a difference.

If 'what works in lessons' is established as a regular item on departmental agendas, the approach will automatically develop through practice. We seem to have moved from an era, some decades ago, when teachers rarely met, to one in which life is an endless series of meetings once the teaching day is over. And yet teachers tell me these meetings rarely focus on what works in the classroom. If this is true of your school, this is an excellent opportunity to change that culture and put what works in the classroom at the top of agendas where it should be. This should make meetings inspiring. If you don't come out of a meeting feeling inspired, or at least resolved to do something that will really make a difference, there's something wrong with the way the meetings are being run. Thinking about how to make meetings engaging and effective should be high on any management agenda.

The various structures suggested in this chapter will help to make this developmental, reflective culture a reality.

In addition, it would be excellent and most logical to engage the students in the development of the approach – after all, it is they who will be on the receiving end. Some schools have successfully managed to create a learning culture in which students are not only invited to reflect on what worked for them in lessons but on how the school could develop to help them learn.

5. Develop a consistent formative assessment approach to marking

As mentioned on page 21, research into the efficacy of formative assessment in supporting effective learning is absolute. This is a truth that some have chosen not to recognise in their desire to put systems in place to raise standards. Many secondary schools still expect teachers to grade every piece of work despite the masses of research showing that using such a summative approach depresses standards. When I first saw the APP units, my heart sank as they seemed excessively complicated with too much focus on assessing where pupils are (summative assessment) and not enough focus on how to move students to the next stage (formative assessment). However, there are excellent elements within the scheme. My suggestion would be that schools select from APP the elements that they have found most useful and add these elements to the approach suggested below as appropriate. This approach has been illustrated throughout this book.

- Co-construct 'toolkits' for each type of work (practical, written or oral) with the students so they know what ingredients to include and develop these as appropriate for each subject.

- Embed students' understanding of these elements by ensuring they are central to your units of work, as illustrated in this book and outlined below, so that the students become increasingly able to talk about their learning and the steps they need to take to make progress.

- As part of this process, ensure writing is regularly shared by pairs of students using the toolkit and the 'good points and key ways it could be improved' approach. The students are then given time to amend their writing as they choose in the light of their peer discussion.

- Introduce a highlighting system to support the approach, e.g. yellow for 'good points' (as in gold) and green for 'could be improved' (green for growth).

- Require all students to write their own comment and highlight their work, using the 'good points and key ways it could be improved' approach, before handing work in to get the dialogue going with their teacher about what was good about the work and what might need more attention.

- Add comments to the student's comment using the same approach and help students identify the steps forward they most need to make progress.

- Provide time to improve work immediately after it is handed back, wherever possible including focused activities based on whatever was identified through the marking process as needing more attention, so students actually look at, and react to, the marking and have the chance again to amend their work in the light of it.

- Select, in addition, up to five misspelt subject-related words that have been corrected for the student to learn. Sometimes begin lessons with a quick spelling test focusing on the key technical words of the unit that are causing the most spelling problems.

- Do not give grades except for the termly/half-yearly assessment pieces, which should be graded in line with summative assessment procedures in the school.

6. Establish a whole-school policy on powerful communication across the curriculum and a means of reviewing and improving it

Now you are in a position to refine the whole-school policy that you will have been developing throughout the process, in the light of practice, and turn it into a meaningful whole-school policy because it is based on practice that teachers support and develop. It can then be given to all new staff members who will be enabled to join in the process because the approach is embedded within how teachers teach in the school and what is discussed in meetings.

Any policy needs a mechanism through which it can be reviewed, so perhaps the exemplar text surgery group could be the conduit through which changes could be considered. This is an important ingredient of the approach because people who are worried about aspects of the policy and how it applies to them need to have someone to listen to their concerns and to recognise that sometimes it might be the policy that needs changing not the teacher.

In this way, we will have got rid of the days when all departments are handed word mats to be displayed on every work surface in every department, which largely consist of the vocabulary of creative writing, or PE teachers at KS3 should somehow incorporate written work within their units. The more staff buy-in to the process because they can see that it will help them teach more effectively, the more effective the policy will be. The more they know that their legitimate concerns are being listened to, the more they will buy-in to the approach.

In addition, this group could become a powerful source of ways to improve teaching and learning within the school, because the more you discuss what works and how teaching approaches can be adapted to make learning more effective, the more progress you make. Exchange of ideas is crucial. For example, following the first training day I provided for a group of cross-curricular teachers in Brighton, Andy Breckenridge, an English teacher, internalised the ideas and adapted them to try to improve writing standards (see pages 144–51). When he presented this at the next training day in Brighton, I was so impressed by the progress made and the techniques used, that I have adapted them to show how you can use A* exemplar text in any subject to raise standards (see pages 152–61 for a science example). Hopefully, you will see ways of further improving these examples. This is what learning is all about; we can all learn from each other.

Conclusion

Teachers who have systematically tried the Talk-for-Writing approach tell me that it has transformed the engagement of their students in their subject and significantly increased their ability to communicate coherently. Even better, where the approach is applied systematically across all subjects, it can raise student achievement across the curriculum. Teachers from all curriculum areas have enthusiastically taken up the approach because they see how it will help them teach their subject as well as contribute to a coherent whole-school approach. It is this that transforms the literacy coordinator's role into an achievable, rewarding task because this approach really does work across the curriculum.

> 'Just thought I would offer a quick update. As planned, we are continuing to reinforce the strategies that you brought to us and ensuring that strategies are implemented across the school. During a recent LA review, the renewed and consistent focus on literacy was highlighted as much improved practice. Thanks again – you have left us with a strong legacy.'
> (Email from a deputy head a few months after a Talk-for-Writing staff training day)

This approach will not only help your school shine when an inspector calls but, more importantly, it will help turn students into more powerful communicators who can present their ideas clearly and achieve better quality written communication in any subject. And, of course, that makes teaching all the more engaging and rewarding.

Try it, it works!

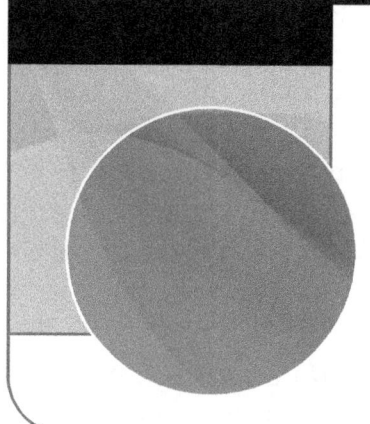

Appendix: A case study of how the Talk-for-Writing approach relates to maths

(This appendix is supported by **Slide 45**, plus the video clip **Part 3: Maths appendix**)

> 'If students don't understand the underlying mathematical concepts they are lost. Making them express concepts in words has significantly helped develop their understanding. They know they've made progress.'
> (Andrew Lyon, KS4 maths coordinator, Queensbury School, from the Bradford Talk-for-Writing pilot)

Maths is different from any other subject on the curriculum because the language of number and mathematical symbols is very different from the language of English. However, the more students can understand the mathematical concepts they are manipulating, and express that understanding in words, the greater their understanding will be. This is why the Talk-for-Writing approach is particularly useful, as it is based on helping students understand the underlying concepts. In, say, English, or almost any other subject, it is a question of establishing a linguistic pattern and then showing the student how to innovate on that pattern so that they can achieve independent application. In maths, it is slightly different, as it is not so much the pattern of expression that is important as understanding the underlying concepts that underpin the mathematical patterns and how to structure your thinking. Establishing understanding of the underlying process and being able to explain it, and then showing the students how to innovate on that pattern enables the students to apply it to any mathematical problem independently.

Warming up the words and concepts of a unit has always been important in maths but now it is increasingly relevant as the quality of written communication (QWC) requirements for maths mean that students have to be able to explain coherently what they have done. When looking at the maths QWC requirements it is comforting to see that it is recognised that spelling, punctuation and grammar are not necessarily relevant when answering mathematics questions, since 'the assessment of the quality of written communication has to be tailored to the subject'.

The maths section of the Edexcel website assures us that 'Questions will NOT be written to specifically address this requirement but will occur quite naturally within the context of traditional questions.' Hence, QWC marks are extended to include:

- *the construction of a reasoned argument such as would be seen in a proof. They will also be seen when work needs to be presented in an ordered way which allows the examiner to follow the work without difficulty*

- *well presented statistical diagrams with clear labelling, scales and/or axes*

- *work where evidence has to be gathered with a clearly stated decision oroutcome.*

One element of the Talk-for-Writing approach that maths teachers have found particularly useful, aside from its focus on explaining the technical language and concepts, is using the boxing-up approach to help structure thinking and how to express answers to mathematical problems.

How the concept of boxing up text helps students internalise how to structure their answers in maths

At the end of 2010, Brighton and Hove set up a Talk-for-Writing pilot to be attended by a range of teachers and advisers across the curriculum. A few months after the first session, I was stunned and delighted to receive the following email from Zeb Friedman, maths adviser in the authority who also teaches maths at Varndean School, Brighton:

My journey into 'Talk for Writing' and how it applies to maths

Suddenly talking about mathematics as a language makes perfect sense. Don't get me wrong I have been going on about this for years. Maths is a language, working out is important, you must structure your answers etc. Students stare back at me distrustfully, 'But Miss, it says on the mark scheme that you get full marks for the correct answer. I know it's right why would I do all of that extra stuff!!?' I know a losing battle when I'm in one.

I was persuaded into going to the session on Talk for Writing in Brighton and Hove and really, although I am always interested in what is happening in other subjects, I was not convinced that there would be anything in it for me or for mathematics beyond 'lets write an essay about the history of maths'. I was starting to feel like my students did when I insisted that they write the working out in their work 'just because'! However, there was something about the 'Talk for Writing' project that struck a chord with me. This was comparing maths to written communication in a direct and explicit way. I had a chat with our science AST and she helped me to see some really important links. Over the last couple of months my thinking has gone something like this:

Maths in secondary schools is facing a huge challenge. How do we as teachers help our students to think about maths more functionally? How can we help them to be better problem solvers when we are being asked to take away scaffolding in the way we assess their work? How can we get them to be more independent in their thinking about maths?

When I thought about this in relation to writing what I realised was that in maths we had been so assessment driven that we were getting students to do questions like 'here is a sentence, what is the missing word?'. Suddenly we had moved to 'Write a mathematical essay where you will be judged on the quality of your written communication'. This was a daunting leap.

Not only were students struggling with this but so were we. Assessment-led teaching had created a generation of de-skilled practitioners in maths. I'm not suggesting that all maths teachers are rubbish, just that for many of us our attention was elsewhere. I had spent several months either with my head in the sand or in a state of paralysis whenever these issues of functionality came up. When I did feel brave enough to look up it felt like an epiphany in the hall listening to Julia Strong explaining about Talk for Writing. This was the answer and as I began to work with aspects of this approach I started to feel as this was the magic wand I had been looking for to move my students and me onwards to the land of written mathematical communication.

The strategy that makes so much sense to me is 'boxing up'. I started talking to my students about maths being a story, an essay. In English lessons they were taught to structure and plan essays it was not enough to just string words together in a muddle. We talked about mathematical stories and what paragraphs looked like in maths. We started with Pythagoras' Theorem and Trigonometry because it is a fairly concrete bit of mathematics which has an obvious structure. I modelled for them how I would do this, then I asked them to do the same. I was insistent about the structure and they really had to follow my steps. So far this is pretty predictable and I was not entirely comfortable as it did not allow them their own approach or any creative methods they might come up with. I am not a 'chalk and talk' or 'follow my method without understanding' type of teacher. However, I persevered.

Students began to produce work like the example below after one lesson of boxing up. Some still needed a bit of convincing. I got them to find the mistake in two pieces of work, one where the work was boxed up and one which was muddled 'old style'. I also made use of the visualiser and got the class to be critical of each other's work. They were all pretty convinced after two lessons.

We looked at our next topic in relation to boxing up and we boxed that up too. Gradually we moved towards a common understanding of the structure behind all mathematics questions and problems.

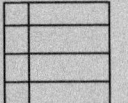

Using boxing up to structure answers to maths problems

What information do I have? What is the question being asked?	
What mathematics do I need to use to do this?	
What calculations/working out do I need?	
Answer – and does it make sense. Have I answered the question?	

This structure is not new to me or to the students but there has been a shift in their work because I now have a way of being very explicit about this structure and its underlying influence on most (all?) maths problems.

Then something which had been bothering me was solved. Students could follow the structure of a mathematical story or essay and understand how to put together the paragraphs but within that structure they had freedom and creativity about the mathematics they used to solve the problem. They were not churning out cloned pieces of work after a while and they were starting to develop individual style and approaches to their work that I was afraid might be lost in the process.

Looking through pupils' books I am for the first time struggling to find examples of sloppy working out.'

As Zeb has so graphically explained, the reason why the boxing-up approach is so useful in maths is because the more you can explain a process, the more you understand it; and the more you understand, the more you will retain the information and be able to build on your understanding. This fortunately fits perfectly with the maths Quality of Written Communication requirements.

Before:
Previously a typical simple maths addition question would have looked like this

289 + 257 =   [1 mark]

After:
But now it has been turned into a problem like this:

- You have an electricity bill where the readings are 289 and 567 units.

- 1 unit of electricity costs 16 pence.

- How much will you be charged for this bill?   [4 marks]

So answers that used to look like this:

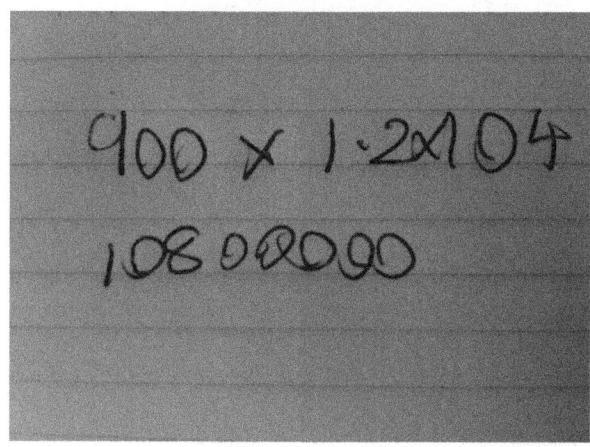

now look more like this:

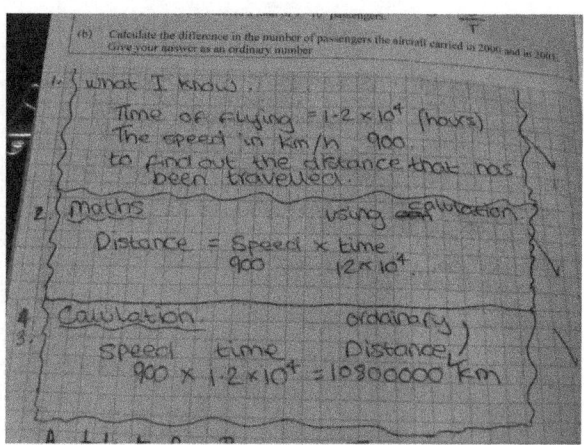

The story behind boxing up

The whole idea behind boxing up – that is, planning any writing task using a basic two- column grid to sort your ideas into order – was to provide a very simple way of students being helped to plan and structure their work.

If you boxed up any typical explanation text for, say, science, history or English, it would basically look like this:

Boxed-up grid for explanation text

Beginning:	• Introduce what is being explained • Include a hook to interest your reader
Middle:	• Put key points in logical order, possibly in several paragraphs • Link points clearly so reader can see how one thing leads to another • Include detail where necessary to make explanation clear
End:	• Conclude your explanation, rounding it off logically in a memorable way

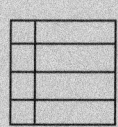

The idea of boxing up is that you use it to understand the structure of any type of text and use the same ingredients to help you structure a similar text. If you apply this approach to any maths problem, when you analyse the questions, the basic structure of what you have to do is always the same.

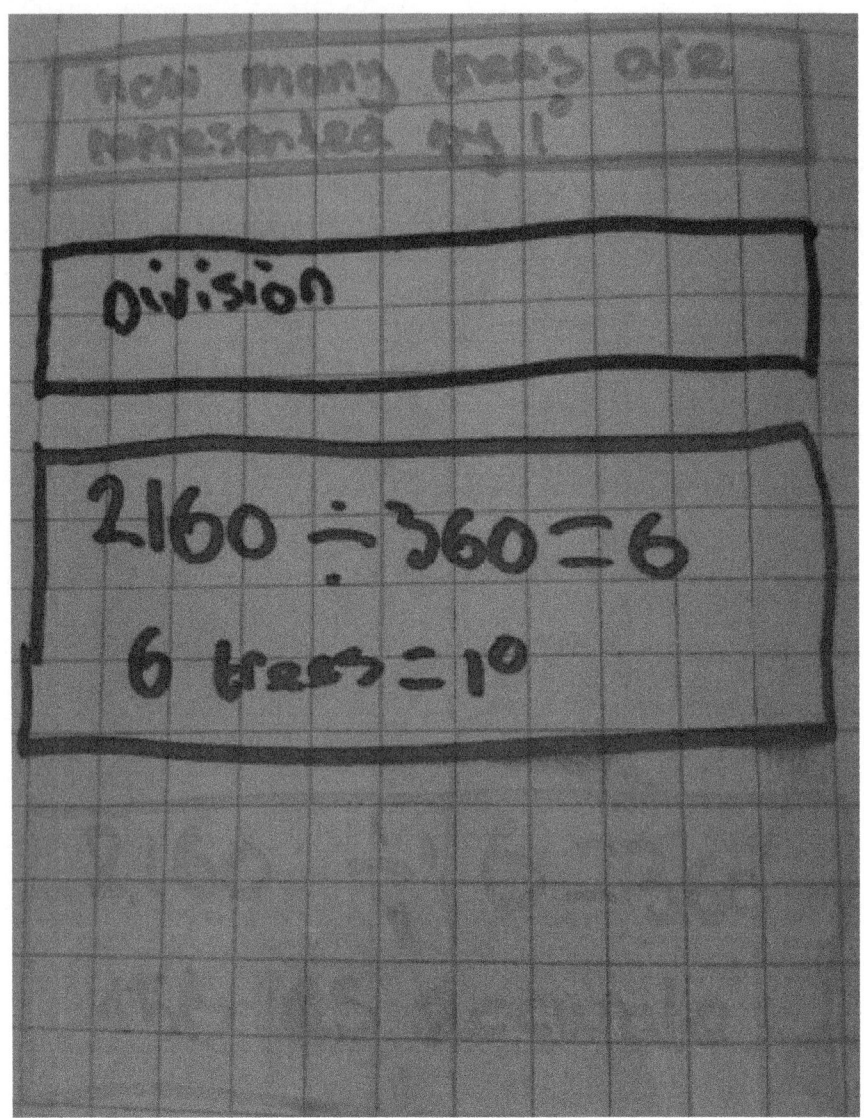

Boxing up

Boxing up maths problems

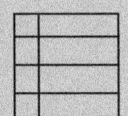

Beginning: – **Plan it**	• What is the question asking me? • What information do I already have?	
Middle: – **Do it**	• What maths will I be using? • What calculations/working out do I need to do?	
End: – **Check it**	• How can I check that my answer is correct?	

In effect, this is the basic maths explanation toolkit.

So let's see how it works in practice. Below is a typical maths problem:

The gas bill problem
Mr Black is looking for the cheapest provider of gas in order to cut his bills. He
has received the following quotes from two companies:

Gascom:
Standing charge per month: £1.00
Cost per kWh: £2.99

Ugas:
Standing charge per month: £3.78
Cost per kWh: £2.38

Mr Black estimates that he will use 4000 kWh in the next 3 months. From which
company would his gas bill be cheaper and by how much?

Below, on the right-hand side, is what the boxed-up answer might look like.

Plan it: **What is the question asking me? What information do I already have?**	Which company is cheaper for 3 months' gas and by how much? Estimated use; monthly standing charges; cost per kWh
Do it: **What maths will I be using?**	$\times + -$
What calculations/working out do I need to do?	*Gascom:* 3 months costs £1 $\times$ 3 = 3.00 Gas costs £2.99 $\times$ 4000 = <u>11,960.00</u> 11,963.00 *Ugas:* 3 months costs £3.78 $\times$ 3 = 11.34 Gas costs £2.38 $\times$ 4000 = <u>9,520.00</u> 9,531.34 Difference 11,963 − <u>9,531.34</u> 2,431.66
	Ugas is cheaper by £2,431.66
Check it:	Check answered question. Check used correct prices. Check calculations

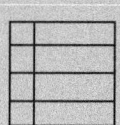

Initially, it's best to get the students to tackle these in pairs so they have to explain
what they are doing. If they regularly have to do this in this manner, they will move

from imitation of the structure to innovation to independent application. They will then automatically be able to apply this method to any maths problem on their own using the template in their head that provides a structure for their thinking but allows them to choose the method that best suits them in solving the problem.

A visualiser, or any equipment that enables you to immediately put up on screen examples of good work, is useful here as you can select the clearest examples of good answers from the students and put them up on screen to discuss what makes them good. The students can then have a look at their work and revise it in the light of this discussion. This will help them recognise the steps they need to take to improve their learning.

At Portslade Aldridge Community Academy in Brighton and Hove, every maths table has the key boxed-up questions permanently on the tables and these questions form the frame for all discussion in maths. When students are introduced to the approach, coloured pens are available on the tables so they can use a different colour

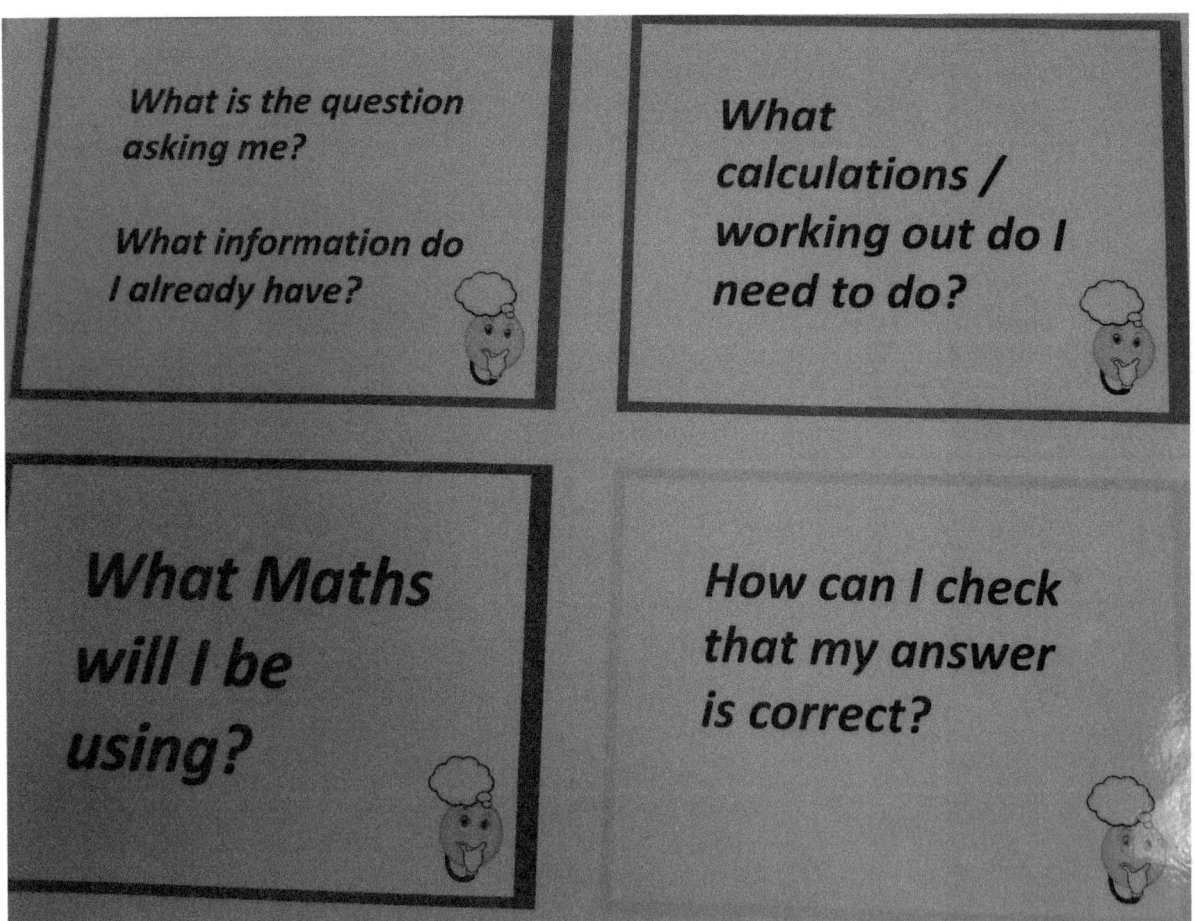

Boxing up in maths

for each stage (using the same colour scheme as the handout) to underline the importance of the stages.

When the students tackle the problems, they do so in pairs, moving swiftly from one problem to another and building confidence in their ability to analyse the question, work out what maths is required, do the maths and check their answers. Most students have found it useful, once they have got over the fact that they have to write more in maths, as evidenced by their responses:

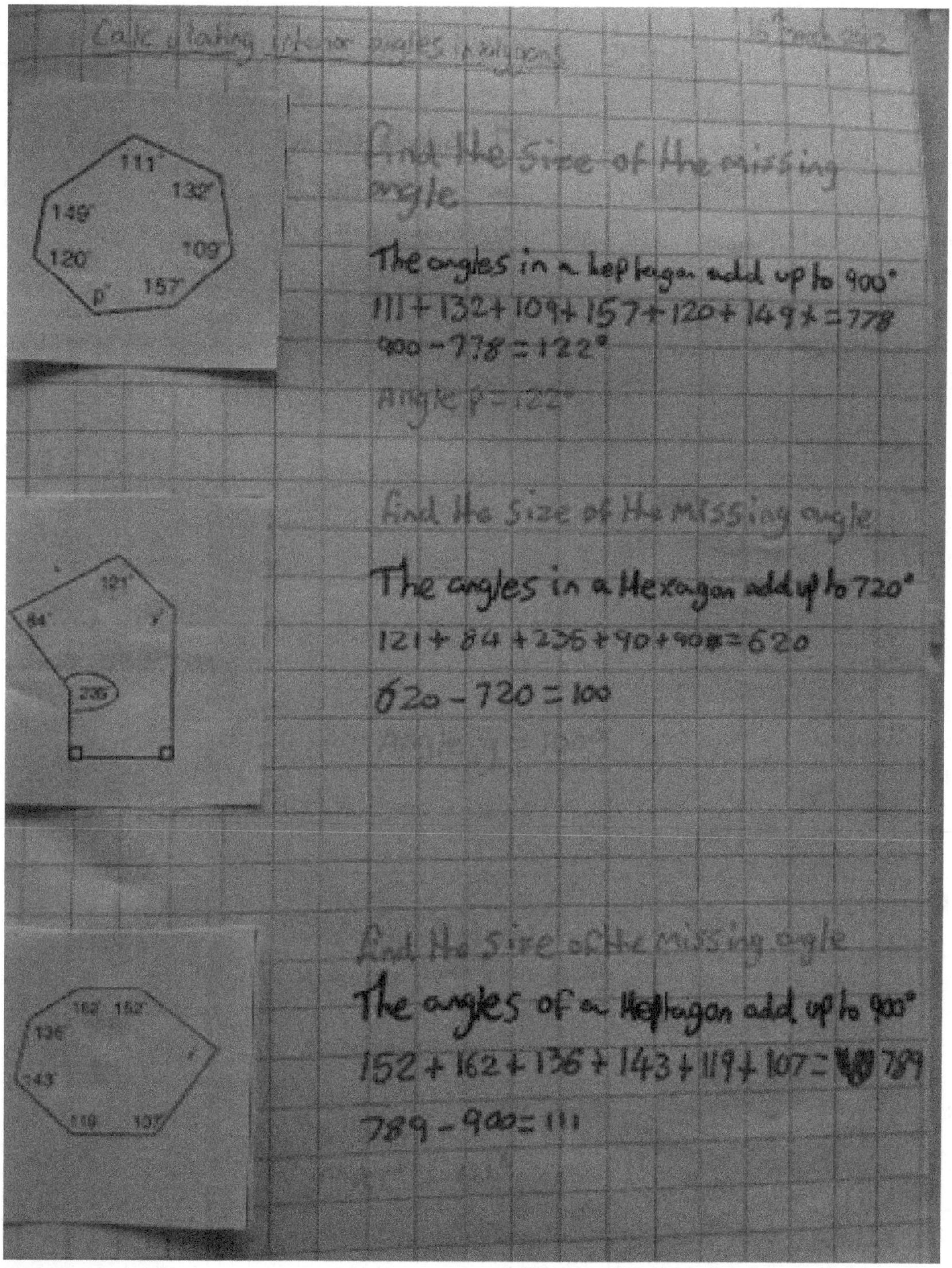

Calculating interior angles in polygons

find the size of the missing angle

The angles in a heptagon add up to 900°

111 + 132 + 109 + 157 + 120 + 149 × = 778

900 - 778 = 122°

Angle p = 122°

find the size of the missing angle

The angles in a Hexagon add up to 720°

121 + 84 + 235 + 90 + 90 = 620

620 - 720 = 100

find the size of the missing angle

The angles of a Heptagon add up to 900°

152 + 162 + 136 + 143 + 119 + 107 = 789

789 - 900 = 111

Working out

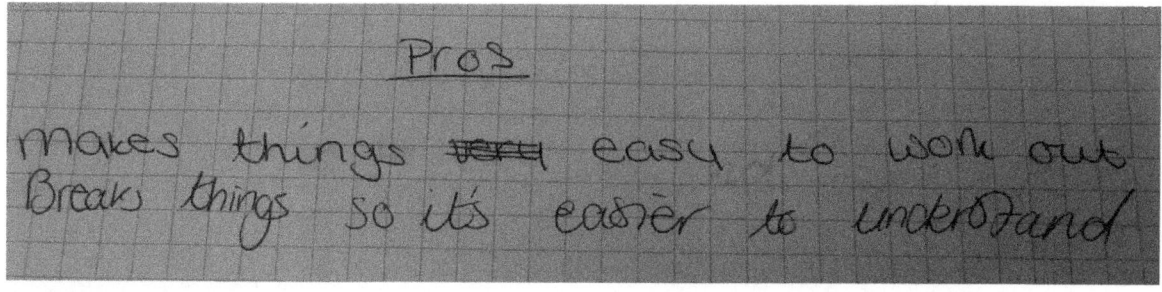

Pros

makes things ~~very~~ easy to work out
Breaks things so it's easier to understand

Student's comment

To spread the approach across the school, maths teachers Helen Hindle and Emma McCrea trained one Year 11 class in the approach and then that class trained the other Year 11s and all the other maths teachers. Then the teachers used the approach with all the other years in the school. The students started to produce work looking like that pictured here.

Where the approach is becoming embedded, students no longer need to work in pairs or refer to the boxed-up stages, as they have internalised the approach and apply it automatically.

A useful way of helping students understand how to structure their maths answers is to get them to compare several different answers to the same question so that they themselves establish 'what = good' and use this to construct their own toolkit of advice for answering questions.

The examples are easy to source, as the examination boards publish exemplar answers online. An even better source is to adapt work that the students have actually done. Obviously you need to alter and adapt the weak examples so the person whose work it is based on does not feel they are being criticised publicly. Devising your own examples means that you can more easily demonstrate the sort of answers you are looking for. It would be useful for students to do this activity for a range of different question types so they can apply their understanding to a range of possible questions.

Ask the class to feed back on their findings and pull their ideas together to create their toolkit for answering maths problems. The class may create a toolkit something like this:

The how to answer maths problems toolkit

Plan it:	• Work out what the question is asking and underline it on the question • Work out what information will help answer the question
Do it:	• Work out what maths to use • Do the working out in order so method is clear • Write down the answer
Check it:	• Check I have answered the question asked • Check calculations • Check answer seems logical given the question and the information provided

Then ask the students to use this toolkit to complete a similar maths problem on their own. Once they have completed their work, ask them to swap their answer with a partner so that they can discuss whether they have followed the class's instructions for how to answer maths problems. Allow time for them to revise their work in the light of the discussions. Again, when you mark the work, check to see if they are all applying the ingredients of the toolkit appropriately and allow time to remedy errors when the work is handed back so the students are not only aware of the steps they need to take to improve their work, but have had a go at putting them into practice.

And, of course, once the students have grasped how to solve particular types of maths problems, model for the class how to be the visiting maths professor who has come to explain how to tackle any maths problem. Then let them practise being the professor in pairs and invite any budding maths professors to present to the whole class. The more they feel they can explain what they are doing, the greater their confidence will be in doing maths problems, and it's entertaining.

You can later present the 'TV professor challenge'. Two professors have a five-minute TV slot to explain how to do maths problems. Challenge them in pairs to come up with a good way of doing this. If some students are good at this, then provide them with classes or groups of students to teach it to.

The complexity of the maths problems will increase as the students move up the school, but the underlying approach remains the same. If the students in the first years of secondary school have internalised the pattern of how to structure their answers to maths problems, and how to use the language of maths coherently, they will then be able to express their mathematical understanding all the more effectively when they take formal examinations; moreover, their ability to develop their understanding will improve significantly.

Interestingly, in November 2012, Zeb and another maths teacher attended the training session at which the online accompanying this book was filmed; they were kindly willing to explain on video how the approach works in maths. At the end of that session, Zeb commented: 'I can now see that it is so much more than boxing up that is relevant.' She estimated that 75% of the approach was directly applicable in helping students think mathematically and express their understanding. This sums up how effective teachers are always reflecting on what processes and practices will best help their students learn and that often we, just like the students, have to experience something several times before we can fully understand it and integrate it effectively into our teaching repertoire so that the students can learn more effectively.